P9-CFW-003

Ciao Italia—
Bringing Italy Home

Also by Mary Ann Esposito

Ciao Italia

Nella Cucina

Celebrations Italian Style

What You Knead

Mangia Pasta!

Ciao Italia—Bringing Italy Home

REGIONAL RECIPES, FLAVORS, AND TRADITIONS AS SEEN
ON THE PUBLIC TELEVISION SERIES <u>CIAO ITALIA</u>

MARY ANN ESPOSITO

ST. MARTIN'S PRESS ✿ NEW YORK

CIAO ITALIA—BRINGING ITALY HOME. Copyright © 2001 by Mary Ann Esposito.
All rights reserved. Printed in the United States of America. No part of this book
may be used or reproduced in any manner whatsoever without written permission
except in the case of brief quotations embodied in critical articles or reviews. For
information, address St. Martin's Press, 175 Fifth Avenue, New York, N.Y. 10010.

www.stmartins.com

Book design by Victoria Kuskowski

Illustrations by Kathryn Parise

Map of Italy by Martie Holmer

641.5945
E SP

Library of Congress Cataloging-in-Publication Data

Esposito, Mary Ann.
    Ciao Italia—bringing Italy home: regional recipes, flavors, and traditions as seen
on the public television series *Ciao Italia* / Mary Ann Esposito.—1st ed.
        p. cm.
    ISBN 0-312-28058-0
    1. Cookery, Italian.   2. Cookery—Italy.   I. Ciao Italia (Television program)
    II. Title.
    TX723 .E8697   2001
    641.5945—dc21   2001019158

First Edition: May 2001

10 9 8 7 6 5 4 3 2 1

This book is in tribute and gratitude to all those who make up the Ciao Italia television production staff—past, present, and future. Your friendship, loyalty, talents, and belief in the program over the years have made you more than co-workers—they have made you family.

Special Acknowledgment

Deep thanks and appreciation to the staff at St. Martin's Press for their professionalism and enthusiasm in embracing this work. I owe special thanks to senior editor Marian Lizzi, art director Steve Snider, interior designer Victoria Kuskowski, associate director of publicity Dori Weintraub, production editor Mara Lurie, copy editor Judith de Rubini, and indexer Elizabeth Parson for capturing the essence of the Italy that I love within the pages of this book. To photographer Bill Truslow, for his excellent work and for once again proving that beautifully photographed food makes a universal statement. To prop stylist Jane Sutton, food stylist Trish Dahl, and culinary supervisor to *Ciao Italia* Liz Hayden, for their dedication to this project.

Contents

Ciao Italia has never won an Emmy award, although it was nominated as one of the best cooking shows on television. *Ciao Italia* has never had a large production budget, yet the quality of the work is as good as on shows that spend much more. *Ciao Italia*'s crew has always worked for modest wages, yet there is always a demand for crew positions. And with all this modesty, *Ciao Italia* has maintained a high profile in the national cooking show line-up for over a decade. I guess you could say that we have beaten the odds.

I owe this success to so many, and I consider myself so very fortunate to have worked with the most dedicated and talented people in the business that just saying thank you seems somehow inadequate. Each time I walk into the studio to tape a *Ciao Italia* segment, I walk into a high-energy field known as the "crew," whose job it is to work with me to turn out a polished television segment from the content to the technical quality. I have never been disappointed. Instead I have been supported by professionalism, enthusiasm, and fun.

I want to recognize them publicly for their work and thank the following who have contributed their creative ideas and energies. To Cynthia Fenneman, who first recognized the merits of producing an Italian cooking show; Paul Lally, executive producer; Kevin Carlson, director; and Sally Northrop, producer. You are the best. To my loyal kitchen staff—Donna Soares, senior supervisor; Ruth Moore, Web site master; and Liz Hayden—I am lucky and privileged to have you as friends. To longtime friend and master food stylist Leslie Ware, who always goes the extra mile for me, thank you so much. To Ward Dilmore, for the wonderful theme music for *Ciao Italia,* which always transports me back to Italy. To the many volunteers without whom the show simply could not function, year after year. To my agent, Michael Jones, Esq., for years of guidance, advice, and friendship. To my husband, Guy, who has followed my career with love and understanding, and who has used his green thumb to plant and maintain my television garden. To my children, Beth and Chris, for sharing their insights and love, and to the underwriters of the series, both present and past, including kitchenetc.com, KitchenEtc., Waring Corporation, Colavita USA, Amtrak, Orthopaedic and Trauma Specialists, Whittier Health Network, Joe Pace and Son Grocer, Nynex (Bell Atlantic), Auricchio Cheese (Bel Gioso), Sini Fulvi Cheese, and King Arthur Flour. Without your financial support, *Ciao Italia* could not be produced. Last, to the *Ciao Italia* viewing family, thank you for spending time with me each week. I have enjoyed your company in the *Ciao Italia* kitchen and I look forward to welcoming you once again *nella cucina* through the pages of this book and in the years to come.

Special Thanks

Believing in something with all your heart is a great feeling, and having friends who believe in your goals and aspirations is pretty special, too. That is why I want to say a special thank-you to the underwriters of the eleventh season of *Ciao Italia,* some of whom have been with the series for quite awhile. To Bob Camp, Larry Job, and John Petrucelli of kitchenetc.com, thank you for your loyal and constant support over the years and for your enthusiasm in helping to make our programs shine. To the Colavita Pasta Company, especially Michele Scasserra, and the Colavita family, especially John Profaci Jr.—who are dedicated to producing authentic Italian products, including Colavita extra-virgin olive oil and pasta—thank you for allowing our series to spread the word about using these quality products in the recipes we create on the series. And a special thank-you to our newest corporate underwriter, Waring Consumer Products, makers of fine small kitchen appliances and other devices for the home cook, and to Lee Rizzuto, Paul Ackels, and Mary Rodgers. Without your sustained help, the lights could not shine in the *Ciao Italia* kitchen. *Mille grazie!*

Television has been called "a window to the world." A piece of phosphor-coated glass that, when excited by electrons, becomes a magically transparent, color-filled cornucopia of sights and sounds representing the world we live in.

For the past ten years, public television audiences have invited an energetic, friendly, warmhearted Italian cook through this "window" and into their homes to share a feast of Italian culture and cuisine. A marvelous mixture of ancient history, ripe plum tomatoes, fine art, superb wines, lots of laughter, and plenty of love—all mixed up into an unforgettable sauce, tossed with pasta, and served immediately.

What makes the creator of this sauce, Mary Ann Esposito, unique, and the book you're about to read equally unique, is that she doesn't even know this phosphor-coated "window" exists. As far as she's concerned, you're with her in her television kitchen when she sizzles the pancetta, tosses the arugula, and tells stories about growing up in an Italian family. You're with her in her books when she writes about Venice, Rome, Palermo, and Milan, and the friendly people and exquisite food she discovers there. You're with her in her world. She's with you in yours.

The way good friends should be.

If you've seen Mary Ann on television or read her many books, you know what I'm talking about. But if you haven't done either, and *Ciao Italia—Bringing Italy Home* is your first experience, then fasten your seatbelt. You're about to "eat" a multicourse meal of a lifetime. Savor each of the over one hundred fantastic recipes she's created. Relish each of the charming essays surrounding them. Oh, and one final suggestion: Don't read this book on an empty stomach. You'll want to go *nella cucina* and start cooking your favorites. Trust me on this, I've already started ("Beatrice's Mushrooms" was my first).

As the executive television producer for *Ciao Italia,* I have the best of both worlds of Mary Ann Esposito. I sit *a tavola* at her house and savor her mouthwatering, home-cooked recipes. I sit in a television control room and watch her prepare those same recipes for you while she looks into a camera and makes a hard job look easy. After more than ten years of working with Mary Ann, I can honestly say that there's nobody like her when it comes to opening up that phosphor-coated "window to the world" and waltzing straight into your heart.

What's her secret? You'll find it when you read this book. You'll find it when you watch her prepare the recipes on television. You'll find it in your own heart if you know where to look. Here's a hint: Just as the secret to Italian cuisine is fresh ingredients and simple preparation, Mary Ann's secret is honesty of soul and genuine love of family. In other words, Mary Ann's secret is Mary Ann.

Just as your secret is you.

Buon appetito, mangia bene e cent'anni.

Paul Lally
Executive Producer, *Ciao Italia*

Italy is my passion, my diversion, my consolation, and my joy. I am happiest when I can be immersed in Italian life, whether it is shopping in the outdoor food markets, having a cappuccino at *il bar,* fighting the traffic on the *autostrada,* or being a spectator at one of the many *sagre* (festivals) that are everyday occurrences. Being a frequent visitor has taught me that there is more to life than what is on our daily schedule of things to do. There is the art of living well, which necessitates the art of eating well. This book showcases some of Italy's culinary art as presented through the television series *Ciao Italia* and reflects over a decade of cooking with you in my television kitchen, with a focus on all-new recipes that are favorites from the regions of the Veneto, Emilia-Romagna, Tuscany, Campania, and Sicily. I chose to organize the recipes this way because these regions generalize the characteristic differences in northern, central, and southern Italian cooking. I also chose to highlight them because these are the regions that viewers of *Ciao Italia* want to know more about.

The major differences in the cooking of northern, central, and southern Italy have been described by culinary historians and food writers using words like *mangiapolenta* (polenta eaters) for the north, *mangiafagioli* (bean eaters) for the center, and *mangiamaccheroni* (macaroni eaters) for the south. These three major staples of cornmeal, beans, and pasta have done much to define regional differences, just as the use of olive oil as a primary cooking fat has defined southern Italian cooking and the use of butter has defined northern Italian cooking. All of this makes perfect sense when one studies the geographic and climatic differences of these regions and realizes that southern Italy is most conducive to the growing of olive trees and the production of olive oil, and the fertile grazing areas of northern Italy are just right for the dairy industry and the production of butter. With these facts in mind it is easy to understand the differences in regional cooking.

Italian home cooks and professional cooks whom I know and respect have never been advocates of complicated foods. Even today, when the culinary world seems determined to globalize and fuse many different tastes together on a dinner plate, it is refreshing to see that Italy keeps her boot firmly on the ground and does not allow shallow theatrics to rule in the kitchen. In almost every *ristorante, trattoria, osteria,* and private home kitchen that I have visited, the urge is strong among cooks to keep tradition alive, keep food preparation simple, and present it in its freshest form.

When my first book, *Ciao Italia,* was published in 1991, I wanted it to be viewed as an intimate look at the way Italian food was carefully prepared at home. When I wrote that book, I was still very much attached to the apron strings of my mother's and grandmothers' southern Italian cooking, and *Ciao Italia* became a library of many favorite family recipes, sprinkled with reminiscences about what it was like to grow up in an Italian home. With my second book, *Nella Cucina,* I untied those apron strings and began a long, investigative culinary journey that has taken me from the top of the boot to the bottom, as well as to the islands of Sicily and Sardinia. In the search for authentically prepared traditional foods I have been fortunate to have had enthusiastic help from many friends in Italy, who spent time with me in public markets and invited me into their kitchens to cook their regional dishes. Many professionals in the food and wine business proudly shared their expertise on everything from the curing of prosciutto di Parma to the making of *nocino* (walnut liqueur). Many days were spent in places where classic foods were made: Modena for balsamic vinegar, Bologna for lasagne, Palermo for *cassata* cake, Florence for *bistecca,* Rome for *abbacchio,* Venice for *riso,* Verona for polenta, and Reggio Emilia for classic ragù. I admired the reverence that Italians had for their regional specialties, their reference to their food as *genuina* (genuine), and their delight in sharing the products of the table with others.

Now, years later, I can reflect on how much I have experienced and grown in my appreciation and understanding of Italian food. It seems natural that I should tell the story of my fascination with Italian food by way of *Ciao Italia*.

Like a fairy tale, *Ciao Italia* began once upon a time on a fall day in 1989. As I sat in front of the television set and watched and listened as the very first episode was aired on public television, I said a silent prayer of gratitude and told myself that when you strongly believe in something dreams can come true. But on the day that I invited viewers into my kitchen for the first time, no one could have predicted that *Ciao Italia* would pique the interest of a national audience and sustain its attention for more than a decade. And it continues to do so!

The series was conceived at a time when I was working toward a master's degree in history, teaching cooking classes, and running a small catering business. That should have been enough on my plate, but I decided that maybe I could interest the local television station in my area in the production of a cooking show about Italian food. The timing seemed perfect. In the late eighties there was an explosion of interest in Italian food as it came to the forefront as the new "in cuisine," with its emphasis on living a healthy lifestyle, which was bolstered by the benefits of including olive oil, grains, vegetables, and fruits in the diet. So I made my move. I was mounting my own personal campaign and learning all that I could about olive cultivation and olive oil production. Frequent trips to Italy led me to small olive-oil-producing plants, and from this exposure it was just a matter of time before I was designing possible television segments based on cooking with olive oil.

In the 1980s professional chefs and editors of food magazines were expounding on the virtues of preparing and eating locally grown foods in season. This came as a great revelation to a lot of home cooks, but it has always been the cornerstone of Italian cooking, and it was this principle that proclaimed Italian cooking as wholesome and good. So my crutch for creating an Italian cooking show was authenticated by the media blitz that Italian food was receiving.

If I had lived in the Boston area, the idea of a television show dedicated to Italian cooking would have generated immediate interest because there were a lot of Italian and Italian-American communities that would have identified with what I wanted to do. But I lived in New Hampshire, the home of lobster and clams, a beautiful place in every way—where one did not come across authentic Italian cooking very often. Still, I was willing to take a chance and extend my enthusiasm and interest in Italian cooking to the community in which I lived. With encouragement from my husband, Guy, I drafted a proposal to the local television station for their review. After waiting for a few months for a reply, I found out what I already had anticipated the answer would be, which was that my proposal was assigned to the ideas-for-later-times file. Wishful thinking, I said to myself, and went back to my catering business, teaching, and traveling in Italy.

But things do happen when you least expect them to and about one year after my original proposal was sent, I received a phone call from the television station asking if I would do a pilot program in my kitchen. Agreeing to do this without any idea of what it actually entailed, I opened my kitchen on a hot August day to a crew of television people, each with a specific job to perform. Before I could comprehend the magnitude of the project, someone was combing my hair, slapping makeup on me, checking my voice level, rearranging my kitchen, removing plants and furniture from their customary places, and putting gel on my windows for the proper lighting. Cynthia Fenneman, the producer, gave me my first pep talk. "Remember," she emphasized, "relate to the camera, think of it as a person. Be natural, be funny, tell us something that we want to hear, and above all, be up, up, up!" It was then that I started to have doubts about what I was supposed to do.

The theme I had chosen was an Italian picnic that featured how to make simple antipasti, then a stuffed Calabrian loaf called a *pitta,* and strawberries in balsamic vinegar for dessert. No one had heard of balsamic vinegar at that time, and the notion of putting vinegar on strawberries . . . well, that's where the insight into Italian cooking was going to come in, and I would relish telling a television audience about the ancient and secret traditions under which this vinegar was made in Modena, Italy.

After what seemed like an eternity to get ready for the segment, I saw the camera zeroing in on me like a missile to a target, and with a lump in my throat and a racing heart, I heard the countdown. Mentally I steadied myself, knowing that in five seconds—no, three—I was on. I focused on the camera, eliminated the notion that hundreds, maybe thousands of people might watch this, and started talking. As I moved along from step to step, I had to keep track of time; I was used to looking at a clock for that, not someone kneeling in front of me out of camera range with black numbered signs that let me know how much time was left. It was extremely hot in the kitchen under the studio lights and we all realized it when one of the cameramen fainted, collapsing on the floor like a deflating balloon. Throughout the day it was stop and go as the television producers decided on angles, shots, pick-up shots, and camera moves, all very new to me. By six o'clock that evening we were still filming, and now we were about to move outside to wind things up on the lawn for our picnic theme. By the time we were all in place for the final shot, I was exhausted but I knew that I had to sell this show. With the food sprawled around me on a checkered tablecloth I mustered what energy was remaining in me, gave my best smile, raised a wineglass, looked into the camera, and said, "Until I see you *nella cucina* again, I'm Mary Ann Esposito, *ciao!*"

That was a wrap. Crew members scrambled to pick up cables, put away lights, gather microphones, shut down cameras, and head for home. It had been a long day for all of us. Cynthia patted me on the back and said, "We'll let you know what happens." I surveyed the disarray in the kitchen. My husband, Guy, had missed the whole event, and when he came home, he bounded upstairs to find me exhausted and huddled underneath the covers and said, "Honey, how was the shoot?" Even he was beginning to pick up television talk. I peeked out from under the covers, shook my head, and said, "Guy, I sure hope they don't do this series. This is just too much work, too many hours, too many people, too much mental strain." But deep down I knew that I wanted to do it; I wanted this challenge at that point in my life. Guy tucked the covers under my chin, gave me a kiss on the forehead, and I drifted off to dreamland and slept like a rock.

A short time later the pilot was aired for viewer comments, and they came back positive, so the search began for funding because this was public television and underwriting would have to come from the private sector.

Slowly I was learning what it took to do a cooking show. It was one thing to demonstrate my cooking at home, but translating it for a television audience would require more than culinary skills; it would require being able to communicate to a large but invisible audience and keep their interest while teaching them techniques, and it would require saturated concentration and stamina.

When the television station called to say they had secured adequate funding and were willing to produce the series, all kinds of projects were set in motion. We had to build a studio kitchen set; we had to assemble a television crew, and a volunteer crew to help in the prep area; we had to get the word out that I was cooking, and I had to think about giving a polished performance each time I stood in front of the camera. At one point I met with Ruth Lockhart, one of the original producers of Julia Child's show, to get some tips on how to "act" on television. Ruth had years of experience to draw on and I listened intently to her; one thing she stressed was for me not to talk too much. "People just like to watch instead of listen all the time," she said. I kept all these suggestions in the back of my mind, but I knew that I had to listen to my heart as well.

A television studio environment can be intimidating—all those lights, cables, cameras, boom mikes, not to mention the number of people it involves. Over the years, some twenty to twenty-five people at a time work on producing the series. Many of these people have been with me from the beginning and we are like a close-knit family.

While my television kitchen was under construction, I thought about what it was that I wanted to teach people about Italian food. I was "the talent" in television talk, a rather dehumanizing term but better than being called a star, which I was very uncomfortable with, and I let everyone know that they could just call me Mary Ann. It was my job to design content and execute coherent, entertaining and, as far as cooking was concerned, doable food segments. Starting with the basics, I developed thirteen show themes and came up with ideas for places where we could film "remotes," another television term referring to the pieces introducing the location of each show. Since our budget was so small, going to Italy was out of the question; I had to bring Italy here. I concentrated on areas around New England that had strong Italian neighborhoods; Boston, Providence, Ellis Island, and my grandmother Saporito's adopted home in Rochester, New York, were some of the destinations. In each locale I found someone whom I could talk to on camera about what I would be cooking later in the studio. These remotes became popular with viewers, so they have always been part of the formula for the series. In the eleven years since the start of *Ciao Italia,* we have filmed remotes from the Napa Valley to the center of Sicily.

I wanted to approach the preparation of Italian food for the television audience from the point of view of the Italians themselves.

Their dedication to freshness and simple treatment of food became my benchmarks. Their attitudes about taking the time to enjoy food at the table with family and friends became a theme that I used often. I wanted the television audience to know that Italians have a wonderful pattern to their meals, eating several small courses. And having traveled so much in Italy I wanted to incorporate their love for the land and vegetable and flower gardens. I felt that I should have at least two garden segments in the series. It was Guy on whom I relied to prepare the garden for these segments. I had no idea how much interest this would spark with viewers, but as soon as I started harvesting different varieties of Italian tomatoes, lettuces, squashes, eggplants, and other vegetables, and showing viewers how to prepare them, the requests came in for buying seeds! I could have started a garden seed business!

The criteria that I used for the series were to make authentic food with fresh ingredients that were readily available and to dispel the notion that the culinary borders of Italy were defined by pizza, lasagne, and spaghetti with meatballs. Instead I approached the series from a regional viewpoint, with the goal of highlighting the twenty regions of Italy; this would certainly keep me going for a while. One of my early statements on the show was "There is no such thing as Italian food, there is only regional food." I began using a map at the beginning of each segment to show the viewer what region of Italy we were cooking from that day.

Of course I had to concentrate on recipes that used ingredients that most people could find in their supermarkets. Not all viewers live in New York City, where fresh mozzarella cheese can be had any day of the week. I had to remember the folks in places like South Dakota and Tennessee, who did not have access to these ingredients, and make appropriate suggestions for substitutions. I was uncomfortable with this since I am a real believer in using authentic ingredients, and fortunately over the years more and more Italian products have become available nationwide and even on the Internet. I had seen too many cooking segments where, for example, the host based a recipe on an exotic ingredient such as a goat head (to make Greek soup)! I had to keep the program user-friendly, so I focused on products that I knew everyone had access to—pasta, vegetables, cheeses, fruits, and fish.

The first season was, as expected, a little bumpy; after all, we were all new at this and it would take time to smooth out the rough spots. We spent a lot of time determining how long the recipes would require to do on camera in "real time." Since I am a from-scratch cook, I had to condense what normally would take an hour to prepare into 26 minutes of real television time. This was manageable if you were making a salad or some simple antipasto, but I wanted to make things like Tuscan bread (*focaccia*), ravioli, and *porchetta* (roasted pork), foods that required prep time. This is where the collective and creative genius of the producers and director came in. One of the people that I am most indebted to and who has been with me for a long time is executive producer Paul Lally. Paul likes to refer to himself as my "television husband." It was he who set me free on the program, allowing me my personal space so that I had the freedom to listen to my heart, to do what I wanted to do. Paul's premise with *Ciao Italia* was that we were telling a story, and his incredible gift for staging the story of Italian cooking translated very well in a cooking program. Before we began taping each show, we would "walk through the recipes." My concern was that we did not cut out crucial cooking steps, and so it became a process of elimination; should we spend time showing how to chop an onion or explaining what "proofing" yeast meant? In other words, what should we assume that the viewer already knew?

Part of my intention was to give some historical background to the recipes and to identify the folklore behind them. So when I did a segment on chickpeas and mentioned that Cicero's name came from the word for chickpea because he had a mole on his nose that resembled this ancient food, people remembered these stories and repeated them to me when I saw them at book signings!

As I began to do multiple series of *Ciao Italia,* Paul made me realize that this was not just another cooking show, that it reached people on a number of levels. I have since come to realize that he was right. I see it in the letters I receive from viewers ranging in age from children to octogenarians, who each have their own story to tell about food and family. When I meet audiences at personal appearances, I hear wonderful stories of how watching *Ciao Italia* has actually brought families together, or delighted a stroke patient, or encouraged a youngster to dream of becoming a chef. In one letter from a mother in Pittsburgh, I relived her tragedy of losing her only son in a car accident. She wrote to tell me that her son loved to cook and was a fan of the show. Experiences like these send shivers up my spine and make me realize the power of television, of cooking, and of course of family.

Since I began the series, I have seen a great number of cooking shows come and go. Surfing through the television channels is like perusing a restaurant menu; you can choose French, Chinese, African, Moroccan, Jewish, Italian, or a host of other cuisines to whet the appetite. All these shows owe a great deal to Julia Child, who opened American minds to thinking about new foods; once Julia began cooking on television, dinner was no longer meatloaf and mashed potatoes. It was monkfish, glazed duck, and puff pastry that excited the television audience. Since then, cooking shows have become a popular form of entertainment in an era when, ironically, less and less cooking is done at home.

Because I am a television cook, I meet many people. When I am among fans I can see the true connection that *Ciao Italia* makes with them; the twinkle in their eyes, their smiles, hugs, and handshakes tell me that what we are doing is right.

I look forward to cooking more regional foods with you in my studio kitchen, and it is my most fervent wish that the cooking of Italy will be preserved for the future. *Buon divertimento!*

Part One

Favorite

Regional

Recipes

from

Italy

Antipasti

Gorgonzola e Marmellata (Gorgonzola Cheese and Marmalade)

Pecorino con Pere e Miele (Pecorino Cheese with Pears and Honey)

Salvia Fritta (Fried Sage Leaves)

Baccalà Mantecato alla Veneziana (Whipped Cod Venetian Style)

Primi Piatti

Risotto all'Amarone (Risotto in Amarone Wine)

Zuppa di Succa al Mascaron (Pumpkin Soup Mascaron Style)

Tortellini di Zucca con Ragù (Pumpkin-Stuffed Pasta with Meat Sauce)

Secondi Piatti

Ossobuco Tre Visi (Veal Shanks with Tomatoes and Porcini Mushrooms)

Cappone Agrodolce (Capon with Sweet-and-Sour Sauce)

Fiori Ripieni di Zucca con Calamari e Salsa di Peperoni Rossi (Stuffed Zucchini Flowers with Squid in Red Pepper Sauce)

Trota Intera al Forno con Patate (Whole Baked Trout with Potatoes)

Insalate

Caprino alle Nocciole con Insalatina di Melone (Hazelnut-Coated Goat Cheese and Cantaloupe Salad)

Insalata di Rucola, Fragole e Noci (Arugula, Strawberry, and Nut Salad)

Insalata di Lamponi, Ravanelli e Zucchini (Raspberry, Radish, and Zucchini Salad)

Dolci

Pandolce di Ezzelino (Ezzelino's Sweet Bread)

Crostata di Limone e Mascarpone con Salsa di Rabarbaro (Lemon and Mascarpone Cheese Tart with Rhubarb Sauce)

Pinza (Venetian Cornmeal Cake)

Torta di Cocco e Noci (Coconut Tart)

Torta di Cocco, Noci e Mascarpone (Coconut and Mascarpone Cheese Tart)

Tortelli Dolci di Amarena (Amarena Cherry Cookies)

Bussolà (Ring-Shaped Venetian Cookies)

Vetelangd (Danish Braided Pastry)

Venice is water, straw hats with red ribbons, gondolas, gondoliers, elaborate palazzi, fish, vaporetti, traghetti, radicchio, music, San Marco, pigeons, bells, high water, bridges, polenta, risotto, zaletti, fogasse, masks, fashion, glass, lions, Prosecco, Bellinis, un'ombra, cichetti, cisterns, campi, mosaics, baccalà mantecato, the Danieli, beautiful people, costumes, serenades, art, mazes, Harry's Bar, gardens, balconies, flags, maps, regattas, monuments, clergy, cappuccino, flowers, tiny grottoes, street shrines, statues, parades, and islands.

Of all the regions of Italy it is the Veneto in the northeast, with the Dolomite Mountains for a backdrop and the gorgeous scenery of Lake Garda, that grips me the most. And it is to the cities of Venice, Padua, Verona, and Vicenza that I am particularly drawn. Venice, *La Serenissima,* intrigues me with its aura of mystery and pageantry. Despite the many times I have been a visitor to this city of delight, each time is one of new anticipation . . . always a surprise. For me it is simply a miracle that this city could exist and thrive on water for centuries. Even more incredible is that, for hundreds of years, Venice has survived the ravages of a staggering number of visitors (myself included) whose very presence grinds down and wears away her underpinnings, walkways, and bridges, strains her natural resources, and tests the patience of the Venetians themselves. Everyone who cares about Venice knows that it is just a matter of time before all of this wear and tear, and the seeping waters that are slowly sinking the city, will have a serious impact.

Still we cannot stay away. Venice draws the visitor like a magnet. There is no perfect time to see it, for Venice cannot be seen the way it must, devoid of crowds so that its magnificent architecture can have the eye's total attention. Venice cannot be seen in one or even one hundred visits. It is a place so rich in culture on every level that it is in need of constant study and understanding. Where should one begin? My choice is the Correr Museum in Piazza San Marco. Many of the historic works of art housed in this fabulous museum give the visitor a visual time line of the history of Venice. You will learn that by the sixteenth century the Venice that we see today was completed. You will learn that Venice is an aggregation of many islands independent of one another, and that it was originally built on wooden pilings driven deep into the mud of the lagoon, and that over time these pilings have petrified. You will learn that Venice is one of the oldest examples of a republic; for more than a thousand years Venice has enjoyed a democratic way of life since the doges who ruled the republic were elected.

I choose to chisel away at seeing the real Venice a little bit at a time. When I am in the city, I make my way onto the crowded *vaporetto* (water bus) and ride down the Canale Grande to the *campi,* the neighborhoods that lurk out of view of the bustle of San Marco and the Grand Canal. It is in these neighborhoods that you will find the real Venetians, learn about their customs, and see how they live. And it is there that you will find the best foods of Venice—real Venetian specialties, not tourist food.

For instance, one of my favorite neighborhoods is Dorsoduro, meaning "hard back," because of the hard subsoil on which the area is built. Here you must visit the sixteenth-century building of Scuola Grande di San Rocco (Grand School of Saint Roch), to see the works of the great painter Tintoretto, who is famous for the technique known as *chiaroscuro* (light and dark) exhibited in his paintings. One of his most moving is the panorama of the Crucifixion. Dorsoduro is also home to many other impressive art museums, including the Peggy Guggenheim.

As far as learning about Venetian foods, the Rialto bridge area is a good place to start. All of your senses will be tantalized here; the fish market is a waterless sea of every imaginable fish, including sea bream, eels, squid, swordfish, flounder, shrimp, shark, soft-shell crabs, and red snapper. A sign at the entrance of the fish market warns that only fish of a certain size can be sold, while a Venetian proverb cautions that fresh fish has a twenty-four-hour life—after that it is simply not edible. From the fish market wander on along the neighborhood canals, where boats laden with vegetables and fruits are anchored for business. Vivid colors await you, from the maroon-red-and-white-striped radicchio di Treviso to the delicate green spring peas used for *risi e bisi* (rice and peas) to exotic-looking pears, peaches, and cherries.

By immersing yourself in the culture of the places you visit, you begin to get a sense of place and a sense of people. Years ago I stopped having daily long lunches in Venetian restaurants and opted for buying the local produce, some cheese and bread, and finding a door stoop where I could just sit and watch people come and go.

I try to incorporate many of the foods that I have enjoyed in Venice into my television series, and have made such classics as risotto, *fegato con cipolle* (liver and onions), and *sbrisolana* (cornmeal cake). It is a good feeling when I can translate the food experiences of travel in Italy to my television kitchen and ultimately to you, the viewer, so we can preserve culinary traditions together.

But I could never leave you with the impression that only Venice is worth seeing in the Veneto; you must also get to Verona to see the Arena colosseum, third largest in the world, where some of the best operatic works are performed with astounding, artistic set designs. Verona is most famous for the story of Romeo and Juliet, and visitors flock there to see her house and the balcony from which she uttered those famous words: "Romeo, Romeo, wherefore art thou Romeo?"

Two other cities in the Veneto worth visiting are Vicenza and Padua; they are not as frequently chosen as tourist destinations but nevertheless are rich in history and good food. Vicenza was the home of architect Andrea Palladio, the sixteenth-century genius whose buildings of clean, symmetrical form not only dot the city proper but the surrounding countryside. One of his most famous achievements is the Villa Rotonda, which also inspired the design of Monticello, Thomas Jefferson's Virginia home.

On a recent visit to Vicenza, I found the city to be eerily quiet. The shops were closed; there was no problem finding a parking space, and the townspeople were conspicuously absent. I wandered into Il Ceppo, a food emporium selling everything from olives to cornmeal cakes shaped like ears of corn. I asked why everything was so quiet. *"Signora, oggi c'è la festa della vergine di Monte Berico."* It was a feast day in honor of the Virgin of Monte Berico. Monte Berico is a fifteenth-century basilica dedicated to the Virgin Mary; a miracle took place there during the plague of 1428, when the Virgin appeared to a young girl to announce that the city had been spared the plague. Since that time the Vicentine have honored the Virgin with a special day, and pilgrims from all over Italy travel here to touch the silver image of the Virgin behind the main altar of the church.

The city of Padua invigorates me on many levels. It has one of the oldest universities in northern Italy, founded in the thirteenth century, and where Galileo taught physics. It has the serene Scrovegni Chapel with its breathtaking cycle of fresco paintings depicting the life of Christ executed by Giotto, the great Florentine artist. It has the impressive basilica of Saint Anthony of Padua, the saint who finds lost articles, and to whom my family regularly prays. It has the eclectic outdoor fruit and vegetable market in Piazza delle Erbe. A day spent in Padua's market becomes a composite look at the foods of the Veneto, with everything that you could possibly crave from Carniroli or Arborio rice that has been mixed and flavored with black truffles or dried asparagus and mushrooms for making risotto to plump and sturdy porcini mushrooms as big as footstools. There are fresh figs so stunning to look at that you cannot bring yourself to eat them, and there are seeds for your garden, and beautiful cut flowers, herbs, and plants.

Adjacent to all of this is the indoor market where vendors sell the popular *carne di cavallo* (horse meat), ground like hamburger, or shaved into small, splinter-like pieces. Fish, olive oils, *torrone,* cheeses, breads, fresh regional pasta, pastries, pizza, honey, cured and fresh meats, wild game, and fowl all exist side by side, and the list is still not complete.

I maintain that you can learn a lot about an area by what foods people buy, and Padua's market provides a wonderful inside look for the visitor. The local shoppers here take great care in selecting their foods. I was reminded of this the day I was looking for *pesca bianca,* the white peaches that I love. The woman who waited on me asked if I wanted hard or soft peaches, and then proceeded to handpick each one from the crate, inspecting every one for any sign of blemish before declaring them perfect and full of flavor. Several others who were waiting for me to finish my transaction complimented the woman for the quality of her fruits and vegetables, and then gave me an explanation of why white peaches are such a favorite in northern Italy. I cannot recall the last time that shoppers in my local supermarket spent time tying up traffic in the produce aisle with animated conversation about the virtues of artichokes and the best way to cook them!

In Italy this is a common occurrence, and watching a scene like this reaffirms my belief that food will always be the glue that keeps Italian culture together and thriving.

Gorgonzola e Marmellata
(Gorgonzola Cheese and Marmalade)

Serves 4

8 small slices good-quality bread, cut ¼ inch thick

8-ounce wedge Gorgonzola dolce, at room temperature

Good-quality jam, such as blackberry, blueberry, or orange marmalade

Gorgonzola cheese is that impressive and curious blue-veined cow's milk cheese that has been made for centuries in the town of Gorgonzola in the region of Lombardia. When aged for three months it is called dolce *for its mild flavor. Longer aging produces a sharper-tasting Gorgonzola known as sta-gionata. It is perfect eaten on its own, but it is also outstanding served with marmalade, as is the practice at alle Vecete, one of fifteen remaining original taverns in Verona. This elegant cheese arrives at your table spread on small pieces of bread with a surprising spoonful of* marmellata di mirtillo *on top. The marmalade is made from the myrtle berry. Simple as this savory antipasto sounds, its success will depend on the freshness of the Gorgonzola; if it smells strongly of ammonia it is past its prime. Have the cheesemonger cut your purchase from the wheel. Make sure the cheese is at room temperature before serving; the flavor will be at its best and it will be easy to spread. And use a good, dense bread like a baguette.*

Preheat the oven to 375°F.

Lightly coat a baking sheet with butter spray and arrange the bread slices in a single layer on the sheet.

"Toast" the slices in the oven until golden brown, about 4 to 5 minutes. Remove them to a cooling rack.

Spread each slice with some of the Gorgonzola and top with a little jam or marmalade. Arrange on a serving dish.

Did you know that Gorgonzola cheese will remain fresher longer if rewrapped in plastic wrap, and then in aluminum foil? Keep the cheese in the warmest part of your refrigerator. Too cold a temperature actually damages cheese flavor. If mold is present on the outside of the rind, cut it off and discard it—the cheese is still good.

Pecorino con Pere e Miele
(Pecorino Cheese with Pears and Honey)

Serves 4

Pecorino cheese is made from sheep's milk and every region of Italy produces its own distinctive variety. The taste varies from locale to locale depending upon the breed of sheep, the type of grasses that the sheep feed on, and the art of the formaggiaio *(cheesemaker). Pecorino cheese made from spring milkings is best because it is when the sheep are feeding on the freshest grasses. The texture and saltiness of the cheese depend on how long it is allowed to age. It is the cheese that is most familiar to Italian-Americans as a grating cheese for pasta and stuffings, but it stands on its own as an eating cheese and fits nicely into a host of dishes from antipasto to main courses to even dessert, as this recipe for Pecorino, pears, and honey attests. You can find regional types of Pecorino cheeses in Italian specialty stores or through mail order (see page 347).*

¼ cup honey

½ pound Pecorino cheese, cut into small slices

2 ripe Anjou or Bartlett pears, cut into slices

Heat the honey in small saucepan until it is hot but not boiling.

Arrange the cheese and pear slices overlapping on a serving dish.

Drizzle the honey over the cheese and pear slices and serve immediately.

Salvia Fritta
(Fried Sage Leaves)

Serves 4

¼ cup cornstarch

⅓ cup unbleached all-purpose flour

½ cup unflavored sparkling water

16 fresh sage leaves, stemmed

Vegetable oil for frying

Fine sea salt (see Note on opposite page)

Alla Borsa, one of my favorite restaurants, is in Valeggio Sul Mincio near Verona. It serves a wonderful antipasto of fried sage leaves—a crispy and delightful surprise, and very addictive. I eat them like potato chips. Make the batter at least 2 hours ahead of time to allow it to thicken sufficiently, and use only fresh sage leaves. Serve with chips of Parmigiano-Reggiano cheese, some cured olives, and a good Pinot Grigio wine. This makes a delicious and effortless beginning to an evening meal.

Sift the cornstarch and flour together into a small bowl. Stir in the sparkling water. Cover the bowl and let it stand for 2 hours.

Add the sage leaves to the batter and coat them well using a spoon.

Heat 1 cup vegetable oil in a heavy-duty saucepan until it reaches 375°F. Use a thermometer to test, or drop a bit of the batter into the oil; if it browns immediately the oil is hot enough.

Drop the leaves a few at a time into the oil and fry them until they are golden brown. With a slotted wooden spoon, remove the leaves to a dish lined with paper towels.

Sprinkle the leaves with salt and serve hot.

A Note About the Use of Sea Salt: I prefer to use sea salt for cooking because it is a natural product, extracted from sea water through evaporation. Sea salt, unlike iodized salt, retains traces of nutritional mineral content and has a clean taste. I find I use less salt in recipes if I use sea salt than if I use iodized salt. Sea salts vary in flavor depending on where they are from; French sea salt, for instance, will have a decidedly different taste from Sicilian sea salt. Sea salt comes in different grinds from fine to coarse flakes. In general cooking, I use the fine grind, but for some types of breads and pizza, I like a coarse grind. As with using salt in general, this is a matter of personal preference. My rule is "Less is more," so if you have a heavy hand with the salt shaker, you may want to add more salt than is called for in the recipes.

Baccalà Mantecato alla Veneziana

(Whipped Cod Venetian Style)

Serves 6 to 8 as an antipasto

1¼ pounds dried cod

1 bay leaf

½ cup extra-virgin olive oil

2 teaspoons finely minced
  Italian parsley

1 clove garlic, minced

Fine sea salt to taste

12 to 14 small baguette-size
  slices of good bread, cut
  ½ inch thick and toasted

This dish made from air-dried cod known as stoccafisso *is a specialty of Venice. Offer it at your next dinner party and listen to the accolades. The recipe's origins go back to ecclesiastical church law, which decreed that no meat could be eaten during the Lenten season. So creative Venetian cooks used dried cod to make this creamy version that is perfect atop little slices of crunchy toasted bread called* crostini. *The idea is to create a smooth emulsion by beating in dribbles of extra-virgin olive oil once the fish has been beaten into a pulp. This is best done with a traditional mortar and pestle. Seasoned with parsley and garlic, whipped cod makes a great antipasto. It will take a day or two to rehydrate the fish before using it in the recipe.*

Place the dried cod in a deep dish and cover it with cold water. Refrigerate. Change the water frequently; refilling with fresh water will allow the fish to rehydrate. It may make take a day or two for the fish to plump up.

Rinse and dry the fish and set it aside.

Place the fish in a pan, cover it with water, add the bay leaf, and cook the fish gently over simmering heat just until it easily flakes with a fork. Drain the fish, let it cool, then remove and discard any skin and cartilage. Cut the fish into chunks. With a mortar and pestle, pound the fish until it is mashed. Then, using a whisk, slowly beat in the olive oil drop by drop until a smooth thickness is obtained. If you don't have a mortar and pestle, use a food processor and add the olive oil slowly through the feed tube. The cod should have the consistency of mayonnaise. Stir in the parsley, garlic, and salt.

Spread the toasted bread slices with some of the cod mixture and serve immediately.

Pasta d'Aglio ed'Olio di Oliva
(Garlic and Olive Oil Paste)

Fulvia Sesani, a native Venetian and well-known cooking teacher, likes to keep a jar of garlic-flavored olive oil in the refrigerator so it is always at the ready. I like to chop garlic cloves as I need them and am always telling students that preminced and stored garlic develops too strong a flavor and smell. Nevertheless, here is Fulvia's recipe for those harried moments in the kitchen when there is no time to chop garlic. Fulvia recommends using a dense and fruity-tasting extra-virgin olive oil from the south of Italy, preferably from Puglia or Sicily. Don't be alarmed by the amount of salt called for in this recipe; Fulvia emphatically points out that the salt is a preservative that allows this garlic paste to be kept indefinitely. Use it in sautés and sauces, on crostini, *and with pasta. How do you know you are buying good garlic? Make sure the bulb feels heavy and has no brown spots. The paper surrounding the cloves should be white and tight around the bulb.*

2 pounds fresh garlic

2 cups sea salt

2 cups extra-virgin olive oil

Did you know that there are no olive trees in Venice because of the lack of sunshine? That is one reason why Venetians began to use butter as their preferred source of fat in their cooking.

With your hands, separate the bulb into individual cloves. Use the flat side of a chef's knife and press down on each clove to separate the garlic from the paper. The paper should easily peel away. Add all the cloves to the bowl of a food processor and pulse until the garlic is coarsely chopped. Add the salt and process for 30 seconds. While the motor is running, slowly add the olive oil through the feed tube until a pastelike consistency is formed.

Transfer the paste to clean sterilized jars; cap them and place the jars in the refrigerator.

The Veneto

Risotto all'Amarone
(Risotto in Amarone Wine)

Serves 4

6 tablespoons unsalted butter

1 tablespoon extra-virgin olive oil

1 white onion, peeled and diced

1 cup Arborio or Vialone Nano rice

2½ cups Amarone wine

1 cup hot chicken or vegetable broth

⅔ cup grated Parmigiano-Reggiano cheese

The Bottega del Vino in Verona is a restaurant noted not only for its regional representation of wines of the Veneto but also for its traditional dishes that use wine as an ingredient. My primo piatto (first course) of risotto all'Amarone (rice with Amarone wine) was perfect. Amarone means a big bitter wine. This is red wine made from dried grapes to concentrate the sugar content. Besides a wonderful flavor, this wine imparts an unusual lavender color to classic risotto. Be sure to use the proper rice for making risotto, one with a high starch content such as Arborio, Vialone Nano, or Carniroli. You can find them in Italian specialty stores and some grocery stores. Or see the mail order sources on page 347.

In a copper or other heavy-clad 2-quart saucepan, heat 2 tablespoons of the butter and the olive oil. When the butter is melted, stir in the onions and cook them over medium heat until they begin to wilt. Do not let the onions brown. Stir in the rice and coat the grains well with the onion and butter mixture. Pour in 1 cup of the wine and cook, stirring constantly, until all the wine is absorbed by the rice. Add the broth, stir, and let the rice absorb all the broth. Add the remaining wine in ¼-cup increments, letting the rice absorb each addition before adding more wine. The rice should be creamy and easy to stir and should flow freely off a spoon. It should not be lumpy or sticky and should not be mushy but *al dente,* meaning firm but cooked through. The Venetians say that the cooked rice must be *all'onda,* meaning "on the wave." In other words, the rice must be free flowing and liquid. The whole process should take about 18 to 20 minutes. Remove the saucepan from the heat, stir in the remaining butter and the cheese. Serve the rice at once.

Variation: Another classic version is to add diced squash (butternut is best) with the onions.

Do you ever wonder how restaurants can have your order of risotto ready in no time at all? The rice is partially cooked ahead of time and finished upon order.

Zuppa di Succa al Mascaron
(Pumpkin Soup Mascaron Style)

Makes 1½ quarts

1¼ pounds acorn squash, quartered and seeded

1½ pounds butternut squash, quartered and seeded

1 cup water

1 tablespoon butter

½ pound (2 leeks), washed, leaves trimmed and bulb sliced thin

2 cups chicken broth

½ cup nonfat half-and-half or light cream

⅛ teaspoon freshly grated nutmeg

Salt to taste

2 ounces radicchio, thinly shredded

Venice is an amphibious city whose aura of opulence evokes magic and mystery—its grand palazzi *are seemingly suspended on water. The food of Venice brings me down to earth; it is honest and homey if you know where to look, and it won't be in Piazza San Marco, where a sea of tourists congregate to marvel at the mosaic encrusted facade of San Marco or the Campanile (bell tower). No, the best food of Venice is found along the narrow streets in the small hidden neighborhoods called* campi. *One such place is al Mascaron Osteria on calle Longa Santa Maria Formosa 5225. The decor is rustic, with wooden tables and chairs that lend family-like atmosphere, and the clientele is strictly local—no English spoken here. So be prepared to practice your Italian while anticipating the arrival of true Venetian food. An outstanding dish is the* zuppa di succa, *smooth and creamy pumpkin soup with just a hint of freshly grated nutmeg that is served with a delicate shredding of cheery radicchio over the top. I have re-created the dish using a combination of acorn squash and butternut squash, which best approximates the taste of this wonderful soup.* Succa *is the Venetian dialect word for* zucca *(pumpkin).*

Preheat the oven to 350°F.

Place the squash quarters in a 15½×10¼-inch pan. Add the water, cover the pan with aluminum foil, and bake the squash for 45 minutes to 1 hour, or until soft. When cool, scoop out the flesh and place it in a food processor. Discard the skins.

In a soup pot, melt the butter over medium heat, then add the leeks and cook slowly over low heat just until the leeks are limp. Stir in 3 tablespoons of the chicken broth and continue cooking until the leeks are very soft. Transfer the leeks to the food processor with the squash and puree the mixture until it is blended. Slowly pour the broth through the feed tube with the motor running and process until the mixture is very smooth.

Transfer the soup to the soup pot. Stir in the half-and-half or cream, nutmeg, and salt. Heat the mixture slowly until hot. Ladle the soup into individual bowls and top with some of the shredded radicchio. Serve immediately.

Tip: To save time, cook and puree the squash several days ahead. Squash can be frozen for future use.

Did you know that radicchio is a member of the chicory family? This dark magenta lettuce with white veining and a slightly bitter taste comes from the Veneto region and is a favorite with Venetians, who use it not only raw in salads but also grilled with olive oil, stirred into risotto, steamed, and shredded as a garnish for fish, vegetables, and soups.

Il Nodo d'Amore

The Love Knot (Or the Legend of the Tortellino)

At the end of the thirteenth century, many wars were plaguing northern Italy, especially in the Veneto region near the banks of the Mincio River. A nobleman by the name of Viscount Giangalezzo, also known as the "Count of Virtue," ordered that a military encampment be set up overlooking the banks of the river that flowed through the town of Valeggio. When not guarding the river against foreign enemies, the troops were entertained by a court jester. One day he retold an old tale of beautiful nymphs who many said lived just beneath the surface of the water, but who because of an ancient curse were changed into horrible-looking witches condemned to live forever in the darkest recesses beneath the water. From time to time these witches broke the spell and emerged from the water to dance on the river's edge.

That night while the soldiers fell into a deep sleep, the witches appeared and danced among them. Only the captain of the troop, whose name was Malco, slept fitfully and awoke to see them. Startled by their presence, Malco tried to confront them, but they began to flee, and as they did one of them lost her cloak and was revealed as the beautiful nymph Silvia. Malco was immediately smitten by her and was cast under her spell, and during the course of one evening they professed their love for each other.

Malco begged Silvia to remain with him forever, but she needed to return to the river before dawn or she would change from a beauty into a haggard witch. Before disappearing she gave Malco a handkerchief tied in a knot as a symbol of undying love.

The next day the count gave a party in the palace for his troops.

He invited three dancers to entertain them. Malco, still reeling from his encounter with Silvia the night before, was stunned as he recognized her as one of the dancers.

Also at the party was the count's cousin Isabella, who had always been secretly in love with Malco. She could sense that something special existed between him and Silvia. She became so jealous that she immediately told her cousin that Silvia was not an invited performer but a witch. The count stopped the entertainment and immediately gave the order to arrest Silvia. Malco, wanting to save his love from harm, impetuously lunged between Silvia and the guards, allowing her time to escape. For his actions, Malco was seized and imprisoned.

That night Isabella came to Malco's prison cell to beg forgiveness from him for betraying Silvia, and while they were talking, Silvia emerged one more time from the river to rescue her beloved. Isabella felt such remorse, seeing their undying love for one another, that she helped them escape. When the news reached the count, an order was issued for the troops to find the lovers and kill them.

Silvia pleaded with Malco to come and live with her beneath the river, because only there could they be together forever. Malco did not hesitate for a moment, and he and Silvia disappeared into the Mincio, while on the banks of the river the troops found a golden knotted silk handkerchief, the symbol of two lovers for eternity.

This story is still retold today on the banks of the Mincio during holidays when a special pasta is made in honor of Silvia and Malco. The dough is golden yellow and as soft as silk. The pasta is cut and stuffed with a delicate filling, then tied into a knot. And this is the legend of the tortellino of Valeggio.

Tortellini di Zucca con Ragù

(Pumpkin-Stuffed Pasta with Meat Sauce)

Makes 12 to 13 dozen

DOUGH

1 recipe tortelloni dough
   (page 74)

FILLING

2 cups pureed pumpkin

½ cup fine bread crumbs

1½ teaspoons fine sea salt

¼ teaspoon freshly grated
   white pepper

1 cup grated Cortland apple

FOR THE RAGÙ
(makes 4½ cups)

¼ pound pancetta (Italian
   bacon)

1 medium onion, peeled and
   quartered

1 medium carrot, peeled

1 medium rib celery

2 tablespoons extra-virgin
   olive oil

1 pound ground pork or beef

Fine sea salt to taste

½ teaspoon freshly ground
   black pepper

½ cup dry red wine

Valeggio Sul Mincio, near Verona, is a quaint and historic town on the banks of the Mincio River. Every June, thousands gather there to take part in La Festa del Ponte (The Bridge Party) and La Festa del Tortellino (The Little Cake Party), which commemorates a battle fought on the bridge by Napoleon Bonaparte. To celebrate, everyone eats tortellini *(little cakes) at long communal tables that span the length of the bridge, and revel in a gigantic fireworks display over the river. One of the restaurants that cooks up its share of tortellini is Ristorante Alla Borsa. Overseeing the whole operation is Albena and her daughter, Nadia. Their tortellini are thin, silky pieces of sunflower-yellow egg pasta stuffed with three types of fillings; the ground beef, veal, pork, and kidney mixture is a wonderful balance of flavors, while the bright green spinach tortellini are a more delicate version filled with smooth-as-cream ricotta cheese. But for me the show-stopper is the plump tortelloni filled with pureed pumpkin and an apple* mostarda *(see page 74 for description of* mostarda di frutta*) served with a long-simmered ragù. The combination of the slightly sweet filling and the rich meat ragù is more than a fitting marriage of flavors. It is sure genius. To make pumpkin-filled tortellini, use pie pumpkin, acorn, or butternut squash. The tortellini can be made ahead and frozen for future use. (See the procedure for* Tortelloni di Zucca *on page 74.) This is a special first course for a fall or winter dinner. To save steps, the pumpkin filling and the ragù can be made several days ahead.*

Follow the procedure for baking the pumpkin in the recipe for Tortelloni di Zucca (page 74).

Mix the filling ingredients together in a bowl and refrigerate until needed.

To make the ragù, mince the pancetta, onion, carrot, and celery together. Set aside.

Heat the olive oil in a medium-size earthenware, cast iron, or other heavy-duty pot. Over low heat, cook the minced vegetable mixture, uncovered, for 30 minutes. Add the ground meat, salt, and pepper and brown the meat completely. Stir in the wine and let it completely evaporate. Stir in the tomatoes, cover the pot, and cook the ragù over very low heat for 45 minutes. Stir in the milk or cream and heat through.

14 ounces tomatoes, peeled and cut into pieces

½ cup milk or cream

Make, cut, and roll the dough as for Tortelloni di Zucca (page 75). To form the tortellini, cut the sheets of dough into 1½-inch circles with a cookie cutter or glass.

Place a scant ½ teaspoon of the filling in the center of each circle. Fold the dough in half over the filling to make a half moon, and pinch the edges closed. Then bring the two opposite ends together and pinch them together.

As you make them, line the tortellini up on cookie sheets as described on page 75. To freeze for future use, follow the directions given on pages 75–76.

For 4 to 6 servings, heat 2 cups of the ragù and keep it warm while the tortellini are cooking. The remainder of the sauce can be frozen or used in other recipes, such as those for cooked rice.

Bring 4 to 6 quarts of water to a boil in a pasta pot. Add 1 tablespoon of fine sea salt and 4 dozen of the tortellini. Cook for no longer than 2 minutes. Scoop the tortellini out of the water and transfer them to a warm, shallow platter.

Pour the sauce over the top and gently mix with 2 large spoons. Serve immediately.

Note: Use a dab of water to help seal the edges of filled pasta dough.

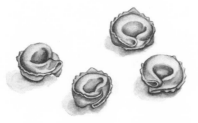

The World of Verona

"There is no world without Verona walls, but purgatory, torture, hell itself." So declared Shakespeare, and that statement was confirmed for me by an extended visit to one of the most famous cities for lovers. Verona, one of the wealthiest and most elegant cities in all of Italy, is situated on the Adige River and deserves all the praise it gets. Many associate it with the tragic love story of Romeo and Juliet, and crowds of tourists make pilgrimages to Verona just to see her house (Casa di Giulietta) at 27 Via Cappello. In the small courtyard below the famed balcony, lovestruck couples pose next to a bronze statue of Giulietta, placing their hands on her right breast, said to be good luck for would-be lovers. The walls of the courtyard and Juliet's house are smeared in a wallpaper of graffiti with names of lovers from all over the world, and odes to loves both won and lost.

I prefer to see the more down-to-earth Verona through the eyes of my good friend Giulia Cocco, who lives there. My fascination with the city started in the Piazza Erbe, the herb square, which is built on the site of an ancient Roman forum. The piazza radiates energy in many forms. It is surrounded by fabulous medieval architecture, buildings that were once the proud residences of the ruling Scaligeri family. Now, beside them, vendors, protected from the heat and sun by umbrella-shaded stalls, sell everything from fruits and vegetables to shoes and leather belts. Giulia piques my interest in the green-as-grass Camone tomatoes, a favorite with the Veronese for salads. Starving artists, some quite good in my opinion, stand with their easels on street corners painting realistic impressions of the city in *acquerello* (watercolors), while curious crowds gather around to critique every brushstroke. Shoppers invade the many chic clothing, jewelry, and gift shops, and enticing pastry shops and *ristoranti* give one the perfect reason to stop for something to eat, drink, and people watch.

Another special square for me is Piazza dei Signori with its pensive statue of Dante Alighieri, medieval author of the *Divina Commedia* (*Divine Comedy*), who was granted refuge in Verona by the ruling Scaligeri family after he was exiled from his native Florence. In college and graduate school, Dante was my hero as I struggled to translate and understand the *Divine Comedy.* Gazing up at his severe face, I feel regret that he was so shunned by his native city but happy that Verona recognized his genius. Giulia says that in the summer this square is filled with people just socializing and retreating from the heat of the day.

In Piazza Bra, one of the most revered sites is the Arena, Verona's Roman amphitheater, which is the third largest of its kind in the world after the Colosseum in Rome and Capua near Naples. Here some of the greatest operas are staged beginning in June. Sitting on the cool stone steps of the Arena I watch, mesmerized, as spectacular sets are erected, re-creating backdrops of faraway cities on the upper levels of the colosseum. When the opera season ends, the Arena becomes an area where the *presepio* (nativity) figures are sold at Christmastime.

One of the nice things about having friends in Verona is that they know where to enjoy the *real* food of the city, and I always make it a point to search out places where there is no English spoken . . . that's where local food, and local color, will be found. And so it was with lunch at Osteria Vecete, one of only fifteen remaining *osterie* left in Verona. Originally an *osteria* was a small inn where men socialized and drank wine, but now it is a small eating establishment frequented mostly by the local clientele. Osteria Vecete has an unpretentious interior with wooden tables and chairs and dark woodwork. On the walls are maps detailing where the remaining *osterie typiche* are located.

We ordered typical local antipasti that included a wonderfully creamy Gorgonzola cheese spread on small pieces of toasted bread called *crostini,* and topped with a marmalade made from myrtle berries (see recipe on page 10). The combination was exquisite. We also sampled *baccalà* (salted cod) served over wedges of polenta, and drank local wines from Azienda Otella Montresor, a winery near Verona and Lake Garda.

After lunch Giulia leads me to another feast, but this one is for the eyes and the soul—the beautiful Giardino Giusti, one of the finest examples of Renaissance gardens in Italy. Upon entering this sculptured sanctuary, a meditative calm soothes and envelops you, a sharp contrast to the noise of the city just beyond the gate. Stately cypress trees soar through the sky and define this beautiful garden started by Agosto Giusti. A maze of perfectly manicured boxwood hedges weaves and curves at every turn with stone statues here and there. There is a palace at the very top of the garden, a private residence, and one's curiosity is teased by the many side paths, grottoes, porticoes, and overhangs as the climb to the top gets steeper. Out of breath upon reaching the top, I am rewarded with the most panoramic vista of the city and of the garden. On the way down there are places to sit and listen to a symphony of birds and take in the perfume of gorgeous lemon trees and other plantings. I leave feeling that I have just had the best massage of the mind.

Hungry again, Giulia suggests that we stop at the Bottega del Vino, a historic and popular local spot featuring the wines of the Veneto and traditional foods. The warm interior is cozy with mustard yellow walls and dark wood paneling. The walls display vintage wines from the Veneto. Giulia tells me that there are sixteen DOC wines from this region. DOC refers to a governing body that sets the standards for wine production. Along with the wines there are sayings written on the walls like "Wine is the soul of poetry" and "Friends and wine need to be old." I am in complete agreement. My favorite wine is Amarone, a gutsy dry red made from Valpolicella grapes. Some of the other famous wines of the Veneto region include Soave, Bardolino, and the sparkling white Prosecco, used to make that popular Venetian drink called a Bellini, which is a mixture of three parts Prosecco to one part peach juice.

Looking at the menu, I am tempted to try the traditional dishes, which include polenta with *salame,* or *pancetta* with Gorgonzola and lard. There is also *bigoli,* a thick type of tubular whole-wheat spaghetti similar to *bucatini* that is served with *anatra* (duck) in a wine sauce, and *Risotto all'Amarone* (page 16), Arborio rice cooked in red wine. I know I am having the risotto. Giulia nods her approval and asks if I have ever had rice cooked in wine with pumpkin, another local specialty. Sounds good, and I scribble in my notebook that I must try making it for an episode of *Ciao Italia.* The risotto arrives and is a shocking lavender color; in a final flourish, the waiter sprinkles it with grated Parmigiano-Reggiano cheese and bids me *buon appetito!*

Now that I am satiated, Giulia insists that I must see the church of San Zeno Maggiore, the sanctuary of Verona's patron San Zeno, the city's first bishop. The church is a masterpiece of Romanesque style, and was built in the twelfth century. The facade jumps out at you with high marble reliefs of biblical scenes, and the miracles performed by San Zeno are depicted on the bronze doors. In the vaulted crypt San Zeno rests, and all who come here pray before his tomb and seek his powerful intercession.

Each day I feel more at home in Verona; I love the drive of the people, the vitality of the city, the progressive thinking, and the sheer elegance of the place. And the more I see the more I agree that Shakespeare made a statement of fact when he said: "There is no world outside the walls of Verona."

Ossobuco Tre Visi
(Veal Shanks with Tomatoes and Porcini Mushrooms)

Serves 4

1 ounce (about ¾ cup) dried
   porcini mushrooms

¾ cup hot water

1 tablespoon extra-virgin
   olive oil

¼ pound pancetta (Italian
   bacon), diced

1 carrot, scraped and diced

1 onion, peeled and diced

1 stalk celery, diced

⅓ cup minced fresh parsley

1 large clove garlic, peeled
   and thinly sliced

2½ pounds veal shanks

One 28-ounce can whole
   plum tomatoes

¾ cup dry red wine

3–4 sprigs fresh thyme

Grinding of black pepper

1½ teaspoons fine sea salt

*I spend a lot of time in Italy gathering all kinds of information for my series, in areas that are not often tourist destinations. One of my favorite places is the city of Vicenza, home of the famous architect Andrea Palladio. It is difficult to walk around this city without feeling his presence everywhere in the magnificent buildings designed by him. One of the most breathtaking buildings is the Teatro Olympico, the oldest indoor theater in Europe. In the Piazza dei Signori Palladian architecture surrounds you and it is clear that the Vicentine are very proud of their native son. They are also proud of their cuisine, and at Ristorante Tre Visi, Corso Palladio 25, the food reflects the cooking of Vicenza and the Veneto region. I had a wonderful lunch there prepared by Chef Luigi, who could not have been more hospitable. For antipasto I sampled air-dried cod (*stoccafisso*) cooked in the Vicentine style with onions, anchovy, and cheese as well as* baccalà mantecato, *dried cod in the Venetian style, made by pounding the cod until creamy while adding extra-virgin olive oil drop by drop. This was served on crostini. The second course was* ossobuco, *veal shank, long simmered in tomato sauce with porcini mushrooms. Ossobuco means "a bone with a hole in it," and the marrow in the center of the bone is considered a delicacy. In this preparation the veal is cooked beginning with the* quattro evangelisti *(see page 124) and then simmered in tomatoes and wine. This is a great dish for company because it can be made several days ahead. Serve it with creamy Polenta (page 262).*

Preheat the oven to 300°F.

    Place the porcini mushrooms in a bowl, pour the hot water over them, and set them aside.

Heat the olive oil in a heavy-duty ovenproof 12×3-inch sauté pan. Stir in the pancetta, carrot, onion, celery, parsley, and garlic, and cook over medium heat, stirring occasionally, until the vegetables just begin to soften.

Push the mixture to one side of the pan and add the veal shanks. Brown the shanks on both sides, then redistribute the vegetable mixture around them.

In a bowl mix the tomatoes and wine together. Pour the liquids slowly over the veal shanks. Add the thyme, black pepper, and salt. Cover the pan and bake the shanks for 1½ to 2 hours.

Halfway into the cooking stir in the porcini mushrooms and their liquid. Cover the pan and continue cooking until the meat is fork-tender. Serve the ossobuco over polenta (recipe on page 262).

Cappone Agrodolce
(Capon with Sweet-and-Sour Sauce)

Serves 6 to 8

SAUCE
(makes 1¾ cups)

½ cup golden raisins

¾ cup honey

Grated zest of 4 oranges

4 tablespoons wine vinegar

½ teaspoon fine sea salt

7 tablespoons extra-virgin
olive oil

FOR THE CAPON

1 pound arugula, stemmed,
washed, and dried

One 9-pound whole capon,
washed and dried

3 ribs celery, washed and
trimmed

2 large carrots, scraped

1 large onion, peeled and cut
into quarters

1 large bay leaf

20 whole cloves

12 whole black peppercorns

Fine sea salt to taste

3 tablespoons minced fresh
parsley

One day, while staying at my friend Giulia's house in Verona, I received a phone call from Marilisa Allegrini, inviting me to visit the Allegrini winery for a private tasting and lunch. What a perfect plan for a picture-perfect day in the Veneto region of Italy. Naturally I said yes, and it did not take much coaxing to get Giulia to come along as well. Marilisa is the sixth generation of her family to make wine, and we sampled Recioto della Valpolicella Amarone, as well as others. Invented by the Greeks, Recioto is a method of picking and drying grapes until they are shriveled; this concentrates the sugar, producing wine with deeper flavor. After the tasting we had a delightful lunch at Trattoria alla Coa. A sampling of the house pastas included homemade tagliolini, *strands of pasta as thin as dental floss dressed in a light tomato sauce. Agnolotti, similar to ravioli, were next; these were filled with a fine mixture of roasted veal and prosciutto di Parma and served in a butter sauce with specks of fresh black truffles grated over the top. When fresh truffles are in season these agnolotti are referred to as* gioielli— *jewels. The second course,* cappone agrodolce, *capon in a sweet-and-sour honey sauce, stays in my mind as a culinary triumph. Capon is a castrated male chicken that, when cooked, produces a delicate-textured meat with mild flavor. The delicacy of the meat paired with the sweet sauce and topped with sharp-tasting shreds of arugula was extraordinary. Order capons from a butcher. If you do not have a butcher, ask your grocery store to carry them or order them by mail from Balducci's (see the mail order list, page 347). This dish can also be made by substituting a free-range chicken such as one from Bell and Evans. Here is my re-creation of this wonderful dish.*

To make the sauce, pour the raisins into a small bowl and cover them with boiling water. Let the raisins soak for 1 hour. Drain the raisins and set aside.

In a separate bowl mix the honey, zest, wine vinegar, and salt. Whisk in the olive oil a few drops at a time until an emulsion, or thick blended sauce, is obtained. Transfer the sauce to a small saucepan and stir in the raisins. The sauce can be prepared up to three days in advance.

To prepare the capon, first stack the arugula leaves in small bunches on a cutting board. Roll the leaves up tightly like a cigar and with a knife cut thin crosswise strips no wider than ⅛ inch. These strips are known as a chiffonnade. Transfer the chiffonnade to a small bowl, cover with plastic wrap, and refrigerate.

Place the capon and the rest of the ingredients—except for the parsley, grapes, and arugula—in a 10-quart soup pan. Fill with water to cover the ingredients. Cover the pot and bring it to a boil. Lower the heat to simmer and cook the capon for 1½ to 1¾ hours, or until a fork inserted near the leg bone can easily detach it. As the soup cooks, use a skimmer to remove any foam that accumulates on the top of the broth.

Remove the capon to a dish and let cool. Strain the soup into a large bowl, pressing on the solids to extract the juices. Discard the solids. Stir in the parsley and adjust for salt. The broth can be used as is, with pasta or vegetables, or frozen for future use.

Cut the capon into serving-size pieces, removing the bones, and place the pieces on a platter.

Slowly reheat the sauce. Stir in the grapes. Transfer the sauce to a sauce bowl. Serve the capon with some of the sauce and sprinkle a little of the chiffonnade over the top.

2 cups seedless green grapes, washed and stems removed

Did you know that capon is a traditional dish served on Christmas Day in Emilia-Romagna and in other regions of Italy, and that it is traditional to have *cappelletti* (little pasta hats) filled with three types of ground meat served in capon broth?

Note: The capon can be cooked a day ahead, removed from the broth and wrapped in foil and refrigerated. Chill the broth overnight to make it easier to remove any fat that has accumulated at the top of the broth.

A Venetian Palazzo

*V*enice hypnotizes me and gives me goose bumps. A place almost too fantastic to be true, it appears like a mirage of sumptuous palaces, and regal churches capped with great domes that are seemingly suspended on water. Venice, Venezia, has been called by many names, from *La Serenissima* to the Disneyland of Italy. My first visit to this city of intrigue was to interview well-known Venetian native and cook Fulvia Sesani, whose mission it was to preserve the art of Venetian cooking and to teach others about it in her ancestral home, known as the Palazzo Morosini. Her cooking classes could be had by anyone with an appetite to know the secrets of making such Venetian specialties as a good risotto, *fegato con cipolle* (liver with onions), or *baccalà montecato* (whipped cod).

Now, years later, I had come back, this time to let the charms of the city and the lagoon envelope me at a slower pace. I had not forgotten how mesmerizing a ride it was by water taxi from Marco Polo Airport down the Canale Grande (Grand Canal). As the expanse of water came into view, palazzi of every description and color—some with brilliant mosaic decorations on their facades—provided spellbinding entertainment and delight on either side of the canal. It was almost too much for the eye to see. Many of the palazzi, some in desperate need of repair, were owned by wealthy foreigners, as many Venetians found them too costly to maintain. Some have been transformed into art galleries, some rented out for private functions, others provided summer vacation rentals, and some were still in family ownership from centuries gone by. One such palazzo, Palazzo Tiepolo in Campo San Polo, gave me the unforgettable experience of what it must have been like to live in grand style centuries ago. Palazzo Tiepolo is lovingly maintained by its present owners, Piero and Silvana Mainardis, and upon entering the great expansive hall, they make quick work of putting one at ease in such gigantic surroundings. Piero is tall with piercing eyes and graying hair that gives him a distinguished look; in his blue blazer and cloud-white shirt, he projects a good example of his profession as an architect and city planner.

Silvana, a tall, handsome woman with fair features, is an art gallery owner, a wine maker, and a fabulous cook. My visit began with a tour of the major rooms of the palazzo. Artwork, both contemporary and traditional, lines the great walls, and delicate and exquisite Venetian glass chandeliers light the way in every room. The walkabout was made more pleasurable while we enjoyed glasses of sparkling Prosecco wine and samplings of *crostini* topped with pheasant pâté.

Dinner was served in a dining room dripping with gilded woodwork and beautiful antique wallpaper that transported me right to the Renaissance. Fragile and intricately made Venetian glass chandeliers in soft hues of blue, rose, and green rained subdued candlelight down on us, and provided the only illumination in the room. On the long dining room table, which spanned the length of the room, was an exceptional fall centerpiece of golden pears, perfect pumpkins, and mahogany-colored chestnuts that set the tone for Silvana's harvest dinner. The dinnerware, also Venetian glass, was an exquisite rosy pink color.

Silvana is a collector of antique Venetian recipes and all the dishes served that evening were prepared by her. We settled in for dinner seated on beautiful antique chairs with rich brocade fabrics. Silvana had thought of everything right down to the calligraphy place cards, and it was my feeling that she and Piero wanted us to experience Venetian hospitality at its best. We began with light and sweet-tasting nuggets of pumpkin gnocchi flavored with nutmeg, a reminder that Venice was the center of the spice trade during the Renaissance, a trade that made her rich, powerful, and envied. *Anatra* (roast duck), our second course, was accompanied by sweet glazed Moscato grapes that were so translucent and fragile-looking that they could almost have passed for Venetian glass as well. A vibrant green salad simply dressed with extra-virgin olive oil and wine vinegar followed, and the meal ended with *Monte Bianco,* pureed chestnuts with sweetened whipped cream that was garnished with whole caramelized chestnuts.

Throughout the meal the conversation was of the foods we were enjoying; it was as if our hosts took us on an analytical and historical tour of the foods of the Veneto, explaining that most of the produce found in the markets comes from the farms in the lagoon. Their appreciation and reverence for the basic necessities of life was profound.

This perfectly executed Venetian dinner was followed by more conversation as we retired to the *salotto* (drawing room), where we sipped espresso and lemon tisans, and I savored what life must have been like in *La Serenissima.*

Fiori Ripieni di Zucca con Calamari e Salsa di Peperoni Rossi

(Stuffed Zucchini Flowers with Squid in Red Pepper Sauce)

Serves 4

Mixing fish with cheese has always been frowned upon in Italian cooking because of the competition in flavors. But in Verona at Osteria la Fontanina, a quaint restaurant with only twelve tables, it is done—and very successfully—with zucchini blossoms stuffed with whipped Provolone and ricotta cheese, served with grilled squid on a bed of sweet red pepper sauce. This luscious dish can be made in stages; the sauce and filling for the zucchini blossoms can be made several days ahead. Buy squid no more than six inches in length; it will be easier to cook and more tender than its larger cousin. Squash blossoms are usually available in the summer months at farmers' markets or in Italian markets. If you grow zucchini you will have your own supply; harvest the blossoms when closed.

To make the sauce, place the peppers on a lightly greased broiler pan and broil them, turning occasionally, until they are blackened all over. Transfer the peppers into a large paper bag, close the bag tightly, and allow the peppers to steam and cool for 20 minutes to loosen their skins.

Peel away the blackened skin and discard it. Remove the core and wipe out the seeds with paper towels. Place the cleaned peppers in the bowl of a food processor and puree until the peppers are smooth. Set aside.

In a sauté pan, melt the butter and cook the garlic over medium heat until it softens. Add the pepper puree and mix well. Lower the heat and gradually stir in the heavy cream or half-and-half. Add the nutmeg, salt, and pepper, and cook for about 5 minutes,

RED PEPPER SAUCE

4 large sweet red peppers

4 tablespoons unsalted butter

2 cloves garlic, minced

1 cup heavy cream or half-and-half

1 teaspoon grated nutmeg

1½ teaspoons fine sea salt

¼ teaspoon freshly ground black pepper

¼ cup finely minced fresh basil or thyme

FILLING FOR BLOSSOMS

8 zucchini blossoms at least 4 inches long, washed and dried

1½ cups ricotta cheese, well drained

½ cup grated sharp Provolone cheese

1 tablespoon finely minced Italian parsley

¼ teaspoon fine sea salt

The Veneto

35

Grinding of coarse black
   pepper

1 egg white

2 tablespoons butter, melted

THE SQUID

8 cleaned whole squid about
   6 inches long

Juice of 2 large lemons

2 tablespoons extra-virgin
   olive oil

¼ teaspoon fine sea salt

stirring occasionally. Stir in the basil or thyme. Keep the sauce covered and warm.

To prepare the blossom, carefully open each blossom, remove the center pistil, and discard it. Set the blossoms aside.

Preheat the oven to 350°F.

Lightly butter a casserole dish and set it aside.

In a bowl with a hand mixer, whip the ricotta cheese with the Provolone cheese, parsley, salt, pepper, and egg white until very smooth and fluffy-looking. With a spoon divide and fill the center of each blossom with some of the filling. Close the petals and place the blossoms side by side in the casserole dish.

Pour the melted butter over the top of the blossoms. Cover the dish with aluminum foil and bake for 30 minutes. Keep warm while the squid is cooking.

To prepare the squid, begin by placing it in a zipper-lock plastic bag with the lemon juice, olive oil, and salt. Close the bag and shake the squid to coat them in the mixture. Set aside.

Preheat an oven broiler or grill. Remove the squid from the plastic bag and place them on a broiler rack or grilltop and cook them for about 5 minutes, turning them once during the cooking time.

Pour half of the red pepper sauce on a serving platter and arrange the squid on top of the sauce. Surround the dish with the zucchini blossoms and serve immediately. Pass additional sauce on the side.

Trota Intera al Forno con Patate
(Whole Baked Trout with Potatoes)

Serves 2

Take the #1 vaporetto (water bus) to Piazza San Marco and head straight for the rooftop restaurant at the Danieli, one of Venice's venerable hotels. Marvel at one of the most spectacular sights in the whole world, the expanse of the Canale Grande, as you take your seat. Order the branzino al forno con patate, *which is a delicate-tasting sea bass baked with paper-thin potatoes. At the Danieli, the fish is presented whole, sitting proudly upright on the potatoes. I asked the waiter how the fish managed to stay upright and not collapse in the oven, and he quickly pulled a whole potato from the slit underside of the fish. What a great idea, and it works! I tried it with farm-raised trout and the results were perfect. This is an effortless and great presentation dish for company since the potatoes can be cut and held in cold water until ready. Any whole fish suitable for baking will do. Have the fish gutted by the fishmonger but leave the head on.*

1 teaspoon plus
    4 tablespoons unsalted
    butter, melted

1 large Russet potato, peeled
    and cut into paper-thin
    slices, and 1 small whole
    potato, scrubbed

1 tablespoon plus 1 teaspoon
    freshly squeezed lemon
    juice

½ teaspoon fine sea salt

¼ teaspoon fine black
    pepper

2 tablespoons minced Italian
    parsley

1¼ pounds whole, gutted
    farm-raised salmon trout
    or sea bass

Preheat the oven to 425°F.

Brush a 14×8×2¼-inch-deep au gratin dish or similar Pyrex baking dish with 1 teaspoon of the melted butter. Use half of the potato slices to make an overlapping layer in the dish.

Combine the remaining butter with 1 tablespoon of the lemon juice, the salt, pepper, and parsley. Pour 1½ tablespoons of butter mixture over the potatoes. Make another layer with the remaining potato slices and pour another 1½ tablespoons of the butter mixture over them.

Open the fish cavity and insert the whole smaller potato. If necessary cut a small piece off the bottom of the potato so it does not roll before positioning it in the cavity of the fish. Place the fish

The Veneto

37

on top of the potatoes in the baking dish and brush the fish with the remaining butter.

Bake the fish for 15 to 18 minutes. Do not overcook it or it will become dry. Use a fork to gently poke the sides of the the fish and if it flakes easily, remove it at once.

Present the dish at the table for all to admire, then take the fish away and place it on cutting surface. Remove the whole potato from the fish cavity and discard it. Cut the head off with a fish knife or a sharp knife and discard it. Gently pull the fish skin away from the body, starting at the tail. It should peel off easily. Discard the skin. Fillet the fish, removing the bones, and serve it with some of the potatoes.

How To Cook an Eel

One cold, dank morning in Venice, I decided to meander through the city's famous market, the Rialto. The bounty of colorful fruits and vegetables was impressive, but it was the fish market that lured me. Here the varied fishes that teem under the Adriatic Sea make a brilliant display in the market, with hues ranging from scarlet red to midnight black. Among the fish on display were sea bream, swordfish, flounder, shrimp, shark, soft-shell crabs, red snapper, and John Dory, also known as St. Peter's fish. I made my way through the crowded market, listening to the fishmonger trying to entice customers to the catch of the day. I noticed a lot of commotion over by the eel vendor. Eel is one of the most delicate fish I have ever eaten. I remember it on the table at Christmas Eve, its snow-white flesh cooked with tomatoes and spices in a light broth. And I'll never forget the succulent taste of roasted eels with myrtle leaves that I enjoyed in Sardinia.

In Venetian dialect, eels are known as *bisato*. Buying them is no easy task, and it takes a critical eye and nose to single out the best ones. In the Rialto market, eels, which resemble black, slippery serpents, slither and swim from side to side in large basins of water, unaware of their impending fate. Customers examine them closely, taking their time to make sure that they are plump and shiny enough. One serious-looking gentleman finally makes a decision, and the fishmonger takes hold of the eel and swiftly cuts off its head. Then he drives a nail into the tail end of the eel to hold it in place, since it continues to squirm long after decapitation. The eel is slit down the center, and the entrails are removed. It is cut into pieces, unskinned to keep it moist for grilling. I asked the man purchasing the *bisato* how he planned to prepare it. His face softened at my interest. He explained that first the pieces must be kept in water and vinegar overnight. The next day the pieces are removed from the water and vinegar solution and dried. They are then brushed with olive oil and sprinkled with aromatic rosemary before being placed on a sizzling hot grill and cooked until the skin crackles and the smell of rosemary fills the air. A squeeze of lemon juice and a little salt is all that is needed to enjoy this delicate fish.

I shake his hand and thank him for the information. Then, in jest, I invite myself to his home for dinner. He lets out a belly laugh, and two strangers share a moment of fun.

Caprino alle Nocciole con Insalatina di Melone
(Hazelnut-Coated Goat Cheese and Cantaloupe Salad)

Serves 8

I have fond memories of this unusual salad of creamy goat cheese encrusted with hazelnuts and served with sweet cantaloupe. This is a nice departure from the more predictable salads where goat cheese is strewn on the top of lettuce. Be sure to use a young, creamy goat cheese.

8 ounces good-quality goat cheese

3 tablespoons finely chopped hazelnuts

1½ cups cantaloupe, diced

1 teaspoon sugar

¼ teaspoon grated lemon zest

1 tablespoon finely minced mint

⅔ cup shredded radicchio

Cut the cheese into eight equal pieces and roll each piece in the hazelnuts to completely coat it. Place the pieces on a dish, cover with plastic wrap, and refrigerate.

In a small bowl combine the cantaloupe, sugar, lemon zest, and mint. Cover and macerate at room temperature for at least 2 hours before serving.

Bring cheese to room temperature at least 1 hour before serving. (It is always best to serve cheese at room temperature for maximum flavor.) Sprinkle some of the radicchio, and then add 1 piece of cheese, to each of 8 plates. Spoon some of the cantaloupe and mint onto each and serve.

Insalata di Rucola, Fragole e Noci
(Arugula, Strawberry, and Nut Salad)

Serves 6

⅓ cup pine nuts or chopped walnuts

¾ pound arugula, stemmed and torn into pieces

12 ounces strawberries, stemmed, washed, dried, and cut in half

1 ripe mango, peeled and cut into small pieces

2 ounces candied citron, diced

½ cup freshly squeezed orange juice

⅓ cup extra-virgin olive oil

½ teaspoon fine sea salt or more to taste

My friends Giulia and Mario Cocco live in Verona and are always gracious hosts. They treat me to large portions of la vera cucina Veronese *and we have a good time talking about food and customs. One day we had a light lunch with a refreshing and elegant-looking salad made with arugula, strawberries, citron, and nuts; it shimmered in a light dressing of extra-virgin olive oil and freshly squeezed orange juice. Arugula is a sharp-tasting green that looks much like the leaves of radish plants and comes in many varieties. My husband, Guy, covets this plant in his garden, growing several types, including a sawtooth variety known as antique arugula. Most people I know mix arugula with other greens in order to tame its outrageous peppery taste, but in this salad it stands alone in the salad bowl, beautifully balanced by the sweetness of the fruit and citron. Citron is available in Italian specialty stores, especially at holiday time, or it can be ordered by catalog (see the mail order section, page 347). If it's not available, substitute golden raisins, or diced, mixed candied fruits.*

Preheat the oven to 350°F.

Spread the nuts on a baking sheet and toast them for about 5 to 7 minutes, or until they are browned. Transfer the nuts to a small bowl.

Fill a bowl with cold water and submerge the arugula in it. Let the arugula soak for 5 to 10 minutes. Drain, and repeat the process one more time to make sure no dirt or sand remains. Drain the arugula, spin it dry in a salad spinner or roll it in a towel, pressing as much water out as possible. Transfer the arugula to a salad bowl. Add the strawberries, mango, and citron. Toss the mixture gently.

Pour the orange juice into a small bowl. Drizzle in the olive oil with a whisk a little at a time until an emulsion is created. Stir in the salt.

Pour the dressing over the salad and toss it gently. Sprinkle the nuts over the top and serve immediately.

_____

Note: Arugula can also be made into a pesto much like the basil version and is delicious over fish or pasta.

Did you know that if you sow arugula seeds in your garden, they will resow themselves year after year? Antique arugula is very hardy and will last in the garden in northern climates into November.

Insalata di Lamponi, Ravanelli e Zucchini

(Raspberry, Radish, and Zucchini Salad)

Serves 4

2 cups washed and dried romaine lettuce leaves, torn into pieces

6 large radishes, washed and thinly sliced

½ cup diced zucchini

1½ cups fresh raspberries

6 tablespoons extra-virgin olive oil

2 tablespoons freshly squeezed lemon juice

1 teaspoon salt

2 teaspoons warm honey

When I serve this salad, friends give me a quizzical look as if to say, "Is that Italian?" And the answer is yes, especially since I first enjoyed it in Valeggio. The combination of radishes, raspberries, and zucchini is delightful and colorful, and a real palate cleanser after fish or a spicy dinner. Use a salad spinner or towel to thoroughly dry the lettuce leaves.

In a medium bowl combine the lettuce, radishes, zucchini, and raspberries. Set aside.

In a smaller bowl, whisk together the olive oil, lemon juice, salt, and honey until the dressing is well blended. Pour mixture over the vegetables and raspberries and toss gently. Serve immediately.

Pandolce di Ezzelino
(Ezzelino's Sweet Bread)

Makes two 1½-pound loaves

H̶ow wonderful the unexpected can be. Such was the case with a visit to Montagnana, a town south of Padua, which bears witness to Venetian rule, when it was changed from a military outpost to an important trading center. In the thirteenth century, the Da Carrara ruling family built the exquisite and beautifully preserved medieval walls that wrap around the town. The remains of the ancient moat that also afforded protection are still visible as well. Steeped in tradition, Montagnana is known for its palio, *a horse race held since the fourteenth century, and for its delicate prosciutto, along with a very special bread. Legend states that one Ezzelino III da Romano, who was the emperor's vicar in Italy and a skillful soldier, saved the town from a great fire but in doing so was badly injured. A country woman made a dough with* leva, *a natural yeast, to which she added lots of honey, walnuts, and hazelnuts from her orchard, and made a sweet bread that restored the health and strength of Ezzelino. The recipe that follows is an adaptation of* pandolce di Ezzelino, *the sweet bread that is synonymous with Montagnana. Today it is made and sold by Giorgio Cuccato, owner of Pasticerria Cuccato, Via Porta 64. With his father, Bruno, Giorgio has researched the history of this recipe for which the citizens of Montagnana are deeply grateful. The life of this bread begins with a sponge or starter made from a little yeast, flour, and honey that is left to rise for 3 hours. The sponge helps the dough to rise beautifully.*

SPONGE

½ cup warm water

¼ teaspoon dry active yeast

½ cup unbleached all-purpose flour

1 teaspoon honey

DOUGH

1 cup warm water (110°F)

1 teaspoon dry active yeast

⅓ cup honey

3 large eggs

2 tablespoons unsalted butter, melted and cooled

2 teaspoons salt

5½–6 cups unbleached all-purpose flour

¼ cup chopped hazelnuts

¼ cup chopped walnuts

2 tablespoons coarse brown sugar (turbinado or Demerara)

Early on the day you plan to make the bread, combine the sponge ingredients in a medium-size bowl. Stir well. Cover the bowl tightly with plastic wrap and set aside for 3 hours. When the sponge is ready it will have increased three times in volume and

The Veneto

look fluffy, with lots of small holes on the surface like the holes of a sponge.

To make the dough, in a heavy-duty mixer or food processor, combine the water, yeast, and honey and allow to proof for 5 minutes. The mixture will look chalky.

On low speed, blend in all of the sponge mixture.

In a small bowl, lightly beat 2 of the eggs and add them to the yeast-sponge mixture.

On low speed, mix in the butter, salt, and 1 cup of the flour. Increase the speed to medium and mix well. Continue adding the flour 1 cup at a time, mixing each addition in well before adding the next. You may not need all the flour. When the dough begins to leave the sides of bowl, increase the speed to high and beat for 4 minutes. Feel the dough. It should feel soft but not stick to your hands. If it is too sticky, add a little more flour until it reaches the right consistency.

Remove the dough from the mixer or processor and knead it a few times on a work surface. Spray a large bowl with vegetable or butter spray, place the dough in the bowl, and cover the bowl tightly with plastic wrap. Allow the dough to rise for 3 hours.

Punch down the dough and turn it out onto a work surface. Stretch it out with your hands. Scatter the nuts over the dough, then fold the dough over several times to enclose the nuts. Cut the dough in half with a knife and knead each piece into a tight ball about 5 inches in diameter. Some of the nuts should be visible on the outside of the loaf.

Place each round on a lightly greased cookie sheet; cover each with a clean towel and allow the breads to rise for 45 minutes to 1 hour, or until nearly doubled in size.

Preheat the oven to 375°F.

Lightly beat the remaining egg in a small bowl. Brush each loaf with the beaten egg. Sprinkle 1 tablespoon of the coarse sugar over each loaf.

With a clean razor blade make an X incision about 3 inches long in the top of each loaf and fold back the four cuts. This will allow for air to escape and prevent the loaves from splitting.

Bake the loaves until nicely browned on top and bottom, about 40 to 45 minutes, or until an instant-read thermometer registers 200°F when inserted in the center of the loaf.

Remove the loaves to a cooling rack.

_____

Note: These loaves freeze well if wrapped tightly in aluminum foil and then in heavy-duty plastic bags.

Variation: Make four smaller loaves to give as kitchen gifts. Wrap each loaf in clear cellophane and tie with a ribbon.

Crostata di Limone e Mascarpone con Salsa di Rabarbaro

(Lemon and Mascarpone Cheese Tart with Rhubarb Sauce)

Makes one 10½-inch tart

RHUBARB SAUCE

1½ pounds rhubarb, trimmed, washed, and cut into 1-inch chunks

1½ cups sugar

Pinch salt

FILLING

1 teaspoon unflavored gelatin

¼ cup water

¼ cup cornstarch

1½ cups sugar

1 cup milk

3 egg yolks, slightly beaten

½ cup freshly squeezed lemon juice

¼ cup unsalted butter

1 cup mascarpone cheese or a good quality cream cheese, at room temperature

Trattoria alla Coa is a charming restaurant not far from Verona. The refreshingly creative menu is the work of Valentina and GiGi Beltramini. From the tagliolini *pasta, cut by hand and as thin as dental floss, to the* Cappone *with Sweet-and-Sour Sauce (page 30), the meal was a crescendo of pure joy and excellence. The desserts were stunners, including this tangy chilled lemon and mascarpone cheese tart served with a sieved rhubarb sauce. The filling can be made a day ahead, and the tart shell can be made and then frozen uncooked for several weeks prior to baking. The rhubarb sauce can also be made ahead and refrigerated, although the tart can stand alone without it.*

In a saucepan combine the rhubarb, sugar, and salt. Cook the mixture over medium heat until the rhubarb is very soft. Transfer the mixture to a fine-mesh strainer set over a bowl. With a wooden spoon stir the rhubarb in the strainer while pushing it through the strainer into the bowl. Discard the solids.

Transfer the rhubarb to a jar and refrigerate.

To prepare the filling, dissolve the gelatin in the ¼ cup water, then transfer it to a small saucepan and stir the mixture over low heat until the gelatin is completely dissolved. Set it aside.

In the top of a double boiler mix the cornstarch and 1 cup of the sugar together off the heat. Slowly pour in and stir the milk until the mixture is well combined. Stir in the egg yolks, lemon juice, and the butter. Place the top of the double boiler over the base pan, making sure that the water line does not touch the bottom of the top of the double boiler. Cook the mixture over medium heat, stirring constantly until the mixture begins to boil and thicken. Cook for 2 minutes. The filling should coat the stirring spoon. Remove the filling from the heat, stir in the gelatin, and transfer the filling to a bowl. Cover the bowl with a piece of buttered wax paper placed directly onto the surface of the filling. Chill the filling for 1 hour.

In a bowl beat the mascarpone cheese with the remaining ½ cup of sugar until smooth. Cover and set aside.

To make the pastry, in a bowl or food processor combine the flour, sugar, and salt. Work in the butter with a pastry blender or pulse until the butter is reduced to fine particles.

In a small bowl lightly beat the egg with the water and lemon juice. Add the egg mixture to the flour mixture and combine until a ball of dough begins to form. If the mixture seems dry, add a few drops of water. Gather the dough up into a rough ball. Flour your hands and press the dough into the base and up the sides of a 10½×1-inch tart pan with a removable bottom. Cover the tart shell with plastic wrap and refrigerate it for 30 minutes or overnight. At this point the tart shell may be wrapped tightly in aluminum foil and frozen for future use.

Preheat the oven to 425°F.

Bake the tart shell for 12–15 minutes, or until it is nicely browned. Transfer the tart shell to a cooling rack and allow to cool completely.

With a rubber spatula spread the mascarpone cheese over the base of the tart shell. Spread the lemon filling over the cheese. Refrigerate the tart for at least 2 hours before serving.

To serve, cut the tart into wedges. Pass the rhubarb sauce separately.

PASTRY FOR TART

1½ cups unbleached all-purpose flour

½ cup plus 2 tablespoons sugar

Pinch salt

1 stick cold unsalted butter, cut into bits

1 large egg

1 teaspoon cold water

1 teaspoon freshly squeezed lemon juice

The Veneto

Pinza
(Venetian Cornmeal Cake)

Makes one 9½×13×2-inch cake

½ cup raisins

2 tablespoons grappa or
  ½ cup warm water

2 cups unbleached all-
  purpose flour

2 cups cornmeal

½ teaspoon fine sea salt

2 teaspoons baking powder

5 cups water

1 cup sugar

6 tablespoons unsalted
  butter, softened

½ cup diced candied lemon
  or orange peel

1 Yellow Delicious apple,
  peeled and diced

1 Bartlett pear, peeled and
  diced

9 or 10 dried whole
  Calamyrna or Calabrian
  figs, stemmed and
  chopped

½ cup chopped walnuts

The Bottega del Pane, adjacent to Padua's fabulous outdoor market, sells delightful breads, pizze, focacce, biscotti, and other pastry delights. You cannot walk in there without succumbing to buying several items. Some of their Venetian specialties include sweets made with cornmeal, since the Veneto region grows a great deal of corn for polenta. Two of my favorites are sbrisolana, *a dense cornmeal cake studded with almonds and hazelnuts that is perfect with coffee or tea, and* pinza, *a cake also made with cornmeal and laden with dried figs, walnuts, and raisins soaked in grappa. Pinza originally was made for the Christmas holidays and was eaten up until the feast of the Epiphany. Now it is enjoyed year-round. There are many versions of this cake; some contain eggs, spices, and a variety of other fruits. In this version, diced pears and apples are also used. This cake is very moist and very hearty. It will keep a week in the refrigerator and is best eaten at room temperature. For best results use a heavy saucepan to cook the flour and cornmeal. I like copper for its even heat distribution. The grappa in this recipe is optional.*

Butter the baking pan and dust it with flour, shaking out the excess, or line the pan with a sheet of aluminum foil, allowing the foil to come up the sides of the pan. Butter and dust the foil with flour. Set it aside.

Pour the water or grappa over the raisins in a small bowl and let them soak for 15 minutes.

Preheat the oven to 350°F.

Combine the flour, cornmeal, salt, and baking powder in a heavy-duty 4-quart saucepan. Slowly stir in the water. Cook the mixture, stirring frequently, over medium-high heat for 15 minutes. The mixture will be very thick. Remove the pan from the heat and stir in the sugar and butter, making sure that the butter melts completely.

Strain the raisins, discarding the water, and stir them into the batter. If using the grappa, add it with the raisins. Stir in the lemon or orange peel, apple, pear, figs, and walnuts.

Pour the batter into the pan, smoothing out the top.

Bake for 1 to 1¼ hours, or until a skewer inserted in the center comes out clean. The top of the cake should be golden brown. Cool the cake completely. If using the foil-lined method, simply lift the foil with the cake out of the pan and, when cool, remove the foil. This will allow for neatly cut slices with no waste at the edges.

To serve, cut into squares.

Tip: For parties, I chill the baked cake, then use small cookie cutters to cut out decorative shapes, which I place in small cupcake papers. They make the perfect dessert finger food for a crowd.

The Veneto

Torta di Cocco e Noci
(Coconut Tart)

Makes one 10-inch tart and one 7-inch tart shell

PASTRY DOUGH

2 cups unbleached all-purpose flour

¼ cup sugar

¼ teaspoon salt

1 stick cold unsalted butter, cut into bits

1 large egg

2 tablespoons water

FILLING

5⅓ cups (14-ounce bag) Baker's sweetened coconut

⅓ cup unbleached all-purpose flour

¾ cup sugar

5 large egg whites, slightly beaten

1 tablespoon almond extract

⅓ cup chopped blanched almonds

½ cup chopped semisweet chocolate

What I love about my stays in Italy are the unexpected pleasures that come along each day. I keep a notebook with me at all times to record such occurrences. One day friends and I decided to visit Padova (Padua) to see the fabulous Giotto frescoes in the Scrovegni Chapel. Afterward we headed for the outdoor market in Piazza delle Erbe. Weary from shopping, we decided to stop at Bottega del Pane for a sweet pick-me-up, where the costumed salespeople know how to make a sale. Seeing our frenzied excitement and animated disagreement over what to buy, they suddenly appear with samples of small pizza, focaccia, biscotti, and bread. We thank them for their kindness—"niente," they reply and smile. And so we succumb to Pugliese bread, fig cake, and this wonderful torta di cocco *(coconut tart). One bite and I could not help but recall the Almond Joy bars of my youth. I have taken a little liberty with the tart, and included bits of semisweet chocolate. The recipe makes enough for one 10-inch tart with enough pastry dough left over to make a small 7-inch tart shell that can be frozen for future use. When serving, cut this tart into small pieces as it is very rich.*

To prepare the dough, in a food processor or large bowl, combine the flour, sugar, and salt. Add the butter and pulse or cut it in with a pastry blender. Pulse or blend in the egg and water until a ball of dough begins to form. The dough should be soft but not dry and should not crumble when pressed between your fingers.

Gather the dough up into a ball and set aside. Overlap two sheets of wax paper on a counter and lightly sprinkle with flour. Place the dough on top of the flour. Sprinkle a teaspoon of flour over the top of the dough and spread it evenly over the top. Cover

The Veneto

52

the dough with another two sheets of overlapping wax paper, and with a rolling pin roll the dough out to a 12-inch circle. Carefully remove and discard the wax paper. Fit the dough in a 10-inch tart-shell pan with a removable bottom, letting the excess hang over the sides. Trim the edges even with the rim of the tart pan. Gather up the extra dough and roll it out to fit a 7-inch tart shell. Freeze the smaller tart shell for future use.

Preheat the oven to 425°F.

To prepare the filling, in a large bowl, mix the coconut, flour, sugar, egg whites, almond extract, chopped almonds, and chocolate together until well blended. Spread the mixture evenly into the tart shell.

Bake the tart for about 30 minutes, or until the coconut is golden brown.

Remove the tart to a cooling rack to cool completely. Carefully lift the tart from the tart pan sides and place it on a serving dish. Cut into thin wedges to serve.

Torta di Cocco, Noci e Mascarpone
(Coconut and Mascarpone Cheese Tart)

Makes one 10-inch tart and one 7-inch tart shell

DOUGH

1 recipe pastry dough for
Torta di Cocco e Noci
(page 52)

FILLING

1¼ cups mascarpone cheese,
at room temperature

1 tablespoon unbleached all-
purpose flour

1 large egg

½ teaspoon almond extract

⅓ cup sugar

3 cups (7 ounces) Baker's
sweetened coconut

2 ounces semisweet
chocolate, cut into small
pieces

Here is a variation on the Torta di Cocco e Noci *(page 52). I make this one with creamy mascarpone cheese, the smooth and sweet dessert cheese made famous as an ingredient in tiramisù. In this version, I fold coconut into the cheese and add a topping of toasted coconut and melted chocolate. After making and eating both, I still can't decide which one I like best. Use the recipe for Torta di Cocco e Noci for making the pastry dough; you will have enough dough left to make a smaller tart shell for future use.*

Prepare and roll out the pastry dough as described on pages 52–53. Freeze the smaller tart for future use.

Preheat the oven to 400°F.

To prepare the filling, in a bowl with a hand mixer, or in a food processor, blend together the cheese, flour, egg, almond extract, and sugar until smooth. Fold in 2 cups of the coconut.

Spread the mixture evenly in the pastry-lined tart shell.

Bake for 20 minutes on the middle rack. Sprinkle the remaining cup of coconut over the top of the tart and continue baking for another 10 minutes. The coconut should brown nicely but not burn. Insert a small knife into the center of the tart as it bakes. When it comes out clean, the tart is done. If the coconut seems to be browning sooner than the filling is set, lay a piece of aluminum foil loosely over the top of the tart.

Cool the tart on a cooling rack.

Fill the base of a double boiler with water but do not allow it to touch the bottom of the top pan. Bring the water to a boil. Turn off the heat. Place the chocolate pieces in the top of the double boiler and allow the chocolate to melt. Stir the chocolate with a spoon until it becomes smooth.

While the chocolate is still warm, using a spoon, drizzle it over the surface of the tart.

Remove the tart pan sides, place the tart on a serving dish, and cut it into thin wedges. Serve at room temperature.

Tortelli Dolci di Amarena
(Amarena Cherry Cookies)

Makes about 3½ dozen cookies

2 cups unbleached all-
  purpose flour

¼ cup sugar

¼ teaspoon salt

1 stick cold unsalted butter,
  cut into pieces

Grated zest of 1 lemon

2½ tablespoons freshly
  squeezed lemon juice

½ cup cherry jam, Amarena
  if possible

1 egg, lightly beaten

2 tablespoons turbinado
  sugar (coarse brown
  sugar)

The train was taking me from Padua to Grisignano del Zocco, and I was grateful for the chance to put my feet up and have a snack while I gazed out the window at the blurred scenery whizzing past. I had purchased some tortelli dolci, *half-moon-shaped cookies filled with Amarena cherry jam. The little cookies were just what I needed to take the edge off my hunger, and I savored every morsel. I wrote in my notebook that I needed to re-create these gems at home, so here is my interpretation. Use regular cherry jam if Amarena cherry jam is not available, or see mail order sources on page 347.*

Mix together the flour, sugar, and salt in a bowl or pulse them together in a food processor. Work the butter into the flour mixture with a pastry blender or pulse it in a food procesor until a coarse texture is obtained. Blend in the lemon zest and enough of the lemon juice to make a soft dough.

Wrap the dough in plastic wrap and refrigerate it for several hours or overnight.

Preheat the oven to 350°F.

Divide the dough in half. On a floured surface, roll the dough out to a thickness of no more than ¼ inch. Use a 2½-inch round cookie cutter to cut circles from the dough. Place about ½ teaspoon of the jam in the center of each circle and fold the circle in half to make a half-moon shape. Seal the edges by pressing on them with a fork dipped in flour. Repeat with the remaining dough. Gather any scraps and reroll them to cut more circles.

Place the cookies on lightly greased cookie sheets, spacing them about ½ inch apart. Brush the tops of the cookies with the beaten egg. Sprinkle the tops with the coarse sugar.

Bake the cookies for about 12 minutes, or until they are golden brown. With a spatula transfer the cookies to a cooling rack and cool completely.

Bussolà
(Ring-Shaped Venetian Cookies)

Makes about 2 dozen

4 cups unbleached all-
  purpose flour

1¼ cups sugar

6 large egg yolks, slightly
  beaten

1 stick unsalted butter,
  softened

1 tablespoon vanilla extract

2 tablespoons freshly
  squeezed lemon juice

2 tablespoons water

Grated zest of 1 lemon

To the uninitiated, these not-too-sweet ring-shaped cookies from the Veneto might seem dull and uninteresting. But Venetians love them and so do I. Called bussolà, *from the word* buca *for "hole," they are perfect with coffee, tea, or dunking in wine. These long-keepers are made from a dense dough that is best made in a food processor. Be sure to measure ingredients carefully, using metal or plastic measures for dry ingredients and glass measures for liquid ingredients. Flour should be lightly spooned into the measuring cup.* Bussolà *can also be formed into S-shapes.*

Add the flour and sugar to the bowl of a food processor and pulse to blend. Add the egg yolks and butter and pulse to combine. Through the feed tube, add the vanilla extract, lemon juice, water, and zest. Process until a soft ball of dough is formed that is not sticky and leaves the sides of the bowl. If the dough crumbles when pressed between your fingers, add a few more drops of water. The dough should hold together and be smooth, not gritty to the touch.

Preheat the oven to 350°F.

Transfer the dough to a work surface. Pinch off small egg-size pieces of dough and roll them under the palm of your hands into a 9-inch rope about the thickness of your small finger. Bring the two ends together and pinch them closed. Place the *bussolà* on lightly greased cookie sheets, spacing them about ½ inch apart.

Bake for about 15 minutes or until they are pale golden brown. Remove the *bussolà* to a cooling rack. When completely cool, store the cookies in airtight containers for up to 2 weeks, or freeze for longer storage.

Lunch at the Lake

*A*lbisano, on magnificent Lake Garda, is a summer getaway for my friend Giulia Cocco and her family. It is here, in a summer home surrounded by lush greenery and chiseled cliffs, that Giulia, a tall, fair-skinned blonde, Danish by birth but married to a Sardinian, relaxes, away from city life in Verona. She has invited an international group of friends to the lake for what she terms a "Danish experience." Even though I never tire of Italian food, I see this as an opportunity for Giulia to expand our view of food in a broader context, a subject that the Italians can discuss for hours.

The view from Giulia's house is hauntingly breathtaking with a peaceful and expansive vista of Lake Garda (Lago di Garda), seemingly clothed in a thin veil of gauze, and ringed by the foreboding and jagged-looking Dolomite Mountains. Lake Garda is a favorite vacation spot for people from all over Europe, and it is easy to see why Giulia and Mario, her husband, love to come here. From our high vantage point, sailboats with brilliant-colored sails can be seen gliding by in silence, while determined windsurfers practice endless ballet-like movements on a stage of shimmering water for as far as the eye can see.

It is a glorious day for our lunch, very warm and tranquil, and a large umbrella shields the outdoor dining area from the merciless midday sun. The table is set on a hillside overlooking the lake; on it a magnificent-looking vase full of wispy summer flowers nods in the breeze, and delicate china and crystal rest on exquisite hand-fashioned Sardinian linens.

The guests number about sixteen, and are from Germany, Denmark, and the United States. We are an eclectic mix to be sure; some

The Veneto

are computer business people, some are winemakers and vineyard workers, some are Giulia's visiting friends from Denmark, and many of the dishes offered have been prepared with their help. It does not strike me as odd that Giulia has prepared a Danish lunch; after all, this may be Italy but she is Danish. What fun to show off her native cuisine! She says it is a way to stay in touch with her homeland, but cautions that Danish food does not measure up to Italian food in her husband Mario's opinion. Mario, strikingly handsome with dark, curly hair and piercing green eyes, is an exuberant man with an inexhaustible supply of energy. He is also a Renaissance man in the modern sense of the word. He speaks five languages fluently, travels all over the world for business, is well read, and is the happiest when he can return for short spurts of rest to his native Sardinia.

Three buffet tables are laden with all sorts of dishes. The first table celebrates Danish herring, including marinated white herring and red herring served with raw onions. There is white herring coated with bread crumbs and fried, then marinated with onions. There is smoked herring in olive oil, and herring marinated in red wine with spices. There is also Giulia's friend Eva's dish of small freshwater lobster.

The second table offers us various types of dried salami, cold rolled pork served with red cabbage and beetroot, and more raw onions. A warm liver pâté is served with brown jelly and mushrooms, and warm meatballs are served with potato salad.

The breads intrigue me; they are dense, rustic brown breads that look artisan made, and when I ask about them, Giulia laughs and says that they are from Sardinia! Not quite a total Danish lunch! Giulia loves Sardinia not only because it is Mario's homeland, but also for its remoteness and unspoiled beauty as well as for its culture, its history, and its food. She knows Sardinia well, spending the summers there in her beach house near the town of Pula. I remember with fondness the day Giulia and I went shopping for handmade Sardinian specialties. We spent a long time admiring colorful handmade baskets and exquisite jewelry, and Giulia succumbed to a pair of long, intricately made gold earrings for her birthday present.

The third table is an international table of sorts with its wonderful display of Danish and Sardinian cheeses, fresh fruits, Sardinian sweets called sospiri, and a real treat for me, panettone from Sardinia, so moist that I covet the loaf for myself. Panettone was originally a northern Italian specialty but now is found everywhere.

Finally we sit down at our carefully thought-out, designated places. Giulia is clever; our place cards have our names written in silver metallic ink on fresh fallen leaves. Each place has its own serving of Danish beer and schnapps, and Mario cannot resist also bringing out Sardinian Cannonau, a wonderful red wine.

Giulia is a wonderful hostess; I admire the way she can communicate, weaving in and out of several languages, talking to everyone and making sure that all feel welcome. I am doing my best in Italian, but I would also like to speak to Eva and the others, and I can sense that they feel the same urge, but we are reduced to our own versions of sign language and facial expressions, and somehow we all feel connected on this gorgeous day, sitting around the table with our commanding view of the lake.

We spend hours sampling everything and asking questions about Danish cooking. Giulia relishes in explaining the various dishes and how they are prepared in Denmark. It is evident that there are some things that she misses about her homeland—not the weather, she assures me, but her family and friends. Her train of thought is broken by Eva announcing that dessert is about to come out of the oven. Giulia surprises us with a jewel . . . warm Danish pastry filled with apples! Eva has brought it frozen and ready for the oven all the way from Denmark! We are like little starving puppies jockeying for position, waiting with dessert plates in hand for a hot wedge of the pastry. Giulia giggles over our enthusiasm, and with satisfaction in her voice says: "Some things you just can't get in Italy."

Vetelangd
(Danish Braided Pastry)

Serves 8 to 10

4 cups unbleached all-
purpose flour

1 package dry active yeast

2½ tablespoons sugar

1 cup plus 1 tablespoon
lukewarm milk

⅛ teaspoon salt

¼ cup unsalted butter,
melted

1 egg

1 egg yolk

¼ cup sliced almonds

GLAZE

1½ cups confectioners' sugar

½ teaspoon almond extract

3–4 tablespoons milk or half-
and-half

Here is Giulia's recipe for braided Danish pastry—perfect after any lunch!

To make the pastry, sift the flour into a large bowl and make a hole in the middle of the bowl.

In a small bowl combine the yeast with 1 teaspoon of the sugar and 4 tablespoons of the milk. Pour this mixture into the hole in the flour bowl and mix in a small amount of the flour from the sides of the bowl to make a small ball of dough the size of a lemon in the hole.

Cover the bowl with a cloth and set aside for about 2 hours, or until the small ball of dough starts to rise. Stir in the rest of the sugar, the salt, butter, whole egg, and all but 1 tablespoon of the remaining milk.

With your hands knead the mixture until a firm and smooth dough is formed. Cover the bowl with a cloth and let the dough rise until it has doubled in bulk, about 45 minutes.

Preheat the oven to 400°F.

Punch down the dough with your fist and transfer it from the bowl to a work surface. Knead the dough briefly, then divide it into 2 equal pieces.

Make 2 strips of dough each about 20 inches long. Place the strips of dough vertically next to each other on a work surface dusted with flour. Pinch the strips together at the top, then braid the strips together. Continue braiding the entire length of the strips. Pinch the ends flat and fold them underneath the braid.

Place the braid on a lightly buttered baking sheet and let it rise, covered, for 15 minutes.

Mix the egg yolk with the remaining 1 tablespoon of milk. With a pastry brush, coat the top of the braid. Sprinkle the braid with the almonds and bake it for 45 to 50 minutes, or until golden brown.

To make the glaze, mix the confectioners' sugar with the almond extract. Add just enough milk or half-and-half to make a smooth glaze that easily flows off a spoon. Drizzle the glaze over the top of the braid while still warm.

Emilia-Romagna

Antipasti

Funghi Fritti di Beatrice (Beatrice's Fried Mushrooms)
Funghi alle Erbe (Mushrooms with Herbs)

Primi Piatti

Maccheroni alla Bolognese (Macaroni with Bolognese Sauce)
Tortelloni di Zucca e Mostarda di Frutta (Pumpkin and Candied-Fruit-
  Filled Pasta)
Tortelli di Coste (Swiss Chard Ravioli)
Gnocchi di Riso (Rice Gnocchi)

Secondi Piatti

Bomba di Riso di Mara (Mara's Rice Bomb)
Coniglio all'Aceto Balsamico (Rabbit in Balsamic Vinegar)
Arrosto di Maiale al Latte (Boneless Rolled Pork Cooked in Milk)

Contorni

Tortina di Patate (Potato Pie)
Erbazzone di Mara (Mara's Swiss Chard Pie)
Insalata di Radicchio e Pancetta alla Trattoria Chilo (Radicchio and
  Bacon Salad Trattoria Chilo Style)

Dolci

Torta di Amarena (Cherry Tart)
Zuccherotti di Polverara (Sugar Puffs from Polverara)
Albicocche Cotte al Vino (Apricots Cooked in Wine)

Emilia-Romagna is prosciutto di Parma, via Emilia, fog, Modena, nocino, balsamic vinegar, bollito misto, mosaics, Ravenna, Dozza, Parma, tortellini, ragù, Bologna, pasticcio, Parmigiano-Reggiano cheese, Lambrusco, lasagne, cappelletti in brodo, cappone, torta di bietole, chizze, piadina, Palazzo Diamonte, Renaissance buildings, Rioveggio, La Rocca, Imola, Piazza Nettuno, arcades, Ferrara, Amarena cherries, passatelli, zampone, Reggio Emilia, university students, fertile plains, tortelli, Dante's tomb, Este dynasty, villas, Museo Schifanoia, Piacenza, Ferrari, faïence ceramics, Po Delta.

$\mathcal{E}$milia-Romagna is positioned between the Adriatic, the Po River, and the Apennine Mountains, and the name of the region comes from the fact that the Romans built via Emilia, a strategic trade road connecting Piacenza in the west to Rimini in the east.

This rich agricultural area is known to many as the region of *buongustai,* or connoisseurs of good eating, and it rightly deserves the title. The region boasts lots of high-quality food due to its abundance of fertile plains. Prized food products include prosciutto di Parma, made from specially bred pigs, and Parmigiano-Reggiano cheese. Both must pass strict production standards before being released for domestic and international sale. A seal is affixed to these artisanal foods, affirming their superior quality.

Another artisanal product, true balsamic vinegar comes from Modena and is made according to ancient family secrets using the unfermented juice of Trebbiano grapes. Each year a competition is held in the town of Spilambarto to judge the best vinegars for that year. There are three grades of balsamic vinegar; the best and most expensive bears the gold seal, followed by the silver and red labels.

My interest in this region started with Massimiliano Iori, a high school student from Reggio Emilia who came with a group of his fellow classmates to the States to study English. Max, as he liked to be called, lived with my family during his month-long stay. I had to curb my desire to cook Italian food for him and remember that *that* was what he ate every day at home; I cooked his requested American favorites, such as hot dogs, tacos, and hamburgers, which ironically my family only ate while he was visiting! I got to know his mother, Lorenza, who was the coordinator for the group, and she and I became instant friends. While the students were visiting, I was in production for our series and I decided it would be a nice twist to get these students' impressions of America on one of our programs. The plan was to film them experiencing a slice of American life at the beach, where they would enjoy an Italian picnic and talk on camera about their impressions of America. It took a lot of coordinating to get the students to the film location, and once there all the food was set out, and before the cameras could roll they were devouring it! I managed to ask a couple of the students who were comfortable speaking English what they thought of American food. Andrea, a handsome fellow with curly hair, did not hesitate a moment and said, "Is better in Italy!" When I asked Nadia, a perky and chatty student, what her impressions of America were, she matter-of-factly announced, "You drive too slow." They were good sports about the segment and by the time we left the beach, they were asking to go to McDonald's!

Emilia-Romagna encapsulates all that is wonderful about regional specialties. Its dishes represent "from scratch" cooking at its best. Wherever I went, from the *salumeria* (butcher shop) to the *panifico* (bread baker's), the pride in creating artisanal foods was abundantly apparent. Shop owners wanted to show me everything. In Montecchio, near Reggio Emilia, I watched the process of making Parmigiano-Reggiano cheese. I learned from the cheese maker that it is a starter, a natural bacteria obtained from the whey of the cheesemaking process, that determines the quality of the cheese. (The whey is the watery liquid that is left after curds start to form.) At Castello di Torrechiara I learned about the process of curing ham with only salt and time to make the world-famous prosciutto di Parma. This ham can only be made around the area of Langhirano. At Panifico Melli, I learned how to make typical breads of the region, including *pane Ferrarese* and braided bread called *treccia.* Stuffed breads included a slightly sweet Swiss chard tart called *erbazzone.* At the Venturini Baldini vineyards in the hills around Reggio Emilia, I learned about the production of Lambrusco wine and balsamic vinegar. At Casalinga, I learned the secrets of making elegant fresh-filled pasta, including such favorites as cappelletti, tortelli, and ravioli.

I absorbed all this information like a sponge, and could not wait to get back to my television kitchen to create these typical dishes for our audience. I could spend a lifetime highlighting the foods of the twenty regions of Italy and never cover it all. I take great satisfaction in knowing that through our series we are beginning to open up a world of Italian food that goes beyond the stereotypic dishes of lasagne and spaghetti and meatballs.

Funghi Fritti di Beatrice
(Beatrice's Fried Mushrooms)

Serves 4

1 pound fresh portobello or button mushrooms

⅓ cup flour

½ to ⅔ cup extra-virgin olive oil

Fine sea salt to sprinkle

Believe it or not, there is an art to cooking mushrooms, as was demonstrated very clearly to me when I was a guest for dinner at the Venturini Baldini vineyards near Reggio Emilia. Beatrice Baldini, one of the owners, is a vivacious woman who is proud of the wine and balsamic vinegar that is produced at Venturini Baldini. Naturally, the food we ate showcased both. The entire meal was exquisite, beginning with three antipasti. Prosciutto di Parma, the prized, raw-cured ham of the region, was served with melon; culatello, cured pork rump, was outstanding served with fresh figs; that was followed by a creamy white pig's fat served on small pieces of bread called crostini. Our first course was tortelli di bietole, small pasta stuffed with Swiss chard. This was followed by fillet of beef with rosemary and olive oil accompanied by the most wonderful porcini mushrooms done in two styles. I loved everything, but the mushrooms were the triumph of the meal. Beatrice cautioned that porcini mushrooms must be picked and cooked the same day, and never stored in the refrigerator. She cooks the mushrooms just before serving so they do not become soggy. Here are the two versions I sampled. Because fresh porcini are not readily available, the recipes were tested using portobello and button mushrooms.

Clean the mushrooms with a mushroom brush or damp paper towels. If using portobello mushrooms, trim the stems and slice the caps into ½-inch slices. If using button mushrooms, do not trim the stems. Cut the whole mushrooms in half lengthwise. Place the mushrooms in a paper bag and add the flour. Close the bag and shake vigorously to lightly coat the mushroom pieces with flour. Set the mushrooms aside.

Emilia-Romagna

In a sauté pan heat ½ cup of the oil, add half the mushrooms, and cook until golden on one side. Turn them over and cook the other side. As they cook, remove the mushrooms to a heated serving dish. Continue cooking the remaining mushrooms, adding more oil as necessary if the pan is dry.

Sprinkle the tops of the mushrooms with salt and serve immediately as an antipasto or as an accompaniment to meat or poultry.

Note: Save the portobello mushroom stems to use in soup.

Funghi alle Erbe
(Mushrooms with Herbs)

Serves 4

1 pound fresh portobello or
 button mushrooms

½ to ⅔ cup extra-virgin
 olive oil

1 large clove garlic, minced

⅓ cup minced mint

⅓ cup minced parsley

Fine sea salt for sprinkling

For this preparation, Beatrice dices the mushrooms and cooks them with mentuccia (wild mint), garlic, and parsley.

Use a mushroom brush or damp paper towels to clean the mushrooms. Trim the woody part of the stems of the portobello mushrooms and discard them. Dice the mushrooms and set them aside. If using button mushrooms, trim off any woody stem parts, then dice the mushrooms and set them aside.

In a sauté pan heat ½ cup of the olive oil, add the garlic, and sauté slowly until it begins to soften. Add the mushrooms and cook slowly until the mushroom pieces begin to soften. Stir in the mint and parsley and continue cooking for about 2 minutes, stirring occasionally.

Transfer the mushrooms to a serving dish, sprinkle them with salt, and serve immediately.

Did you know that mushrooms are celebrated all over Italy? In the fall it is not unusual to see *festa di funghi* signs along the roadsides, advertising outdoor fairs where you can order a plate of just-harvested mushrooms. And you can eat to your heart's content because mushrooms are very low in calories; they also contain vitamin D.

Maccheroni alla Bolognese
(Macaroni with Bolognese Sauce)

Serves 4 to 6

This robust Bolognese sauce made with ground pork, pancetta, and chicken livers is perfect for short cuts of pasta such as rigatoni. The sauce ingredients simmer for 30 minutes; this is in sharp contrast to other types of Bolognese sauces that need to cook slowly for at least two hours or until they are very concentrated. Resist the temptation to add too much salt to this sauce, as the pancetta provides just enough.

In a 10- or 12-inch sauté pan combine the butter, pork, pancetta, onion, carrot, and celery, and cook the mixture, stirring often, until the pork has turned gray in color and the onions have softened.

Sprinkle the flour over the mixture and stir in. Pour in the chicken broth, cover the pan, and simmer the mixture for 30 minutes. Uncover the pan, stir in the chicken livers, cover the pan again, and cook for an additional 5 minutes over low heat. Season the sauce with salt and pepper to taste. Set it aside and keep it warm while the pasta is cooking.

Cook the pasta in 4 to 6 quarts of salted, boiling water until it is al dente; pasta should retain its shape and not collapse on itself and when cut into, no trace of white flour should remain. Drain the pasta and transfer it to a serving dish. Pour the sauce over the top and toss it well. Sprinkle on the cheese and serve immediately.

1 tablespoon butter

1 pound lean ground pork

¼-pound piece pancetta, diced

1 onion, peeled and diced

1 carrot, diced

1 rib celery, diced

1½ tablespoons flour

1½ cups hot chicken broth

4 chicken livers, washed and diced

Fine sea salt to taste

Grinding of coarse black pepper

1 pound short-cut pasta, such as rigatoni or ziti with lines

4 tablespoons grated Parmigiano-Reggiano cheese

Emilia-Romagna

Tortelloni di Zucca e Mostarda di Frutta
(Pumpkin and Candied-Fruit-Filled Pasta)

Makes at least 6 dozen

FILLING

1 to 1½ pounds butternut or acorn squash

¼ cup water

1 teaspoon fine sea salt

⅓ cup crushed (12 small) amaretti cookies

¼ cup diced mostarda di frutta or dried apricots

DOUGH

4 large eggs

1 teaspoon fine sea salt

3 to 3½ cups unbleached all-purpose flour

Tortelloni are large-size tortellini (little cakes). On many visits to Italy, in the regions of Emilia-Romagna, Lombardia, and the Veneto, I have enjoyed various preparations of tortellini, tortelloni, and tortelli. My favorite? The pumpkin-filled tortelloni served at ristorante Ochina Bianca on via Finzi in Mantua. Not only are they gorgeous to look at, but the unusual sauce of melted butter, diced tomato, and slivered almonds is a terrific compliment to the pumpkin filling, which is sweetened with crushed amaretti cookies. I have changed the recipe slightly, adding mostarda di frutta, *a fine dice of candied fruits in sugar syrup that is also used in many Lombardian dishes. Mostarda di frutta is made up of such small whole fruits as cherries, apricots, pears, apples, and quinces. Mostarda di frutta and amaretti cookies are available in Italian grocery stores or by mail order (see page 347). If you cannot find mostarda di frutta, use dried apricots. To save time, make the filling two days ahead. These are just about the most elegant first course I know, so I make them ahead and freeze them. The sauce proportions given below are for two dozen tortelloni; double or triple the sauce ingredients depending on how many servings you need.*

Preheat the oven to 350°F.

To prepare the filling, cut the squash in half and remove and discard the seeds. Place the squash cut-side down in a baking dish and add the water. Cover the pan tightly with aluminum foil and bake the squash until fork-tender, about 40 to 50 minutes.

Remove the squash from the pan and when it is cool scoop the flesh from the shell into a bowl. Mash the squash with a fork until it is smooth. You should have about 2 cups of packed squash. Stir in the salt, cookies, and mostarda di frutta. Mix the ingredients well. Cover and refrigerate until needed.

To prepare the dough in a food processor, whirl the eggs with the salt until the eggs are foamy. Add the flour 1 cup at a time until the mixture forms a ball of dough that leaves the sides of the processor. You may not need all of the flour—it will all depend on how the flour was measured (3.5 to 4 ounces per cup) and the size of the eggs. Feel the dough. If it is too sticky, add a little more flour 1 tablespoon at a time. If the dough is too dry, you will not be able to seal the edges of the pasta to hold the filling. Add a little water if dough seems dry.

If making the dough by hand, beat the eggs in a bowl, then begin adding the flour 1 cup at a time, mixing it in with your hands until a ball of dough is formed. Knead as above.

Remove the dough from the bowl of the food processor and knead it by hand on a work surface for about 4 minutes. Place the dough on a lightly floured surface, cover it with a bowl, and let it rest for 30 minutes. This step will relax the gluten in the dough and allow it to be easily rolled out.

Divide the dough into four equal pieces. Work with one piece of dough at a time and keep the rest covered to prevent the pieces from drying out. Use a hand-crank pasta machine or a rolling pin and roll each piece of dough out into 5- or 6-inch-wide strips that are not more than $\frac{1}{16}$ inch thick; this is a number 7 or 8 setting on a standard pasta machine. Another indicator of thinness is being able to see your hand behind the thinned-out sheet. Do not roll the dough so thin that the filling will pop through it.

Use a 3-inch round cutter and cut circles from the dough. Place a measured teaspoon full of the filling in the center of each circle. Fold the dough over the filling to create a turnover and seal the edges with your fingers. Mark all around the outside edge with the tines of a fork. As you make the tortelloni, place them in single layers on towel-lined cookie sheets. Gather up the scraps and make more tortelloni. To freeze the tortelloni for future use, cover

SAUCE

1 stick unsalted butter

¾ cup skinned, seeded, and diced fresh plum or cherry tomatoes

¼ teaspoon and 1 tablespoon fine sea salt

⅓ cup slivered almonds

Did you know that the pumpkin is the symbol of the city of Mantua in the region of Lombardia?

Emilia-Romagna

the towel-lined trays loosely with aluminum foil and place them in the freezer for several hours. When the tortelloni are hard, transfer them to double-lined, heavy-duty, plastic zipper-lock bags and store them until needed. When ready to boil, take out what is needed and cook them frozen; do not allow them to thaw.

To prepare the sauce, in a saucepan, melt the butter over medium heat; do not allow it to brown. Stir in the tomatoes and ¼ teaspoon sea salt and cook just until the mixture is hot. Do not allow the tomatoes to disintegrate; they should hold their shape. Keep the sauce warm while the tortelloni are cooking.

To cook 2 dozen tortelloni, bring 4 quarts of water to a boil in a pasta pot. Stir in the remaining 1 tablespoon of salt. Gently add the tortelloni to the water. (I shake them from the towel into the water.) Cook uncovered for 2 to 3 minutes, but no longer, as fresh pasta cooks very quickly. With a strainer, scoop the tortelloni out of the water, shaking off the water, and place them in a shallow platter. Pour the warm sauce over the tortelloni. Sprinkle on the almonds and toss the mixture several times with two large spoons. Serve immediately.

Tortelli di Coste
(Swiss Chard Ravioli)

Makes approximately 7 to 7½ dozen 2-inch tortelli

Serves 10 to 12

Along with its sister cities of Bologna, Parma, and Modena, Reggio Emilia is a mecca for some of the most wonderful foods of the region of Emilia Romagna. Of course, it is the tortellini, tortelloni, *and* tortelli *(all forms of ravioli) that are the stars from this region, and these ricotta cheese and Swiss chard–filled tortelli are a good example of the deliciousness of the cuisine. At one time in Parma it was a tradition to make and eat these tortelli on the eve of the feast of Saint John (June 23–24), when green walnuts were harvested to make* nocino, *a smooth and powerful-tasting walnut liqueur. To ensure success, make sure the Swiss chard is well squeezed and the ricotta cheese well drained. There are no eggs in the filling, and if you need to cut down on fat, substitute skim-milk ricotta. Make the tortelli ahead, then freeze them in single layers on baking sheets to prevent them from sticking together before transferring them to freezer bags.*

To make the filling, fill a large soup pot with water and bring it to a boil. Add the Swiss chard and push it into the water with a wooden spoon to submerse it. Cook, uncovered, for 3 minutes. Drain the Swiss chard into a colander and with the back of a spoon push on it to squeeze out the excess water. Place the Swiss chard on a cutting board and let it cool. Mince it with a knife and place it in a bowl. Mix in the ricotta cheese, salt, pepper, and grated cheese. This should be a fairly dry mixture. Cover the bowl and refrigerate until ready to use.

To make the dough, in a large bowl or food processor, beat the eggs with the salt until smooth. Add the flour 1 cup at a time, mixing until a dough is formed that moves away from the sides of the

FILLING

2 pounds Swiss chard, well washed, stems removed

2 pounds ricotta cheese, well drained

1½ teaspoons fine sea salt

½ teaspoon coarsely ground black pepper

½ cup grated Parmigiano-Reggiano cheese

DOUGH

5 large eggs

¼ teaspoon fine sea salt

3 to 3¾ cups (15 ounces) unbleached all-purpose flour

SAUCE

2 sticks unsalted butter, melted

¾ cup grated Parmigiano-Reggiano cheese

bowl or food processor. The dough should feel soft and should hold together. It should not feel tacky or sticky—if it does, add a little more flour.

Knead the dough with your hands on a very lightly floured surface for about 3 or 4 minutes and let it rest for 30 minutes. It should be smooth and show no signs of flour. Divide the dough into four or five pieces and work with one piece at a time. Keep the rest covered.

With a rolling pin flatten each piece into a rectangle roughly 6×7 inches. Using a hand-crank pasta machine, thin the dough into a strip that is roughly 5 inches wide. (You can also use a rolling pin, but you will have more control over the thinness of the dough if you use a standard hand-crank pasta machine on the thinnest setting.)

Divide the strip into two equal pieces. Starting ¼ inch from the top edge of the strip, evenly space 6 tablespoons of the filling along the length of the strip. Make a second row of filling below the first, leaving about a ½-inch space between the rows. Cover the strip with the second piece of dough and, with the side of your hand, press down in between the filling lengthwise and crosswise to seal it.

Use a pastry wheel to cut between the sealed tortelli and place them on a floured baking sheet in a single layer. Repeat the process with the remaining dough, including the scraps.

To make the sauce, melt the butter in a saucepan, stir in ½ cup of the cheese, and keep the sauce warm while cooking the tortelli.

Bring a pasta pot with 6 to 8 quarts of water to a boil. Carefully transfer the tortelli with a slotted spoon to the water and cook them for 2 to 3 minutes, or until they are tender but not mushy. With a slotted spoon transfer them immediately to a platter. Pour the sauce over the top, toss them gently with two serving spoons, and sprinkle the remaining ¼ cup of cheese over the top. Serve immediately.

For cooking half of the tortelli, reduce the amount of sauce ingredients by half.

Did you know that Swiss chard is one of the most popular vegetables in Italy?

Emilia-Romagna

Gnocchi di Riso
(Rice Gnocchi)

Makes about 1½ dozen gnocchi

The idea of making gnocchi conjures up fear in some people. Most have eaten potato gnocchi, small bits of a flour and potato dough that is rolled off the tines of a fork, but they are hesitant to make them for fear the dough will be too tough. In our series I have introduced many types of gnocchi, including those made with spinach, pumpkin, and ricotta cheese. This Emilian version of rice gnocchi is not as well known. It is made with Arborio rice, the same short-grain, starchy rice used to make risotto. This recipe will work with leftover Arborio rice as well. The gnocchi can be made and refrigerated for a day before baking.

Bring the water to a boil in a 4-quart nonstick saucepan, add the salt, and stir in the rice. Cook the rice, uncovered, over medium heat, stirring occasionally, until the rice absorbs most of the water. This will take about 20 minutes. Transfer the rice to a bowl and let it come to room temperature, or refrigerate it for several hours to make it easier to shape into balls. Stir in the bread crumbs, 3 tablespoons of the butter, the nutmeg, ⅓ cup of the cheese, and the eggs.

Grease a baking dish with 1 teaspoon of the butter and set it aside. With your hands form balls the size of a small lemon. Roll each ball in flour and place in the baking pan. Melt the remaining 3 tablespoons of butter and pour it over the gnocchi. Sprinkle the remaining cheese over the top and season with more salt to taste. At this point the dish can be covered and refrigerated and baked the next day.

When ready to bake, preheat the oven to 350°F. Bake the gnocchi until they are nicely browned, about 35 minutes. Serve immediately.

6 cups water

1 teaspoon fine sea salt

1½ cups Arborio rice

¼ cup fresh bread crumbs

6 tablespoons plus 1 teaspoon unsalted butter, at room temperature

½ teaspoon grated nutmeg

⅔ cup grated Parmigiano-Reggiano cheese

2 eggs

Flour

Did you know that there is no such thing as salted butter in Italy? All butter is unsalted. If you are using salted butter in the recipe, adjust the amount of salt called for, to taste.

Emilia-Romagna

Bomba di Riso di Mara

(Mara's Rice Bomb)

Makes one 9-inch mold

½ pound boiled ham, cut
  thinly into approximately
  4½×6-inch-long slices

1 ounce dried porcini
  mushrooms

Warm water for soaking
  mushrooms—just enough
  to cover them

1 carrot, peeled and cut into
  chunks

1 stalk celery, cut into
  chunks

1 small onion, peeled and cut
  into chunks

1 tablespoon extra-virgin
  olive oil

1 tablespoon butter

1 clove garlic, minced

1 pound ground beef

1 tablespoon tomato paste

1 pound (2¼ cups) canned
  peeled tomatoes

2 tablespoons minced
  parsley

Fine sea salt to taste

Grinding of coarse black
  pepper

Emilia-Romagna

80

When I was first introduced to bomba di riso, *a rice bomb, I was very amused by the choice of words used to describe this impressive molded rice dish that is a staple in the kitchen of my friend Mara Neviani, who lives in Cavriago. The origins of this dish are said to trace back to the town of Piacenza, where it is still prepared for the Feast of the Assumption on August 15, known as Ferragosto. The procedure calls for the use of Arborio rice, the short-grain starchy rice used to make risotto. The rice is boiled in either chicken or beef broth, then packed into a ring mold that is lined with overlapping slices of cooked ham. The center of the mold is filled with a meat* ragù. *The contrasting tastes of delicately flavored rice and intensely flavored* ragù *is a delight. This dish makes a great presentation for company. The* ragù *can be made days ahead and the rice mold assembled a day prior to baking.*

Lightly butter a 9×2¼-inch ring mold. Line the mold with the ham slices, overlapping them slightly so no gaps appear, and allow a 2-inch overhang over the rim of the mold. Cover the mold loosely with plastic wrap and refrigerate it until ready to fill.

Place the mushrooms in a bowl, cover them with warm water, and let them soak for 30 minutes. Drain the mushrooms, reserving the liquid. Dice the mushrooms and set them aside.

Mince the carrot, celery, and onion together with a chef's knife.

Heat the oil and butter in a saucepan, stir in the carrot, celery, and onion and cook the vegetables over low heat until they are soft. Stir in the garlic and cook it until it begins to soften. Stir in the ground beef and cook it until it loses its pink color.

In a bowl mix together the tomato paste, tomatoes, and ½ cup of the reserved porcini liquid and add it to the beef mixture. (Save the remaining porcini liquid to use when making soups or stocks.) Stir in the parsley, salt, and pepper. Cover the pan and simmer the ragù for 1½ hours. Ten minutes before the ragù is cooked, stir in the mushrooms. The consistency of the mixture should be very thick with almost no liquid. Keep the ragù warm while the rice is cooking.

Bring the broth to a boil in a soup pot. Stir in the rice, cover, and cook it, stirring occasionally, until all the broth is absorbed. Stir in the cheese, butter, and cream.

Preheat the oven to 350°F.

Pack the rice evenly into the mold. Place the mold in a baking pan large enough to hold it and carefully pour hot water into the baking pan, allowing it to come up to about 1 inch along the sides of the ring mold. Bake for 25 minutes, or until the rice is hot. Remove the mold from the water bath, and run a butter knife around the inside edge of the mold to loosen the ham and ensure that it will unmold. Place a serving dish larger than the mold over the top and invert the mold onto the dish. Fill the center of the mold with some of the ragù. Put the remaining ragù in a bowl to pass separately. To serve, cut the mold into wedges and spoon some of the ragù on the side.

FOR THE RICE

6 cups chicken or beef broth

2½ cups Arborio rice

5 tablespoons grated Parmigiano-Reggiano cheese

1 tablespoon butter

¼ cup heavy cream

Did you know that a water bath, or a *bagnomaria* in Italian, is used when heat needs to be evenly distributed slowly when cooking some types of foods, like the *bomba di riso* or delicate custards and cheesecakes?

Emilia-Romagna

Coniglio all'Aceto Balsamico
(Rabbit in Balsamic Vinegar)

Serves 2

1 tablespoon butter

1 red onion (4 ounces),
  peeled and thinly sliced

¼ cup balsamic vinegar

1 tablespoon olive oil

¼ pound pancetta, thinly
  sliced

Fine sea salt to taste

Freshly ground black pepper
  to taste

2 pounds rabbit pieces,
  washed and dried

2 cloves garlic, minced

2 large shallots, peeled and
  minced

1¼ cups dry red wine

1 tablespoon minced fresh
  rosemary

Some say it has healing properties; others regard it as highly as a fine port. For me, it's the wonderful taste that aged balsamic vinegar imparts to game and poultry that makes it so special. Osteria di Rubbiara, in Modena, near Parma and Reggio Emilia, is the place to go to enjoy the finest rabbit cooked with wine and balsamic vinegar. The food is straightforward and is proudly prepared and served by owner Italo Pedroni, along with his wife and daughter. This rustic-looking inn with low beamed ceilings and wooden tables and chairs was originally a place where only men went to drink wine. Bottles of award-winning balsamic vinegar are on display along the walls, and the smells coming from the kitchen immediately tell you that the prized vinegar is a key ingredient in the cooking. Don't expect a menu, just follow the suggestions of Italo, who will whet your appetite with offerings of the classic tortellini in brodo, *or penne in a rich* salsa Bolognese *to start. For the second course the choices are even harder; roast pork and chicken or rabbit cooked in wine with balsamic vinegar were my favorites. When I asked Italo about the preparation of the rabbit, he smiled but would not divulge the recipe. What follows is an adaptation of the original. For best results use fresh domestic rabbit or chicken and cook the meat slowly to ensure tenderness without dryness. Because rabbit is so lean and bony, allow 1 pound per person for a serving. Bacon can be substituted for the pancetta, but the flavor will not be quite the same.*

In a heavy-clad sauté pan melt the butter over medium heat. Stir in the onions and sauté them, stirring occasionally, until they are limp and glazed looking. Stir in the vinegar and continue to cook, allowing most of the vinegar to evaporate. Remove the onions and any juice to a bowl. Add the oil and pancetta to the pan and cook until the pancetta is crisp. Remove the pancetta with a slotted spoon to the bowl with the onions. Rub salt and pepper all over the rabbit pieces. Add the rabbit to the pan along with the garlic and shallots and cook over medium heat, browning the rabbit evenly on all sides. Add ½ cup of the wine and continue cooking for 3 to 4 minutes. Return the onion mixture to the pan, add the remaining wine, and cook uncovered over low heat for 20 to 30 minutes, turning the rabbit pieces occasionally. The rabbit is cooked when a knife is easily inserted into the meat. Sprinkle the rosemary over the rabbit and serve immediately.

Did you know that the production of balsamic vinegar has a long history and that it is made from the unfermented Trebbiano grape must? The best aged *aceto balsamico,* which is at least twelve years old, and sometimes a hundred years old, never leaves Modena, and there is a tasting contest each year in the town of Spilamberto. Each vinegar is an artisanal product and will differ slightly in taste. Aged balsamic vinegar is syrupy and dark mahogany in color. The taste is sweet and acidic. Do not be fooled by imitations, of which there are many. Most vinegars bought in America are young vinegars, no more than five years old. These are fine for cooking. Look on the label to see if the product comes from Modena or Reggio Emilia; the label will have the abbreviations *Mo* for Modena or *RE* for Reggio Emilia. These are the two areas where the vinegar is made according to the rules of a *consorzio* that controls its production.

Arrosto di Maiale al Latte
(Boneless Rolled Pork Cooked in Milk)

Serves 6

2 tablespoons fresh
  rosemary needles

5 fresh sage leaves

2 cloves garlic, peeled

3 pounds boneless pork
  roast, tied

1 teaspoon fine sea salt

1 teaspoon coarsely ground
  black pepper

1 tablespoon butter

1 tablespoon olive oil

4 cups milk

2 tablespoons flour

Reggio Emilia is known for its wonderful food shops that sell superior food products such as prosciutto di Parma, Parmigiano-Reggiano cheese, tortellini, lasagne, and a host of other specialties. It is also home to our dear friends Lorenza and Sandro Iori. Their house, a beautifully restored villa, has all the right touches—antique clocks, delicate glass, and blue and white china. One night Lorenza made a typical Emilian meal for us. The star attraction was a succulent, boneless pork roast cooked in milk, which resulted in a wonderful gravy. Lorenza cautioned that in order for this dish to be successful, the pork must be fresh, rosy pink in color, and uniformly shaped. Make the dish a day ahead.

Mince together the rosemary, sage, and garlic on a cutting board. Transfer the herbs to a large plastic zipper-lock bag and set it aside.

Wipe the roast with paper towels. Rub the salt and pepper evenly all over the roast. Place the roast in the plastic bag with the herbs. Close the bag and roll the roast in the bag to evenly coat the meat with the herbs. Set it aside.

Heat the butter and olive oil in a 10×4-inch-deep Dutch oven or similar pot just large enough to hold the roast. Brown the meat on all sides over medium-low heat; this will take about 20 to 30 minutes and is the secret to flavorful meat.

Slowly pour in the milk almost to cover the roast. Cover the pot and cook over low heat for about 2 hours. As the roast cooks the milk will start to coagulate. When the meat is cooked, remove it to a dish and let it cool. Remove the strings, wrap the roast in aluminum foil and place it in the refrigerator.

Allow the remaining liquid in the cooking pot to cool. Place the covered pot in the refrigerator. The next day skim off any fat that has accumulated on the surface and discard it.

Return the pot to the stove top and cook the liquid down until it is reduced by one-third. As it cooks it will turn a deep brown color. Remove ½ cup of the reduced liquid from the pot to a small bowl, and, with a small whisk, beat in 2 tablespoons of flour until the mixture is smooth. Return the mixture to the pot and stir to blend the ingredients. Cook slowly for 2 minutes. Cover and set aside.

Cut the pork roast into ¼-inch slices and return them to the pot. Slowly heat the meat in the gravy until hot and serve immediately.

Tip: To remove rosemary needles from the stem, hold the stem from the tip end and run your fingers down it, stripping the needles as you go.

Tartufesta (Truffle Festival)

I scribbled in my journal *il tempo fa male oggi* (the weather is bad today) as I sat in the country home of my friend Luciano Berti in Polverara, a little hamlet near Sasso Marconi. But the rain and fog did not deter my curiosity to see what was happening at the *tartufesta* (truffle festival) in nearby San Benedetto Val di Sambro. Luciano was more than happy to take me there on such a dreary day, and the ride through the valley along winding roads was beautiful despite the weather. The trip was made more interesting by the number of old stone towers, once defensive sentinels, that lined the way, and the foliage was just beginning to tease the eyes with a color change that signaled a harsher season to come.

San Benedetto Val di Sambro that Sunday morning was just starting to come alive with people seeking to be near intoxicating black truffles, and as soon as we opened the car doors that unmistakable earthy odor surrounded us. I quickly whipped out my umbrella to repel the driving rain and headed for the makeshift tent city that had been set up in a hurry to protect the vendors and their precious displays of black nuggets from getting soaked. Boxes of the wrinkled black beauties, with dirt still clinging to them, were displayed on tables and guarded like the crown jewels. When I asked if I could buy some, the answer was no; these truffles were already spoken for and were merely for display! I consoled myself by heading to the cooking tent with only one mission: to have a taste of finely shaved black truffles over something—risotto, tagliatelle—or a smidge of intense-tasting truffle paste smeared on a slice of crusty bread. I could hardly believe my eyes when I scanned the menu: polenta with sausage, bean soup with ragged cut noodles called *maltagliati,* even *taralli* (small, hard ring biscuits flavored with pepper)—but no truffles!

I felt as bleak as the weather and ordered the *minestra con fagioli* (bean soup) and joined a group of the local residents sitting at a long table. They were curious about me. No one but the local citizenry ever came to San Benedetto's truffle festival. So we ate, drank Barbera wine, and talked of Italy and truffles. After lunch, and feeling better now that I had met new friends, I wandered through the rest of the festival, stopping to look at locally made honey, homemade breads, and local celebrated artist Pietro Romagnoli's exquisite bread sculptures made from flour and water. They included vases, flowers, and even a farm scene, all fashioned by hand. The constant smell of truffles became more intense as time went by. I stopped to talk to a vendor from Sardinia who was selling a young Pecorino cheese embedded with flakes of black truffles. The cheese was for sale, and I did not hesitate for a moment to buy a wedge to take with me. This was the closest I was going to get to having truffles from the tartufesta! On the drive home, truffle odor filled the car and I anticipated cracking open a bottle of wine and cutting into that cheese as soon as I reached the house.

No sooner had I taken off my coat than I was looking for a knife to cut into the cheese. It was smooth and semisoft and those tiny truffle flecks packed so much flavor into each bite that it was difficult to stop eating. But a wedge lasts only so long, I reasoned, and I wrapped the remaining cheese carefully in paper and put it in the refrigerator. When I returned to it the next day, the odor of truffles had permeated everything in the refrigerator; it was as if I were standing in the woods where black truffles had just been unearthed. It was hard to believe that these small chips of black gold could create such an intense smell. And for days after the last morsel of cheese was gone, the memory of it lingered on each time I opened the refrigerator door.

Emilia-Romagna

Tortina di Patate
(Potato Pie)

Serves 4 to 6

6 tablespoons unsalted
  butter, softened

½ cup toasted bread crumbs

1 pound Yukon Gold
  potatoes, peeled and cut
  into chunks

1¼ cups milk

⅓ cup grated Parmigiano-
  Reggiano cheese

2 tablespoons flour

½ teaspoon salt

¼ teaspoon grated nutmeg

3 tablespoons finely minced
  parsley leaves

2 eggs

At first this sounds like just another mashed potato recipe, but the dish is elevated to something more with the addition of a cream sauce that is folded into the potatoes before being baked. Parmigiano-Reggiano cheese and a whiff of nutmeg complete the nice balance of flavors. Serve this with roasted chicken or with steak.

Use 1 tablespoon of the butter to grease an 8-inch baking pan. Sprinkle ¼ cup of the bread crumbs over the butter and set the pan aside.

Put the potatoes in a saucepan, cover them with cold water, and cook the potatoes until they are soft. Drain the potatoes and return them to the saucepan. Heat the potatoes briefly on low heat to "dry them."

Transfer the potatoes to a ricer and rice them over a large bowl, or mash them with a hand masher until they are smooth. Stir in ¼ cup of the milk, the cheese, and 1 tablespoon of the butter. Cover the bowl and set aside.

Preheat the oven to 350°F.

In a small saucepan melt 2 tablespoons of the butter over medium heat. Whisk in the flour to form a smooth paste. Slowly pour in the remaining milk, whisking continually. Cook the mixture until it thickens slightly, just enough to coat a spoon. Remove the sauce from the heat and stir in the salt, nutmeg, and parsley. Stir in the eggs, one at a time, and blend well.

Transfer the sauce to the bowl with the mashed potatoes and combine the two until the sauce and the potatoes are well blended.

Emilia-Romagna

Spread the mixture in the prepared pan. Sprinkle the remaining bread crumbs evenly over the top of the potatoes and dot with the remaining butter.

Bake for 25 to 30 minutes, or until heated through and the top is nicely browned. Serve immediately directly from the pan.

Erbazzone di Mara
(Mara's Swiss Chard Pie)

Makes one 9-inch pie

FILLING

¼ cup raisins or candied citron, diced

1¾ pounds Swiss chard or spinach, stemmed and washed

One 15-ounce container skim-milk ricotta cheese, well drained

½ teaspoon fine sea salt

½ teaspoon grated nutmeg

2 tablespoons sugar

PASTA FROLLA
(PASTRY DOUGH)
(makes 12 ounces dough)

1¼ cups unbleached all-purpose flour

¼ cup potato starch

¼ teaspoon fine sea salt

¼ cup sugar

4 tablespoons unsalted butter, cut into bits

2 large eggs

2 tablespoons water

This recipe for erbazzone, *a specialty of Reggio Emilia and Piacenza, comes from longtime friend Raffaella Neviani's mother, Mara, who lives in Cavriago, not far from Reggio Emilia. Mara made this savory, country* torta *(pie) one night when I came to visit. It is usually made with Swiss chard or spinach. When it is encased in a slightly sweetened pastry crust it is called erbazzone, and when made without a crust it is called scarpazzone. This pie actually has an ancient history going back to Roman times. Of course there are many variations of the recipe; some use a pastry made with only lard, water, and salt. The filling can be flavored with pancetta, or onions and parsley. Mara's filling included ricotta cheese and raisins. Cook the Swiss chard or spinach dry in a soup pot with only the water clinging to its leaves after cleaning it. This rustic pie is delicious served hot or at room temperature. It also makes an unusual picnic food.*

To prepare the filling, soak the raisins in warm water for 30 minutes. Drain and dry them, then dice them and place them in a large bowl.

Put the Swiss chard or spinach in a soup pot with no additional water. Cover the pot and cook over medium heat just until the leaves wilt down; this will take about 4 or 5 minutes. Drain the leaves in a colander and squeeze them with the back of a spoon to extract as much water as possible. Coarsely chop the greens and add them to the bowl with the raisins. Stir in the drained ricotta cheese, salt, nutmeg, and sugar. Mix well, then cover and refrigerate while you make the dough.

To prepare the *pasta frolla,* in a food processor or bowl, mix to-

Emilia-Romagna

gether the flour, potato starch, salt, and sugar. Pulse in the butter or use a pastry blender to reduce the butter to small bits. Add 1 of the eggs and the water and pulse or mix until a ball of dough is obtained that is moist but holds together. If the dough seems dry, add 1 drop of water at a time until you get the right consistency. Flatten the ball into a disk and wrap it tightly in plastic wrap. Refrigerate for 1 hour.

Preheat the oven to 375°F.

Lightly butter or spray a 9-inch tart pan with a removable bottom. Set it aside.

Divide the dough in half. Roll out each half on a floured surface to a 12-inch circle. Fold one dough circle in quarters, then lift it and unfold it, draping it into the tart pan. Trim the dough even with the top edge of the tart pan.

Add the filling to the tart pan, spreading it evenly. Fold the second piece of dough in quarters, place it on top of the filling at the center, then unfold the dough and trim it even with the edges. Reroll the scraps of dough and use a cookie cutter to make cutouts for the top of the pastry. Beat the remaining egg slightly and with a pastry brush paint the top crust evenly with the egg wash. With a scissors make a V in the center of the crust.

Bake the pie for 35 to 40 minutes, or until the crust is golden brown. Cool the pie on a rack for 20 minutes before serving.

Did you know that the best way to separate Swiss chard from its stem is to fold the leaves back on themselves and tear them away from the stem? Save the stems to use when making soup.

Insalata di Radicchio e Pancetta alla Trattoria Chilo

(Radicchio and Bacon Salad Trattoria Chilo Style)

Serves 6

¼-pound chunk pancetta, diced

1 large onion, peeled and diced

4 tablespoons balsamic vinegar

½ pound (two small heads) radicchio, washed, drained, and torn into pieces

¼ teaspoon fine sea salt

2 tablespoons extra-virgin olive oil

Shavings of Parmigiano-Reggiano cheese

Outside the main gate to Ravenna's old city center is an inviting little restaurant called Trattoria Chilo. My husband Guy and I dined there outside on the patio surrounded by brick walls and climbing plants. The owner, Rita Pezzi, is a vivacious person who gives cooking lessons in her spare time. She is lots of fun to talk to about Emilian cuisine. Our first course was cappellacci, fresh pasta stuffed with a mixture of fragrant herbs and Parmigiano-Reggiano cheese. After that we were offered un' assaggio, a tasting of paper-thin lasagne sheets with a mixture of vegetables nestled between them, and a plate of grilled vegetables, including the elongated radicchio di Treviso. After all that, Guy was still hungry, so he ordered rabbit cooked with grapes, lemon, and parsley. I opted for a refreshing radicchio salad that was flavored with fried bits of pancetta (Italian bacon) and onions that had been cooked in a young balsamic vinegar. I was glad I did!

Cook the pancetta without any additional fat in a sauté pan set over medium heat until it is crisp. Drain the pancetta on brown paper and set it aside.

Wipe out the sauté pan with a paper towel. Add the onion and the balsamic vinegar and cook over medium heat until the vinegar has evaporated. Stir the onion once or twice during the cooking. Transfer the onion to a dish and set it aside.

Put the radicchio in a salad bowl and mix in the pancetta and the onions. Toss the mixture with the salt, then with the olive oil.

Use a vegetable peeler to make long, thin shavings of Parmigiano-Reggiano cheese on top of the salad. Serve immediately.

The Town of Murals

I just like the way it sounds. Dozza. The name of a sleepy little town, southeast of Bologna, that is anything but dull. Dozza has the distinction of being one of the oldest towns in Italy. I had read about it years ago and when I finally visited it, I made a mental note that this would be the ideal place to come back and film a segment of real Italian life for *Ciao Italia*.

With a population of less than a thousand, Dozza is my kind of town. It has gorgeous, pastoral scenery; it has La Rocca, the impressive fortress that was once the home of the ruling Sforza family and now serves as a cantina for all of the wines produced in the region of Emilia Romagna; and it has amazing, vibrantly painted walls in canary yellow, sky blue, and coral. As I walked down its quiet, narrow streets I noticed that the walls were covered with murals (*muri dipinti*) depicting every artistic subject imaginable from still life to geometric designs. Did this have some significant meaning? I had to know.

I found a *tabacchi* that was open. The signora behind the counter could not have been more gracious. She was surprised to see Americans, she said, since no one but the folks from the surrounding towns ever came to Dozza to sample the wines like Albana, Malvasia, and Lambrusco. The murals, she proudly explained, have been in existence since 1960 and are the work of over 150 itinerant artists. Every two years these artists come to Dozza and leave their signature works of art on the town's walls. The people of Dozza take it all in stride, she said, and always have something nice to look at. It's a permanent outdoor art museum.

I asked her where I should have lunch. She pointed toward La

Emilia-Romagna

93

Rocca and said *"La, c'è Ristorante da Marino."* The restaurant was on a hillside overlooking the wine-growing valleys below and had a great view of La Rocca. The menu featured all homemade pasta. I had tagliatelle with prosciutto, followed by grilled chicken with specks of fresh herbs and a spritz of lemon juice, simple but flavorful. For dessert I had *dolce fritto,* a combination of pear and apple chunks that were mixed together in a batter and fried. They were served with confectioners' sugar.

I could have stayed in Dozza longer, just listening to the local chatter and the soothing call of the church bells, browsing for hours through its streets, and looking at those amazing murals. Dozza is definitely on my list of places to return to.

Torta di Amarena
(Cherry Tart)

Makes one 10¼ × 1-inch tart

All the cares and stresses that each day brings seem to evaporate once Italians step into their local pasticceria *(pastry shop) and indulge in something sweet like a* cornetto, babà au rhum, *or a slice of glistening* torta di frutta. *And when they are invited to someone's home for dinner, they bring cakes, tarts, or cookies from the pastry shop all beautifully wrapped and tied with a bow. I like to duplicate many of these sweets in my kitchen. Fruit tarts are a favorite, like this Amarena cherry tart. Amarena cherries are small, dark red, and slightly sour, and take their name from the word* amare, *which means "bitter." They grow around the cities of Bologna and Modena and are preserved in a sugar syrup, which makes them perfect for drizzling over a plain cake, or topping off a dish of vanilla ice cream. When ground to a paste and set in a sweet pastry crust, Amarena cherries make such a dense and intense-tasting tart that a mere sliver of a wedge will make you swoon. Amarena cherries are very expensive, so make this tart for a special occasion. One export company, Fabbri, sells them in beautiful blue and white glass jars. These are available in Italian specialty stores or by mail order (see page 347).*

PASTRY DOUGH

2 cups unbleached all-purpose flour

¼ teaspoon salt

½ cup sugar

6 tablespoons cold unsalted butter

2 large egg yolks, slightly beaten

2 to 4 tablespoons or more ice water

FILLING

3 cups (2¼ pounds) drained Amarena cherries

2 tablespoons milk for brushing top of dough

1 tablespoon turbinado (coarse brown) sugar

To prepare the dough, in a bowl or food processor, mix the flour, salt, and sugar together. Work in the butter with a pastry blender or pulse it several times in the food processor until the mixture resembles coarse meal. Blend in the yolks and water, or add them through the feed tube and pulse to blend, until a ball of dough is formed. If the dough seems dry, add a little more water. Divide the dough into two pieces, one slightly larger than the other, and wrap in plastic wrap. Refrigerate for 1 hour.

Emilia-Romagna

To prepare the filling, put the drained cherries in a food processor and pulse until a smooth, thick paste is obtained. Alternately use a blender. There should be about 3¼ cups of smooth cherry paste. The drained syrup can be saved to spoon over fresh fruit, ice cream, or sherbet.

Lightly butter a 10¼×1-inch-deep tart pan with a removable bottom. Set it aside.

Preheat the oven to 425°F.

On a floured surface, roll out the larger piece of dough to a 14-inch circle. Lightly dust the top of the dough and fold it loosely into quarters. Lift the dough and position it in the tart pan with the point of the fold in the center of the pan. Carefully unfold the dough and fit it to the pan, trimming off the excess at the top edges. Any pastry dough scraps can be rerolled and used to line small tart pans for jam tarts.

Spread the filling over the dough and set it aside.

Roll the second piece of dough into a 12-inch circle. Use a pastry wheel to cut twelve ½-inch-wide strips. Lay six of the strips vertically over the top of the filling, spacing them evenly. Lay the remaining strips horizontally over the first strips, spacing them evenly. Trim and pinch the ends to seal.

Brush the strips with the milk and sprinkle the turbinado sugar evenly over the top.

Bake for 30 to 35 minutes, or until the crust is golden brown. Cool the tart completely on a wire rack, remove the sides of the tart pan, then transfer the tart to a serving dish. Cut with a sharp knife into thin wedges and serve.

Variation: Serve the tart with a little sweetened whipped cream or a small scoop of vanilla ice cream.

Did you know that in an Italian *pasticceria,* customers make their selections and pay for them first, before being served?

Zuccherotti di Polverara
(Sugar Puffs from Polverara)

Makes 12 puffs

Polverara, a tiny hamlet near Sasso Marconi, is a relaxing country re-treat where my friend Luciano Berti has a wonderful rustic home. There I take over his kitchen and happily cook Italian food to my heart's content. One of his favorite recipes is zuccherotti di Polverara, *fried and sugared puffs of yeast dough. Luciano says the recipe comes from his grandmother's servant, who made them for his afternoon* merenda (snack) *after school. They were served with* karkade, *a tea made from hibiscus flowers. I love them as a treat on Sunday morning, slathered with marmalade. The dough can be made a day ahead of time in a food processor, mixer, or by hand, left to rise, then punched down, placed in a plastic bag, and refrigerated. In the morning divide the dough into small balls, let them rise for about 1 hour, then fry them up and serve them hot. It is very important that the vegetable oil be the proper temperature in order for the puffs to fry quickly. Test the temperature by dropping a marble-size piece of dough into the oil. If the oil sizzles and the dough browns and rises immediately, it is hot enough.*

½ cup warm milk (110°F)

1 tablespoon active dry yeast

1 cup plus 2 tablespoons sugar

3 eggs, slightly beaten

7 tablespoons unsalted butter, softened

3½ to 4 cups unbleached all-purpose flour

1 teaspoon fine sea salt

1 tablespoon wheat gluten (optional)*

5 cups vegetable oil for frying

In a food processor with dough blade inserted combine the milk and yeast. Alternately mix the ingredients in a bowl by hand, or use an electric mixer. Pulse or stir in 1 cup of the sugar, the eggs, and butter. Add 2 cups of the flour, the salt, and wheat gluten to the bowl and process to combine, or mix with your hands in a bowl. Add enough of the remaining flour to create a ball of dough that moves away from the sides of the food processor, or does not stick to your hands. The dough should be soft and pliable, but not sticky. Adding too much flour will result in heavy-tasting puffs.

Transfer the dough from the bowl onto a lightly floured work

Emilia-Romagna

surface and knead it until smooth and soft. Place the dough in a bowl. Cover the bowl with plastic wrap, and allow the dough to rise for 2 hours. Punch down the dough, transfer it to a work surface, and knead it again for a few minutes. Divide the dough into 12 equal pieces and roll each piece under the palm of your hand to form a tight ball about 2 inches in diameter.

Place the balls on a clean towel, cover, and allow them to rise for 1 hour. They should be double their size when ready to fry.

Meanwhile heat the vegetable oil in a deep fryer to 375°F. Or use a heavy-clad pot and a thermometer to gauge the temperature of the oil.

Fry the balls a few at a time until they are puffed and golden brown. Remove them with a slotted spoon, and allow them to drain on brown paper.

Place the warm puffs in a heavy-duty paper bag and add the remaining sugar. Close the top of the bag and shake the bag to coat the puffs with the sugar.

Transfer the puffs to a serving dish and serve warm.

Note: For miniature-size puffs, divide the dough into 24 equal pieces before shaping them into balls.

*Wheat gluten is found in the baking section of grocery stores and is used to promote yeast growth, and give added strength to rising dough.

Albicocche Cotte al Vino
(Apricots Cooked in Wine)

Serves 4 to 6

Fresh apricots simmered in dry white wine was my choice for a refreshing dessert at Osteria di Rubbiara. Select apricots that feel heavy, yield gently to the touch, and have no brown spots. Once the apricots are cooked, they can be used in a variety of ways, including serving them as is, or as a sauce over ice cream or lemon sherbet, or over a plain cake. Fresh basil complements the taste of the apricots. They also make a great hostess gift when spooned into a decorative jar and covered with wine syrup.

2 cups dry white wine, such as chardonnay

½ cup sugar

One 5-inch piece vanilla bean

1¼ pounds fresh apricots, washed, stemmed, cut in half, and pitted

2 or 3 sprigs of fresh basil leaves

Heat the wine in a 10×2-inch-deep sauté pan. Stir in the sugar and cook gently until the sugar dissolves. Add the vanilla bean and the apricots cut-side down in a single layer in the pan. Lower the heat and simmer the apricots for about 4 minutes. Do not overcook them or they will turn mushy and not hold their shape.

With a slotted spoon remove the apricots to a serving bowl. Continue cooking the wine for about 10 minutes, or until it is slightly syrupy. Remove the vanilla bean and pour the syrup over the apricots. Add the basil leaves. Let the apricots cool to room temperature before serving.

Did you know that cutting a whole apricot along the side where there is an indentation line and then twisting the fruit will result in two perfect halves?

Note: The apricots can be made ahead and kept in the refrigerator for a week.

Emilia-Romagna

Tuscany

Antipasti

Pomodori Ripieni d'Emma (Emma's Stuffed Tomatoes)
Crostini Toscani (Tuscan Crostini)
Pane Toscano (Tuscan Bread)

Primi Piatti

Zuppa di Funghi (Mushroom Soup)
Zuppa di Verza, Patate e Fagioli (Cabbage, Potato, and Bean Soup)
Cannellini con Fettuccine e Salvia (Cannellini Beans with Fettuccine
   and Sage)

Secondi Piatti

Carciofi Ripieni di Maiale (Pork-Stuffed Artichokes)
Peposo (Tuscan Tilemakers' Stew)

Insalate

Insalata di Messalina (Messalina's Salad)
Insalata di Funghi Freschi con Formaggio (Mushroom Salad with
   Cheese)

Dolci

Biscotti di Prato
Spumini Mandorlati (Almond Foams)
Schiacciata alla Fiorentina (Florentine Flat Cake)
Nocciolata (Nutty Squares)

Tuscany is light, cypress trees, Ponte Vecchio, Michelangelo, porchetta, Chianti, sunflowers, Giotto, biscotti di Prato, Palazzo Davanzati, the Medici, San Lorenzo market, leather, Florentine paper, Palio, focaccia, Pecorino cheese, fettunta, Uffizi, David, cannellini beans, Nanini, panforte, bistecca, Vespa, gold, olive trees, Carrara marble, Arno River, Renaissance, ribolitta, Leaning Tower of Pisa, trippa, pappardelle, alchermes, Maremma, San Gimignano, Brunello di Montalcino, Etruscan, Santa Croce, Sforza, Baptistry doors, Torre di Mangia, red poppies, hay, schiacciata, Dante, Pitti Palace, Ghirlandaio, Brunelleschi, Fiesole, cenci, ricciarelli, cavolo nero, cacciucco.

Tuscany was one of the first regions I visited in Italy. It was on my list of must-see regions, because I am a big fan of Dante Alighieri, the fourteenth-century author of *The Divine Comedy,* whose work I had struggled with in college and graduate school. Here was a complex man exiled from his native Florence with a price on his head for his political thinking. Dante never returned to Florence, seeking refuge in places like Verona, and upon his death was buried in Ravenna adjacent to the Romanesque Church of San Francesco, where he often prayed and where his funeral was held. To this day, the Florentines are still trying to bring his body back to Florence.

There is nothing simple about living in Florence. It is a giant of a city for Tuscan achievements, a city saturated with so much art, history, and culture that it is prey to tourists day after day. Florence was home to many greats in the arts and sciences and to major ruling families like the Medicis. There are so many famous names associated with Tuscany that a list of them would read like a litany of saints. Who determined that so many great minds and achievements would come from this one area?

Michelangelo was a Florentine. I read his life's story in Irving

Stone's book *The Agony and the Ecstasy*. After that I had to see some of his masterpieces, especially the *David* in the Academy of Art. All the power and determination of the human spirit is captured in this single sculpture of David.

Florence and some of the other major tourist areas of Siena, Pisa, Lucca, and San Gimignano can overwhelm the visitor. I like to get away from all the activity and get a simpler perspective of life in Tuscany in the smaller cities, towns, and rural communities. Cortona and Arezzo in eastern Tuscany are two places I recommend.

Tuscan food is unfussy and straightforward. Simple grilled meats, fowl, and fish brushed with olive oil, maybe a squirt of lemon juice, a little salt, a few herbs, and that's it. Tuscan cooking uses no elaborate sauces or complicated ingredients. One of the first specialties highlighted on my series was Tuscan bread, round or elongated loaves of saltless bread that become the canvas for a spread of pureed cannellini beans, or chicken livers with fresh sage, or chopped tomatoes with fresh basil. The bread is cleverly used as a thickener in soups too. After that show aired, I did a book signing in Boston, and met a little girl not more than eight years old, who came with her mother. The mother began telling me how much her daughter watched *Ciao Italia*—so much in fact that one day while the two of them were shopping, the mother asked the girl if she was hungry, and would she like to stop at a pastry shop for something. "Yes," came the reply, and when the clerk asked her what she wanted, she blurted out, "A loaf of Tuscan bread!"

What is Tuscany without vineyards? They blanket the region. I often feature wine in our televised segments. What I have come to tell viewers is that Italians regard wine as a food, an integral part of the meal, not just a beverage treated like the occasional cocktail. I have also explained that the production of wine is a very complex process that starts with weather, soil, and type of grape. The best way to learn about Italian wines is to read about what wines come from what regions, and to train your palate to look at, smell, and taste a variety of regional wines. I encourage the viewer to cook with wine and use the same wine for cooking that would give pleasure sipped from a glass.

In a host of books on Tuscan cooking, the words *cucina povera* (poor cooking) are used to describe the food. If what this means is economical cooking with locally grown ingredients, then I agree. For example, grapes are pressed into sweetened yeast dough to become a delicious flat cake; chestnuts are gathered and ground into flour for making cakes and pasta; cannellini beans are dried after harvesting and saved for winter soups; when pigs are butchered, use is made of the whole animal, including the blood, for a pudding called *sanguinaccio*. Wild mushrooms are turned into hearty soups and made into a sauce for pasta. These are the kinds of foods that typify Tuscans' "poor cooking."

Giovanni Lodovico, a Tuscan wine and food writer who is also a friend, wrote a book on Tuscan cooking in which he says that the characteristics that set Tuscan cooking apart from other regional cooking are the patience of the cook and the care with which foods are prepared. I think what he means is that it takes more skill to cook simple food well than to cook complicated "gourmet food."

Pomodori Ripieni d'Emma
(Emma's Stuffed Tomatoes)

Serves 6

6 fresh plum tomatoes (1¼ pounds), washed

1 cup packed Italian parsley, leaves only

2 cloves garlic, peeled

4 to 5 tablespoons extra-virgin olive oil

¼ teaspoon fine sea salt

⅓ cup diced mostarda di frutta or mixed candied fruit

⅓ to ½ cup extra-virgin olive oil

12 small slices bread

One day while sitting in my friend Emma Berti's kitchen, I quizzed her about what she liked to cook. Emma is Neapolitan by birth but lives near Florence. I expected her to shower me with information about Neapolitan cooking when she said: "Let me show you my quick tomato sauce." Out came a well-worn pan. I expected the tomatoes, olive oil, and garlic to be next, but Emma surprised me when she poured milk into the pan and heated it, and then took a whole tube of tomato paste and squeezed it into the milk! A little salt, some minced parsley, and the sauce was ready! But for me the real triumph in her kitchen was the baked plum tomatoes stuffed with a parsley and garlic pesto, and topped with a dice of mostarda di frutta, a delicious mixture of such whole fruits as pears, cherries, and plums preserved in sugar syrup. Mostarda di frutta can be found in Italian specialty shops or purchased by mail order (see page 347). If it is not available, substitute diced candied fruits. Serve this dish warm as an antipasto.

Preheat the oven to 350°F.

Core the tomatoes, cut them in half lengthwise, and squeeze out the seeds. Or use the handle of a teaspoon to scrape out the seeds.

Spray a 12-inch baking dish with vegetable spray. Place the tomato halves in the dish, cut-side up. If the tomatoes do not sit level in the dish, shave a small amount off the bottom of the tomato with a small knife.

Put the parsley and garlic in the bowl of a food processor. Grind the mixture until it is coarse. With the motor running, add the olive oil, a little at a time, until a paste the consistency of pesto sauce is obtained. Transfer the mixture to a bowl and stir in the salt.

Fill the tomato cavities with some of the parsley mixture.

Bake the tomatoes, uncovered, for 25 to 30 minutes, or until they soften but hold their shape. Remove the tomatoes from the oven and spread a little of the diced fruits over the top of each one.

While the tomatoes are baking, heat the olive oil in a sauté pan and brown the bread slices on both sides. Transfer them to a towel-lined dish.

Place each tomato half on a slice of the bread and serve immediately.

Crostini Toscani

(Tuscan Crostini)

2 to 2½ dozen crostini

½ cup extra-virgin olive oil

2 medium onions, peeled
and sliced

2 pounds chicken livers,
washed and dried

2-ounce can anchovies in
olive oil, oil drained

¼ cup capers in salt, rinsed

½ cup brandy

Juice of 1 lemon

¼ teaspoon salt

Small slices of bread, about
2 inches in diameter

Sage leaves for garnish

Cherry tomato slices for
garnish

Crostini are small pieces of toasted bread with various toppings. A popular one in Tuscany features chicken livers with capers. This recipe makes a lot and is great for a party. This is best made in a food processor.

Heat 3 tablespoons of the olive oil in a sauté pan over medium heat. Stir in the onions and sauté them until they begin to soften. Do not let them brown. Add the remaining olive oil and the chicken livers and sauté them, turning them occasionally. Use a small knife to pierce one of the livers as they are cooking; when the center is no longer red-brown in color, stir in the anchovies and the capers and cook for another 2 minutes. Pour in the brandy and allow it to evaporate. Turn off the heat and stir in the lemon juice and salt.

Transfer the mixture to a food processor and process until a paste is obtained. Transfer the mixture to a container and refrigerate.

When ready to serve, bring the liver mixture to room temperature. Toast small pieces of bread and spread some of the liver mixture over the top of the slices. Garnish with a small sage leaf and a cherry tomato slice. Serve the crostini at room temperature.

Pane Toscano
(Tuscan Bread)

Makes 1 large loaf

Tuscan bread has its roots in history. It seems that the people of Tuscany refused to pay a tax levied on salt in the thirteenth and fourteenth centuries. As a result, when bread was made it contained no salt, and to this day Tuscan bread is saltless. But Tuscans are clever about their bread, making up for the lack of salt by using a grating of fresh garlic and a drizzle of olive oil for seasoning. They smother slices with chicken livers and fresh sage, or place thick slices in the bottom of a soup bowl to add texture and bulk to soup. The bread dough begins by making a starter or sponge that needs a day to bubble and brew before combining it with the rest of the ingredients. I like to bake this bread on an oven baking stone, but you can also use a baking sheet.

SPONGE

1 teaspoon active dry yeast

½ cup warm water (110°F)

1 cup unbleached all-purpose flour

DOUGH

1½ teaspoons active dry yeast

1¼ cups warm water (110°F)

4 to 4½ cups unbleached all-purpose flour

To make the sponge, sprinkle the yeast over the water in a bowl. Stir to dissolve the yeast and allow it to get foamy. Add the flour with a spoon and mix well. The mixture should have the consistency of a soft dough. Cover the bowl with plastic wrap and allow to rise in a warm, draft-free place for 24 hours.

To make the dough, in a large bowl sprinkle the yeast over ¼ cup of the water and let it proof until foamy. Add the remaining cup of water and the sponge and mix them together well with your hands. Add 3½ cups of the flour and mix well, then add enough of the remaining flour to make a soft ball. Turn the dough out onto a floured surface and knead it until the dough is smooth and not bumpy looking. Place the dough in a lightly greased bowl. Cover the bowl tightly with plastic wrap and allow to rise for 3 to 4 hours.

Tuscany

Turn the dough out onto a floured surface and gently form it into a round or oblong loaf. Place the loaf on a baker's peel lined with parchment paper, if using the baking stone, or place the dough on a greased baking sheet. Cover and let rise for 35 minutes, or until nearly doubled in size.

Preheat the oven to 400°F.

Make three quick slashes across the top of the bread with a clean razor blade or lame (bread slasher tool), about 3 to 4 inches long and ¼ inch deep, to allow gas to escape and prevent the bread from splitting as it bakes.

If using the baking stone, set it on the bottom rack of the oven to preheat for 30 minutes. If using the stone, slide the dough with the parchment paper from the peel onto the stone and bake for 35 to 40 minutes, or until the bread is evenly browned and the bottom crust is hard. If baking on a baking sheet, bake for 40 to 45 minutes, or until the bread is nicely browned and hollow sounding when tapped on the bottom.

Remove the bread from the oven to a cooling rack and cool completely before serving.

Zuppa di Funghi
(Mushroom Soup)

Serves 4 (makes 1 quart)

Funghi (mushrooms) are near and dear to the hearts of Italians. I am in awe of their knowledge of all types of wild mushrooms and of their determination to seek out the best that the countryside has to offer. One of my favorite episodes of Ciao Italia *dealt with foraging for porcini mushrooms in the hills around Napa Valley, California. I learned to look for telltale signs of where they were lurking—under oak trees, where little mounds of earth erupted. In Italy, mushroom gathering is a national pastime, and while staying in Cortona, I did my best to seek out and cook all kinds of mushrooms. Mushrooms should be cooked as soon as you get them so they will be at peak flavor. I use just a damp paper towel or mushroom brush to clean them, preferring not to soak them in water. To add more flavor to this mushroom soup, I add leftover meat juices from roasts that I have saved and frozen, as well as red wine. But you can substitute beef bouillon for the meat juice if you wish. Just be more sparing with the salt, since bouillon tends to have more than enough salt.*

I use a variety of mushrooms and serve the soup over slices of toasted Tuscan Bread (see the bread recipe, page 109).

1¾ pounds mixed assorted fresh mushrooms— portobello, shiitake, crimini, button

2 tablespoon extra-virgin olive oil

1¼ cups (4 ounces) diced leeks

1 large clove garlic, minced

2 tablespoons minced Italian parsley leaves

¾ cup meat juice or bouillon

¼ cup dry red wine

1 teaspoon fine sea salt

Grinding of coarse black pepper

1 tablespoon fresh thyme

4 slices bread, toasted

Extra-virgin olive oil for drizzling on bread slices (optional)

Clean the mushrooms with a mushroom brush or damp cloth. Trim the stems and cut the mushrooms into thin slices. Heat the olive oil over medium heat in a 4- to 6-quart saucepan or soup pot. Add the mushrooms and the leeks and cook them together, stirring frequently. Stir in the garlic and continue cooking until the mushrooms begin to exude their juices. Don't worry if the mushrooms seem crowded in the pan; as they cook they will wilt down.

Stir in the parsley, the meat juice or bouillon, wine, salt, and

Tuscany

111

pepper. Cover the pot and cook the soup for 10 to 12 minutes. Stir in the thyme.

To serve, place a slice of bread in each of 4 soup bowls. Ladle the soup over the bread and drizzle with a little extra-virgin olive oil, if desired. Serve piping hot.

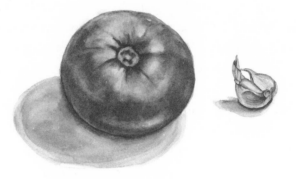

Zuppa di Verza, Patate e Fagioli
(Cabbage, Potato, and Bean Soup)

Makes 3 quarts

While visiting Prato I stopped to have lunch at Osteria La Farnacia dei Sani. The rustic walls of this tavern, which is also an enoteca *(wine shop), are lined with bottles of regional wine. The patrons dine* faccia a faccia *(face to face) at long wooden tables seated on rock-hard benches. There is no menu; the waiters just rattle off the kitchen's offerings like drill sergeants. My choice,* zuppa di verza, patate e fagioli *(cabbage soup with potatoes and beans), was served in deep bowls accompanied by hunks of Tuscan bread and a flask of extra-virgin olive oil for drizzling on the soup. One of my favorite techniques for flavoring this soup is to crumble chicken bouillon cubes over the sautéing vegetables instead of dissolving the cubes in liquid first. I also like to add the cheese rinds from Parmigiano-Reggiano cheese. Start the process the night before by soaking the beans in water. The recipe makes a lot and the soup can be frozen for future use.*

The night before making the soup, soak the beans in 2 cups of water. The following day, drain and rinse the beans, put them in a pot and cover them with 3 cups of water. Cook the beans for 20 minutes, then drain them and set them aside.

In a soup pot, heat the olive oil, stir in the crumbled bouillon cubes, cabbage, carrot, and onion. Cover the pot and cook the vegetables over medium heat for 20 minutes. Uncover the pot, stir in the beans, potatoes, water, and cheese rinds (if using), and cook, covered, over low heat for 45 minutes, or until the beans are tender, hold their shape, and are not mushy. Stir in the parsley, salt, and black pepper.

1 cup dried cranberry or Great Northern beans

1 tablespoon extra-virgin olive oil

4 chicken bouillon cubes, crumbled

1 pound cabbage, washed, cut in half, core removed, and leaves cut into ¼-inch strips

1 medium-size carrot, shaved into strips with a vegetable peeler

½ pound of onions, peeled and diced

½ pound all-purpose potatoes, peeled and diced

7 cups hot water

4 ounces cheese rinds (optional)*

¼ cup minced Italian parsley leaves

1 tablespoon fine sea salt

Grinding of black pepper

Extra-virgin olive oil to drizzle over soup

Tuscany

Remove the cheese rinds with a spoon and with a small knife scrape off the cheese and return it to the pot. Discard the rinds.

Serve the soup hot in soup bowls with a drizzle of olive oil over the top.

Variation: Place toasted slices of Italian bread in the base of individual soup bowls and ladle the soup over the bread.

See tip about use of cheese rinds on page 261.

Did you know that one of the best things to buy in Italian grocery stores are bouillon cubes? They are made by Knorr but are much larger than the bouillon cubes available here, and they have a more concentrated flavor. I always make a habit of buying a few boxes to bring home.

Cannellini con Fettuccine e Salvia

(Cannellini Beans with Fettuccine and Sage)

Serves 4 to 6

Dried beans were historically considered "poor man's meat" and have been one of the main sources of protein in Italy and worldwide. So it is not surprising to see so many dishes made with beans. In Tuscany, and in particular in Florence, cooking beans is serious business. Beans are to Florentine cooking what rice and polenta are to Venetian cooking. Beans cooked in a flask, beans served at room temperature with onions and olive oil, beans pureed into soup, and beans spread over crusty bread and drizzled with extra-virgin olive oil are but a few of the ways to prepare them. Cannellini beans are white and creamy in texture; they are used both fresh and dried. For this recipe, use dried beans instead of the canned supermarket variety, which is very salty and just not as good a representation of the real taste. If not available, substitute dried white kidney or Great Northern beans. Soak the beans overnight to save time when making this dish.

1 cup dried cannellini beans

3 cups water for soaking beans, then fresh water for cooking them

⅔ cup extra-virgin olive oil

1 medium red Spanish onion, diced

⅓-pound chunk of pancetta, diced

3 tablespoons minced fresh sage leaves

1 teaspoon salt

½ teaspoon coarsely ground black pepper

1 pound fettuccine

¼ cup reserved pasta cooking water

Grated Pecorino cheese for sprinkling

Soak the beans overnight in 3 cups of cold water. Next day, drain the beans, which will have swelled in size, and place them in a 2-quart saucepan and cover them with fresh cold water. Bring the water to a boil, lower the heat to medium-high, and cook the beans until a knife is easily inserted into them. Do not overcook the beans or they will split and disintegrate in the water. Drain and set aside.

In a sauté pan, heat ⅓ cup of the olive oil. Stir in the onions and pancetta and sauté until the onions are soft and the pancetta is browned. Stir in the sage and sauté, stirring frequently, for 2 to 3 minutes. Add the beans and stir them gently to coat them with the

Tuscany

115

oil and sage. Season with the salt and pepper. Turn off the heat and set aside while the fettuccine is cooking.

Cook the fettuccine in 4 to 6 quarts of rapidly boiling water to which 1 tablespoon of salt has been added. Cook just until the fettuccine is *al dente,* meaning that the fettuccine is cooked through, retains its shape, and is still firm, not mushy. Drain the fettuccine into a strainer and add it with the reserved cooking water directly to the sauté pan. Stir in the remaining olive oil and quickly reheat the mixture, stirring constantly until hot. Transfer the mixture to a serving platter and serve at once. Pass grated Pecorino cheese on the side.

Note: Do not be alarmed at the amount of olive oil used in this recipe. The beans absorb a lot of it so if you want to cut down on the amount of oil, remember that the dish will be drier in taste.

Did you know that Tuscans have Central America to thank for introducing cannellini beans into Italy? Beans were imported to Italy in the sixteenth century. Look for these beans under the name of white kidney or Great Northern beans.

Carciofi Ripieni di Maiale
(Pork-Stuffed Artichokes)

Serves 4

If you are in Florence in early spring, take a moment to admire the piles of gorgeous purplish-green and wine-colored artichokes at the Mercato Centrale near San Lorenzo. They are so tender that they can be cut into thin slices and eaten raw in salads. Ask the vendors how they like to cook them, and you could get enough versions to write a cookbook. I have grown artichokes in my own garden to my great surprise but the season is usually not long enough, and the plants were started early in the greenhouse. Use globe artichokes, which are not anywhere near as tender as Italian varieties, but knowing how to cook them yields good results. In this recipe the artichokes are boiled briefly, then hollowed out to remove the hairy choke and filled with ground pork and baked in the oven with fresh tomatoes.

4 large artichokes (about 2 pounds)

1 pound ground pork

⅓ cup diced onion

2 tablespoons minced Italian parsley leaves

1 teaspoon fine sea salt

Grinding of coarse black pepper

1 teaspoon dried oregano

½ cup grated Parmigiano-Reggiano cheese

1½ cups fresh crushed plum tomatoes

With a knife, remove the stems of the artichokes and discard them. With your hands, pull off the first layer of artichoke leaves at the base and discard them. Cut ¼ inch off of the tops of the artichokes, and with a scissors snip any needle-like points off the leaves. Rinse the artichokes, place them in a saucepan just large enough to hold them snugly upright, and cover them with water. Bring the artichokes to a boil, cover the pan, and boil them for 10 minutes. With a slotted spoon remove the artichokes to a cutting board. When cool enough to handle, use a melon baller to scrape out the hairy choke from the center of the artichoke, and pull away the palest-looking innermost leaves. Set the artichokes aside while you make the filling.

Preheat the oven to 350°F.

Heat a dry sauté pan over medium-high heat. Stir in the pork and cook until it begins to exude its fat. Discard most of the fat. Stir in the onions and continue cooking until the onions have wilted and the meat begins to brown. Transfer the meat mixture to a bowl. Stir in the parsley, salt, pepper, oregano, and cheese. Allow the mixture to cool slightly.

Fill the cavities of the artichokes with the meat mixture, packing it in gently. Place the artichokes in a deep casserole dish just large enough to hold them. Pour the tomatoes over and around the artichokes. Cover the pan with a cover or a piece of aluminum foil.

Bake for 30 to 35 minutes. Halfway through the cooking time, check to see if the bottom of the pan is dry; add a little water if necessary.

Serve the artichokes hot.

Tip: To keep artichokes upright while cooking, position chunks of potatoes between them in the pot.

To Market to Market to Buy a Porchetta

*L*ive and eat like the Italians. That is my advice to anyone contemplating a trip to Italy. Whenever I am in Italy, I enjoy doing the daily things that Italians do, like shopping for local ingredients and cooking a meal. I try to find out what is going on in the area where I am staying so that I can have as meaningful an experience as possible. I stopped staying in hotels long ago and decided that renting a place was not only cheaper, it immediately made me feel right at home and gave me the freedom to really experience Italy away from the often staid environment of a hotel.

One of my fondest memories is shopping on market day in the town of Camucia near Cortona in eastern Tuscany. Camucia's outdoor market is similar to many found throughout Italy and, in fact, many of the vendors travel with their goods from town to town. Every town has a designated market day, and Thursday was the big shopping day in Camucia. I had heard the local people in a bar talking about getting to the market early so they could be first in line to buy *panini* (sandwiches) stacked with thin slices of spit-roasted pork known as porchetta. As I came to find out, porchetta is the most popular item at the market. I decided to be there early too. The vendors have a unique system for setting up shop with their portable stores on wheels that seem to unfold with no effort. Husband-and-wife teams and whole families steer you toward their goods as their singsong voices resonate over the crowd. Early on a sunny morning people begin to mingle among the vendors after their cappuccino at a nearby bar. The biggest decision they will make this morning is what to eat for a *merenda* (snack), and what to buy for *cena* (supper).

Because market day is *the* main event of the week, it has a carnival-like atmosphere. Just the anticipation of what will be offered is enough to get everyone's curiosity, and it is an occasion to see old friends and catch up on all the news. On benches nearby, elderly women and gentlemen, who are in no hurry, watch the scene unfold. Smartly dressed women in short skirts and high heels, with pretty-colored scarves at their necks, push baby strollers with children who are so perfectly dressed that they could easily be on the runway of an Italian fashion show. The men, in dark sunglasses and many with *telefonini* (cell phones) glued to their ears, are more interested in the women passing by than the price of fruits and vegetables.

A large line begins forming near the porchetta man's truck, and the air around it is thick with the smell of rosemary and other spices. Resting on the counter like a golden calf is a whole pig with sprigs of rosemary stuck in its ears and a whole lemon in its mouth. Its skin is so shiny and uniformly tanned that I think to myself that any lifeguard would be envious.

The skin is crackling, the meat is lean, and it is cut into thin slices and layered on good, saltless Tuscan bread. Customers wave their hands like fans at a rock concert, waiting to get their hands on precious tickets so they can be next to shout out their orders. As soon as sandwiches are made they are snatched up and eaten on the spot. I buy one too; it is succulent and flavorful and worth standing in line for. This same scene will be played out again every Thursday, as long as there is a market day in Camucia.

It is easy to get lost in a sea of people in the market; there is much to look at. Flowers of every description make a colorful backdrop for the market; gladioli, daisies, roses, and carnations are some of the most popular varieties. Fresh fish, whole or gutted, anchovies in salt, octopus, squid, and fish whose names I have never heard of get lots of attention from market-goers; the vegetables are varied and numerous, and the variety of dried beans is dizzying as well. As soon as I see the garden seeds I am weak in the knees. I always buy too many seeds; it is a link from Italy to my home garden. I buy eggplant, lettuce, bean, squash, and fennel, and a host of others I know that I will never plant. Hard candy, *torrone,* nuts, packaged cookies and cakes, shoes, T-shirts, wallets, purses, slippers, pots and pans, cheeses, linens, pocketknives, scarves, and jewelry—it is all here. Sometimes there is livestock as well.

The linen truck is where I search for towels and tablecloths to bring home as gifts. I am careful to look at where things are made; not everything in the market is from Italy. In fact, a lot of the clothing and linens are from China. One item that really surprises me are the hanging quilts! I consider them a uniquely New England item. "*Mi dica, Signora,*" comes the command from a young man selling kitchen tablecloths. I buy kitchen towels embroidered with grapes, apples, and pears that say *uve, mele,* and *pere.* "*Sono regali*" ("they are gifts") I tell him, and he nods his head and wraps them in tissue paper and ties them with ribbon. Even in the market, the Italians do things with style.

I look down at my bags and take inventory. So far I have made purchases of huge, sugar-sweet, pale yellow moscato grapes, a wedge of Pecorino cheese, and some marinated artichokes that will make a nice al fresco lunch. The spit-roasted chickens look good too, so I buy one of them as well as fennel and some fresh porcini mushrooms, which I plan to grill.

Now loaded down with a good representation of Tuscan food in each hand, I walk back to the house, blending in perfectly with the rest of the local shoppers, who are also juggling bulging bags of produce, clothing, and kitchen gadgets as they make their way out of the market.

Sitting in the midday sun, my feet propped over a chair, I savor the moscato grapes. The thought of ever again having to shop for groceries in my local supermarket back home has no appeal whatsoever.

Peposo
(Tuscan Tilemakers' Stew)

Serves 4 to 6

1 carrot, scraped and cut into quarters

1 medium onion, peeled and quartered

1 rib celery, cut in half

3 large sprigs parsley

4 cloves garlic

4 whole basil leaves

2 tablespoons fresh thyme

2 tablespoons fresh marjoram

1 tablespoon fresh mint

2 tablespoon fresh rosemary needles

4 whole sage leaves

⅓ cup extra-virgin olive oil

1¾ pounds stew beef, trimmed of all visible fat and cut into 1-inch cubes

1½ teaspoons fine sea salt

1 tablespoon coarsely ground black pepper

1 cup vin santo or moscato wine

2 cups hot beef broth

Beef stew with pears? Absolutely delicious when made by my friends Giovanni and Iris Lodovici. This antique Tuscan recipe is known as peposo *(from the word* pepe *for "pepper") and its origins go back to tilemakers who prepared a* calderone *(big pot) of stew and placed it at the mouth of the* fornace *(oven) while they made tiles. They left the stew to cook for many hours which resulted in deliciously tender meat in a beautiful sauce made with* vin santo *(holy wine). In today's Tuscan kitchen pears have been replaced by tomatoes and the dish is more commonly referred to as* peposo dell' Impruneta, *taking its name from the town of Impruneta near Florence, where the tiles that are famous all over the world (*cotto dell'impruneta*) are still made. In this dish the true worth of the four evangelists of Italian cooking (see page 124) is evident. Vin santo is made in many areas of Italy and is a beautiful amber-colored, high-alcohol dessert wine. If it is not available, use a good moscato wine. For quick work in the kitchen use a food processor to mince the vegetables and herbs. Make the dish several days ahead and refrigerate, to really meld the flavors.*

In a food processor or with a chef's knife mince together the carrot, onion, celery, parsley, garlic, basil, thyme, marjoram, mint, rosemary, and sage. Set it aside.

In an ovenproof 10½×2½-inch sauté pan heat 2 tablespoons of the olive oil and stir in the minced vegetables and herbs. Sauté them, stirring occasionally, until they soften, but do not let them brown. Transfer the ingredients to a dish and set it aside.

Preheat the oven to 300°F.

Dry the meat with paper towels; sprinkle the meat with salt and pepper. Add the remaining olive oil to the pan and when the oil begins to shimmer, add the meat and sauté, turning the pieces frequently to brown them. When there is no more liquid in the pan, raise the heat to high, add the wine and allow it to reduce by half. Lower the heat and pour in the beef broth to cover the meat. Return the vegetable mixture to the pan and stir in the peppercorns and the lemon zest. Add the bay leaf. Cover the pan and bake in the oven for 1 hour.

Peel and core the pears. Dice 2 of the pears, then cover and set them aside. Puree the remaining pear in a food processor or blender until it is smooth.

Stir the pureed pear into the meat mixture. Cover the pan and bake for an additional 1½ hours, adding more broth if necessary. Five minutes before the meat is done, add the diced pears and remove the bay leaf.

Serve immediately. This stew can also be refrigerated for several days.

1 tablespoon whole green peppercorns in vinegar, drained

Grated zest of 1 lemon

1 whole bay leaf

3 ripe William, Anjou, or Bartlett pears

Tuscany

I Quattro Evangelisti

The Four Evangelists

I arrived in Florence for dinner with Giovanni and Iris Lodovici. Giovanni is a Tuscan wine and food expert and has written a brilliant book on Italian food called *Anche Gastrea è una Musa.* More than a cookbook, it is a meditative look at Italian food. Giovanni calls it Mediterranean yoga. Giovanni's wife, Iris, is the other half of this passionate team—a fabulous cook and a great conversationalist—so I knew I was in for a special evening.

Their apartment, part of a fourteenth-century palazzo, is conveniently located near the center of the city. Florence is full of beautiful, history-filled palazzi, and I was delighted that, finally, I would get a peek at what lurks behind those intricately carved, colossal wooden doors that hide so many palazzi from public view. I lifted a beautiful bronze lion's head door knocker to announce my arrival while marveling at how much the Italians show fashion flair in every detail, even stunning door knockers in the whimsical form of angels, serpents, hands, flowers, and faces.

Giovanni and Iris warmly greet me like a family member as we ascend the long marble staircase with its chunky balustrade. I have brought a cake from a nearby *pasticerria* and hand it to Iris; she seems touched by this gesture.

The apartment is spacious, filled with artwork and antiques. There is even a small chapel, originally the private chapel of one of the first owners, and the ceiling is especially beautiful with its painting of plump little cherubs known as *putti.* Even the walls of the chapel are decorated with paintings of various saints.

In the cozy and dimly lit living room, antipasti await and include crostini with dried tomatoes and a focaccia with chopped, vibrant-looking green olives. Both are delicious and I settle in for an evening of good food and conversation. It always amazes me how involved Italians are with food. Giovanni brings up the name of Pellegrino Artusi, a Romagnolo by birth, who wrote *The Art of Eating Well,* and who, according to Giovanni, changed the way that Italians eat. Once we are seated in the dining room, more antipasti arrive, and I am in awe of the *fagianella in gelatina,* a shimmering mold holding delicate pheasant and perfect-looking bay leaves in suspension, and as if that were not elegant enough, the whole affair is surrounded by thinly sliced Scamorza cheese and smoked salmon with black olives. Sheer joy! I conjure up in my mind just how Iris made the pheasant mold and vow to make it the first thing when I get home.

Our first course is pappardelle, very light-tasting, homemade wide ribbons of Tuscan pasta that are served with fresh cannellini beans, extra-virgin olive oil, and crushed pine nuts. The beans are so creamy that they seem to disappear in your mouth. I tell Iris that only the dried variety are available at home and that I would like to try her recipe using them. Her eyebrows arch to Gothic heights and she gives me a faint smile. Giovanni, trying to be diplomatic, remarks that for his palate there are enough pine nuts and beans in the dish, but more extra-virgin olive oil is needed.

I soon sense that talking about food is a very serious connector for the Lodovicis. Giovanni asks me if I know about *i quattro evangelisti* (the four evangelists) and I wonder what that has to do with the train of the conversation, but I immediately say yes and begin to spout off the names of Matthew, Mark, Luke, and John. Giovanni throws back his head, releases a loud laugh, and interrupts me to say that he meant the four evangelists of Italian cooking, a term I had not heard before. Curious to know more, I ask him to explain.

"*Allora,*" he begins, narrating with his hands in midair as if conducting a symphony orchestra. "The four evangelists are onions, celery, carrots, and parsley, the very foundation for cooking Italian food with the best flavor." Of course, I should have known, and I do know them by another name. They are *gli odori*, the flavor boosters that are the point of departure for beginning a *soffritto* (a slow sauté) for sauce, stews, and soups.

"And," he emphasizes with excitement in his voice, "as the *evangelisti* cook together in a finely diced assembly, they lose their individuality to become one flavor essence. When that is achieved, the dish is in harmony." What an interesting way to look at food. I guess you could say it is a meditative view. Iris excuses herself to get the next course, a wonderful smelling *peposo*, a beef stew with pears and whole black and green peppercorns (page 122) in which the four evangelists have played a big part. It would never have occurred to me to use pears in a beef stew, but it was magical and I made a mental note to make this dish as well.

Iris knows how to pace the meal and after all, as Giovanni states so well in his book, the whole point of being at the table in the first place is not just to eat but to reflect on the dining experience, and that takes time. Being at table with the Lodovicis is like enjoying a long Thanksgiving dinner, except that here it is an everyday experience.

After a long pause, the most wonderful and delicate-looking tray of tiny mandarin orange shells makes their appearance; they have been cut in half, the juice extracted and made into sorbet, then put back into the mandarin halves and frozen. Iris cuts them while frozen into quarters. What a nice idea, and a nice presentation. There was also silky smooth vanilla gelato with a velvety chestnut sauce. I am more than satiated but have left no visible trace of these two desserts on my plate.

Time is growing late when we finally leave the dining room and move into the parlor to have espresso and *vin santo* (holy wine) that Giovanni has made from Malvasia and Trebbiano grapes. Iris brings out the fruitcake that I have brought her and tells me to try it with the vin santo. She is right, a perfect match!

It is hard to say *buona notte* (good night) after such wonderful hospitality and I thank my hosts profusely for their kindness. Descending the grand staircase, I envy their knowledge and enthusiasm about food, and a bemusing thought comes to mind . . . Where else but in Italy can one pose the question "Do you know who the four evangelists are?" and get a divine interpretation of Italian foods.

Insalata di Messalina
(Messalina's Salad)

Serves 6 to 8

½ cup good prepared
mayonnaise

2 tablespoons ketchup

3 tablespoons heavy cream

2 tablespoons minced Italian
parsley leaves

3 navel oranges, peeled and
cut into pieces

2 Red Delicious apples, cut
into cubes

2 slices fresh pineapple, cut
into cubes

2 small bananas, cut into
¼-inch rounds

¼ cup coarsely chopped
almonds

I have learned a lot of things about Tuscany and Tuscan food from my friend Luciano Berti, who lives in Florence. Whenever we get together the subject of food is front and center of our conversations. Luciano is a busy bachelor who eats a lot of meals in restaurants, but he is a good cook too, which was evident the day we prepared and cooked dinner for his parents' wedding anniversary. This fruit salad with a mayonnaise dressing is one that Luciano likes to prepare. It is a departure from what one normally thinks of as an Italian salad, which is typically made up of greens and vegetables, with a dressing of extra-virgin olive oil, lemon juice, or red wine vinegar. This colorful salad is named for Messalina, the wife of the Roman Emperor Claudio, and well known in Rome for her licentious behavior, for which she was condemned to death.

In a bowl whisk together the mayonnaise, ketchup, and heavy cream. Stir in the parsley and set aside.

Combine all the fruits in a salad bowl. Pour the dressing over the fruit and mix well to coat them in the dressing.

Divide the salad among 6 salad plates. Divide and sprinkle the almonds evenly over the salads. Serve immediately.

Insalata di Funghi Freschi con Formaggio
(Mushroom Salad with Cheese)

Serves 4

Foraging for wild mushrooms is both an art and a dark secret among Italians. In the fall it is common to see people heading to the woods, baskets in hand, to stake out their territorial domain and scour the ground in search of porcini, the most prized of the mushroom family, as well as for other types, including ovoli (egg), and finferlo (turkey cock, or chanterelle). Those who forage are very knowledgeable about mushrooms, and caution is advised for amateurs because many types of mushrooms are poisonous. The preparation can range from grilled to sautéed to stewed. Many are delicious uncooked. In this salad, the domestic portobello or button mushrooms are best. It is important that the mushrooms be thinly sliced in order for them to "cook" in the lemon and olive oil marinade. Make this salad several hours before serving. Look for mushrooms whose caps are smooth and uncracked and have no soft spots. Turn the mushrooms over and inspect the stems. They should not be separating from the cap or show any spaces, and the gills should not look dried out.

½ pound fresh mushrooms, stems removed

1 tablespoon fresh squeezed lemon juice

5 tablespoons extra-virgin olive oil

½ teaspoon salt

Shavings of Asiago or Parmigiano-Reggiano cheese

Grinding of coarse black pepper

Wipe the mushrooms with a damp paper towel or use a mushroom brush to whisk away any dirt. If you wash them in water be sure to dry them well or the marinade will not coat them properly.

Slice the mushrooms thin and place them in a shallow salad bowl. In a separate small bowl whisk together the lemon juice, olive oil, and salt. Pour the mixture over the mushrooms and mix well. Cover the bowl and allow the salad to marinate for several hours at room temperature.

Just before serving use a vegetable peeler to make long cheese

> Did you know that you should allow mushrooms to breathe in a paper bag as opposed to a plastic bag when storing them in the refrigerator? Plastic bags trap moisture and will cause the mushrooms to deteriorate rapidly.

Tuscany

curls from a wedge of Asiago or Parmigiano-Reggiano cheese. Sprinkle the curls over the mushrooms. Grind the pepper over the salad and serve.

Variation: Add ¼ cup minced Italian parsley leaves to the mushrooms with the lemon juice and olive oil.

Zuppa di Succa al Mascaron (Pumpkin Soup Mascaron Style), page 18

Tortellini di Zucca con Ragù
(Pumpkin-Stuffed Pasta with Meat Sauce), page 22

Trota Intera al Forno Con Patate
(Whole Baked Trout with Potatoes), page 37

Caprino alle Nocciole con Insalatina di Melone
(Hazelnut-Coated Goat Cheese and Cantaloupe Salad), page 41

Crostata di Limone e Mascarpone con Salsa di Rabarbaro

(Lemon and Mascarpone Cheese Tart with Rhubarb Sauce), page 48

Bomba di Riso di Mara

(Mara's Rice Bomb), page 80

Erbazzone di Mara (Mara's Swiss Chard Pie), page 90

Albicocche Cotte al Vino (Apricots Cooked in Wine), page 99
and *Pizzelle Colorate* (Colored Pizzelle), page 312

Torta di Amarena (Cherry Tart), page 95

Pomodori Ripieni d'Emma (Emma's Stuffed Tomatoes), page 106

Peposo
(Tuscan Tilemakers' Stew),
page 122

Biscotti di Prato, page 135,
and *Spumini Mandorlati*
(Almond Foams), page 137

Piramidi di Melanzane alla Nonna Galasso
(Grandma Galasso's Eggplant Pyramids), page 146

Calamaretti in Brodo
al Pomodoro Piccante
(Baby Squid in Spicy
Tomato Broth), page 163

Torta al Limone (Lemon Curd Cake), page 180

Insalata di Zucchine, Peperoni Rossi e Ricotta Salata
(Zucchini, Red Pepper, and Ricotta Salad), page 217

The Charisma of Cortona

On a sparkling September day, I arrived in Cortona in eastern Tuscany, about 62 miles south of Florence. I had rented a country house with friends and was anxious to settle into the old place on the *strada bianca* (white road). Cortona, important as a powerful Etruscan city-state, was originally settled by the Umbrians. The city rises to a height of 2,132 feet high atop Mount Sant'Edigio. Cortona was important as an agricultural center. As the car ascended to this ancient city evidence of Umbrian and Etruscan handiwork presented itself at every hairpin turn. Massive and imposing defensive fourth-century B.C. stone walls encircled the city. Etruscan tombs called *melone* were numerous in the countryside nearby, and the Museo Palazzo Casali within the city walls itself housed a wealth of Etruscan artifacts from intricately fashioned jewelry to bronze lamps to the stone foundations of Cortona's buildings.

Finally the house came into view, an inviting rose- and peach-colored stone building perched on a precipice with looming Etruscan walls as its backdrop. The house endeared itself to me immediately: its crooked green shutters were tilted slightly off their hinges, brilliant red geraniums in terra-cotta pots billowed over the tiny balcony above the doorway, and unruly deep purple bougainvillea flowers conquered and outlined the corners of the house. The grounds boasted pear and fig trees, herbs of every description, fragrant lavender bushes, and porcelain-like roses in soft kaleidoscopic colors.

I felt comfortable amid this natural splendor, and for a moment, I stood captivated by the beauty that surrounded me. Gazing at the almost surreal landscape below, I was struck by the light—Tuscan light, a magical light, a light that gave the landscape a spiritual and sensual feel. From my vantage point, the great expanse of the lush Val di Chiana could only be described as a masterfully executed pastoral painting by Pinturicchio. The neat landscape was vividly defined by different hues of green created by the sunlight reigning haphazardly in selected areas, casting shadows of light and dark here and there that were, in a word, dramatic. From where I stood, stone houses with their quilted-looking red clay tiled roofs appeared like toys nestled among the cypress, chestnut, pine, and olive trees. There was stillness too, as in a sanctuary.

The terraced hillsides around Cortona gave evidence of the careful use of the land, and in the verdant valleys vines hung heavy and low with grapes that were ready for the *vendemmia* (the harvest). Fields and fields of sunflowers with their heads seemingly bowed in prayer waited to be harvested for making sunflower oil. Row upon row of tobacco plants swayed rhythmically in the gentle breeze while the whiff of precious mushrooms lurking in their secret hiding places teased one's senses.

My plan was for total immersion into Cortonese culture and that of its nearby environs. There are five gates through which to enter the city of Cortona today, although in ancient times there were at least nine. Each day I made my way *a piedi* (on foot) through the Porta Colonia gate and down via Dardano to buy food and whatever mementos there were to take home as a reminder of my visit. Chills ran up and down my spine when I pondered the age of this city, with its beautifully preserved medieval and Renaissance buildings, that was functioning just fine in a twenty-first-century world. My first stop: the *fruttivendolo* (fruit market) to buy *pesca bianca,* my favorite peaches. Their pale yellow and green color belie their intoxicating aroma and flavor. Next stop, the *pastificio* to get some *pici,* the local pasta that is similar to a square-cut spaghetti, then some Tuscan bread from the *panificio,* and from the *pasticerria* those wonderful biscotti called *cantucci* to dip in glasses of vin santo wine.

Soon I had the routine of living in Cortona. Eventually the shop-keepers came to know me as la Signora Americana. I inquired about the weekly outdoor market day, since every town has one when locals and traveling merchants set up shop in the city center. Cortona's market was on Saturdays in Piazza Signorelli, named in honor of its famous son, Renaissance painter Luca Signorelli, and in Piazza del Duomo.

In addition to all the history, art, architecture, and wonderful food, Cortona provided the ideal location from which to explore such wonderful cities as Perugia, Orvieto, Arezzo, Florence, and Siena and afforded the opportunity to visit the surrounding vineyards and wineries to learn about and sample some delicious and famous wines, such as Chianti Classico and Brunello di Montalcino, and buy the area's artisanal foods to accompany these wines, such as *salame locale* and Pecorino cheese.

Tuscans celebrate and honor their local foods with style, and they do so with a *sagra,* or festival. In fact, hardly a month goes by that food is not being celebrated in some region of Italy. I did not have to wander too far from Cortona to experience several *sagre.* In Monterchi, a town famous for Luca Signorelli's endearing painting of the *Madonna del Parto* (the pregnant Madonna), La Festa della Polenta was in full swing. I watched with great interest as the townspeople wearing green and yellow colors came together to celebrate the corn harvest by making their beloved polenta in great cauldrons and then dramatically spilling out the yellow gold onto wooden boards, where it was sold to people who had brought a hodgepodge of different containers, bowls, and pots in which to carry the cooked cornmeal home. Many came to just eat it on the spot with *sugo* (sauce) or grilled on a wood fire.

Not far away in Palazzo del Pero, it was La Festa del Fungo—The Mushroom Festival—that had everyone's mouth watering for fresh porcini and *ovoli* mushrooms. The way to buy them is to bargain with the locals, who stand on street corners with baskets of just-picked, warm-from-the-earth *funghi.* I could not resist and I bought a crate of *porcini freschi,* which I intended to use with fresh tagliatelle. Heading back toward Cortona with a full stomach, I noticed a Festa dell'-Uva (Grape Festival) sign strung across the highway, but wisdom intervened and I tabled the idea for another time.

Living in Cortona, experiencing its culture, beauty, history, and art, has left lasting impressions and taught me many lessons: the art of keeping things simple, the influence of the past on the present, the power of community pride, and the need to preserve one's heritage. Cortona is a rare Tuscan jewel encased in Umbrian-Etruscan stone that has lasted for centuries and shines as brightly today as it did centuries ago.

Biscotti di Prato

Makes 2½ dozen biscotti

What do Tuscans have for dessert after a meal? Biscotti di Prato dunked in vin santo. The city of Prato has special meaning for me since it was the home of one of Tuscany's most influentials citizens, Francesco di Marco Datini, whose palazzo I visited, and whose life I read about in the book The Merchant of Prato *by Iris Origo. Datini was a wealthy textile merchant who had great influence in political circles. In his daily diary, he talked about the deals he made and the debts he owed. He also made many notations about the foods he enjoyed and those that were forbidden to him by his doctor. It is a fascinating look at life in Renaissance Tuscany. Not far from Datini's palazzo is the shop of Antonio Mattei, in via Ricasoli; this old establishment has been making and selling biscotti di Prato since 1858.*

½ cup blanched and slivered almonds

2 cups unbleached all-purpose flour

1 teaspoon baking powder

¼ teaspoon salt

¾ cup sugar

3 large eggs

1 tablespoon vanilla extract

Preheat the oven to 350°F.

Spread the almonds on a baking sheet and toast them in the oven for 7 to 10 minutes, or just until they begin to brown at the edges. Transfer the almonds to a bowl and allow them to cool.

In another bowl mix together the flour, baking powder, and salt.

In another bowl mix together the sugar, eggs, and vanilla. Add the sugar and egg mixture to the flour mixture and mix with your hands to form a dough. Fold in the almonds. The dough will be stiff.

With floured hands transfer the dough to a sheet of wax paper and shape it into a 10×5½-inch-long loaf. Wrap the dough in the wax paper and refrigerate it for several hours or overnight.

With a sharp knife, cut the dough in half lengthwise and place each half, cut side down, on a parchment-lined baking sheet, spacing them 2 inches apart. Reshape the loaves slightly.

Bake the loaves for about 18 minutes, or until they are firm to the touch but still pale looking. Remove the baking sheet from the oven and allow the loaves to cool for 10 minutes.

With a sharp knife cut diagonal ½-inch thick slices from each loaf. Lay the slices on their sides and return the baking sheet to the oven. Toast the biscotti on each side for about 5 minutes, or until they are golden brown. Remove the baking sheet from the oven.

Transfer the biscotti to a cooling rack. These cookies should be hard in texture. Serve them with vin santo or other dessert wine or with coffee and tea.

_____

Note: These are "long keepers" if stored in an airtight tin. They can be frozen successfully for several months.

Spumini Mandorlati
(Almond Foams)

Makes about 4 dozen cookies

What I love about these bite-size meringue and almond cookies are their delicateness and their almost ethereal texture and taste. And I also love the name given to them by my Tuscan friends and super cooks Giovanni and Iris Lodovici, spumini mandorlati, *the literal translation of which is "almond foams." This exquisite cookie calls for only four ingredients, is quick to put together, but requires a 45-minute baking time to produce a dry, crisp* spumini *that literally melts in your mouth like foam.*

1 cup whole blanched almonds

2 large egg whites, at room temperature

¾ cup sugar

¼ cup unbleached all-purpose flour

Preheat oven to 225°F.

Line 2 baking sheets with parchment paper and set aside.

Grind the almonds in a food processor until very fine and transfer them to a medium-size bowl.

In an electric mixer whip the egg whites until they are foamy. Gradually whip in the sugar, a little at a time, until the egg whites begin to form peaks and appear shiny. Whip in the flour a little at a time. Fold the nuts into the egg-white mixture until they are well blended.

Use 2 teaspoons to spread small rounds of batter onto the parchment paper, spacing the *spumini* about ½ inch apart. They will spread a little. Or fill a tipless pastry bag with the batter and pipe out 1-inch rounds.

Bake the *spumini* without opening the oven door for about 45 minutes, or until crisp. They should remain pale in color.

Allow the *spumini* to cool completely on the baking sheets, then carefully remove them from the parchment paper.

Note: These are perfect to serve with fresh fruit, ice cream, or sherbets.

Tuscany

Schiacciata alla Fiorentina
(Florentine Flat Cake)

Makes 1 cake

¾ cup unbleached all-purpose flour

¼ teaspoon salt

1 teaspoon baking powder

2 eggs

½ cup sugar

¼ cup extra-virgin olive oil

⅔ cup milk

Grated zest of 2 oranges

This easy-to-prepare schiacciata (flat cake) from Florence has an interesting, moist texture, and pleasant orange taste. As the name implies, this cake is only about ½ inch high after it bakes. Cut it into squares or rounds, or use cookie cutters for a more festive look.

Preheat the oven to 325°F.

Lightly butter a 7½×11½-inch glass lasagne pan or similar pan and set aside.

Sift together the flour, salt, and baking powder. Set aside.

In a separate bowl with a hand mixer, beat together the eggs and sugar until thick and foamy. On low speed, beat in the olive oil and milk. Stir in the orange zest.

On low speed, beat the flour mixture into the egg mixture until the batter becomes smooth. It will be the consistency of pancake batter.

Pour the mixture into the prepared pan and bake for 35 to 40 minutes, or until the cake springs back when touched with your finger.

Remove the pan to a cooling rack and cool completely.

Turn the cake out onto a serving dish. Cut into squares or other shapes. This cake is delicious as is, but for a festive look sprinkle the top completely with confectioners' sugar. Also try the cake topped with fresh fruit.

Nocciolata
(Nutty Squares)

Makes about 40 squares

The late Tuscan chef Edgardo Sandoli was an authority on Italian rice, and it was a great pleasure of mine to teach cooking classes with him in Montalcino, an ancient Tuscan town with a pristine landscape famous for its production of Brunello di Montalcino wine. Edgardo's cooking was all about efficiency and quick work in the kitchen. To this day, whenever I am in a hurry and need something fast for dessert, I make nocciolata, *rich shortbread-like textured squares chocked full of nuts. They are perfect with ice cream or a fresh fruit salad. They keep away the winter chill with a cup of tea or coffee. Edgardo used only hazelnuts, but I use a combination of walnuts, almonds, hazelnuts, and pecans.*

¾ cup walnut halves

¾ cup shelled whole almonds

¾ cup shelled hazelnuts

¾ cup pecan halves

5 cups unbleached all-purpose flour

2½ cups sugar

1 pound unsalted butter, melted and cooled

Preheat the oven to 350°F.

Place the nuts on a baking sheet on the middle oven shelf and toast them for 8 to 10 minutes. Transfer the nuts to a bowl and allow them to cool. Coarsely chop the nuts and set them aside.

In a large bowl combine the flour and sugar. Pour in the butter and combine the mixture well. Stir in the nuts. The mixture will be stiff. I find it best to do this by hand.

Spread and pat the mixture out evenly onto a 17×11½-inch nonstick baking sheet.

Bake on the bottom rack for 25 minutes, or until the top and edges are nicely browned.

Cool slightly, then cut into 2-inch squares.

Campania

Antipasti

Piramidi di Melanzane alla Nonna Galasso (Grandma Galasso's
  Eggplant Pyramids)
Pizza Rustica con Olive (Country-Style Pizza with Olives)
Pizza con Gorgonzola e Pomodori Secchi (Gorgonzola and Sun-Dried
  Tomato Pizza)
Pizza di Scarola (Escarole Pizza)

Primi Piatti

Riso del Mezzogiorno al Mario (Mario's Mezzogiorno Rice)
Frittata di Zucchine (Zucchini Omelet)
Peperoni Imbottiti (Stuffed Peppers)
Spaghetti alle Cozze (Spaghetti and Mussels)
Calamaretti in Brodo al Pomodoro Piccante (Baby Squid in Spicy
  Tomato Broth)

Contorni

Scarola e Fagioli (Escarole and Beans)
Melanzane alla Parmigiana di Zia Anna (Aunt Anna's Eggplant
  Parmigiana Casserole)

Secondi Piatti

Pollo Scarpariello (Shoemaker-Style Chicken)
Pollo alla Cacciatora (Hunter-Style Chicken)
Sartù (Neapolitan Rice, Pork, and Vegetable Mold)

Dolci

Biscottini d'Anice di Mamma (Mom's Little Anise Cookies)

Pastiera (Neapolitan Ricotta and Rice Pie)

Torta al Limone (Lemon Curd Cake)

Sfogliatelle Ricce (Rich Flaky Pastry)

Sfogliatelle Frolle (Tender Flaky Pastry)

Ripieno per Sfogliatelle (Flaky Pastry Filling)

Campania is Greek temples, Roman ruins, mosaics, Pucinella, Caserta, Palazzo Reale, pizza Margherita, limoncello, bird cages, laundry, tomatoes, fusilli, heat, Salerno, Amalfi Coast, vongole, Naples, Capri, sfogliatelle, Benevento, torrone, graffi, Strega, eggplant, Sorrento, ragù napoletana, Ravello, Vietri ceramics, maccheroni, Alianico grapes, San Gennaro, mozzarella di bufala, Bourbons, feste, anchovies, babà, bougainvillea, timballo, lovers, laughter, Bay of Naples, frutti di mare, Via Appia, mountains, figs, Blue Grotto, villas, fountains, traffic, beaches, olives, la musica, Castel dell'Ovo, Vesuvius, cloisters, museums, coral, torta caprese, presepio, frittata, spumone, mezzogiorno, mountains, Arch of Trajan, Sophia Loren.

---

*S*omeone once referred to Campania as all the world in one region and a unique museum in the open. Greek in origin, this region was expanded under the Romans and later felt the impact of foreign domination by others, including the Normans, French, and Spaniards. Campania has everything from the unpredictable and formidable Mount Vesuvius to the sandwiched layers of archeological treasures of Pompeii and Herculaneum to the stunning waters of the Blue Grotto of the island of Capri. Campania, the most densely populated region of Italy, enjoys an enviable and captivating position on the Mediterranean Sea, extraordinary fertile soil, an ebullient cuisine, fascinating artisanal crafts, and a people who have a personal warmth and zest for life found nowhere else in Italy.

Meaning *country,* Campania is aptly named; its foods emerge from precious lands made fertile by volcanic ash. From it come some of Italy's best vegetables and fruits, and it would be unthinkable not to highlight the contribution that the tomato has made in Neapolitan cuisine for rich meat ragùs, fresh and light tomato sauce, exuberant insalata caprese, topping for the classic pizza Margherita, and the foundation for many soup and pasta dishes. Its coastline teems with fish that find their way into excellent seafood dishes, from *cozze* (mussels) generously covered with black pepper and flavored with parsley and garlic to dense fish soup (*zuppa di pesce*) served over crusty bread. One of my favorites is *calamaretti,* small squid cooked in a light, spicy tomato broth (see page 163).

In Campania, citrus trees intoxicate the air; sunny lemon trees dot the countryside and the fruit offers the cook endless opportunities, including the famous limoncello liqueur, an elixir for relaxation. It is truly a cook's dream to live in Campania; everything is available and preparation is kept extremely simple since there is no need to tamper with the clean, fresh flavors of its foods.

For me there is a special bond with this region because it was the ancestral home of my maternal grandmother, Anna Galasso, who grew up in the province of Avellino, an earthquake-prone area that saw a lot of destruction in 1980. Anna was an olive picker and she taught me so much about Neapolitan specialties. I have come to realize that there is more to know about what comes from this blissful region other than what has been epitomized and defined as Neapolitan food, namely pizza and spaghetti. This narrow focus persisted in American society at the end of World War II when returning GIs came home with mouthwatering stories about eating their fill of spaghetti and pizza.

I came to Campania to be close to my origins, to get to know some long-lost relatives, and to experience the culture and the food. My first impression was one of frenzy, everything and everyone moving at phenomenal speed, whether on the streets of Naples or in a relative's kitchen in Benevento. Watching the *pizzaiolo* (pizza maker) stretch and whirl pizza dough all in a matter of seconds confirmed this frenetic, almost trance-like energy. And there was the even quicker work of composing the toppings for a variety of trademark Neapolitan pizza, including pizza Margherita and pizza napoletana, all done with precision.

Attempting to drive in Naples requires more than nerves of steel. Suspend any notion of orderly traffic with rules and regulations. Alternating defensive with demolition driving is what it's all about. Outside the city, driving is slightly more manageable, but it's still a congested traffic nightmare that draws on quick thinking to survive.

My husband's family came from Benevento, one of the five provinces of Campania and an important agricultural area for the ancient Romans. On our last visit we drove for miles through lush fields of tobacco plants grown for export. Mountains surround the entire basin and the province is famous for its super-sweet Strega liqueur, a must for relaxing after dinner or to salute some special occasion. *Torrone,* a nougat confection seen at all the street fairs and a treat always to be found in Christmas stockings, is also a Benevento specialty.

The provinces of Caserta, Avellino, and Salerno along with Benevento and Naples tell much of the story of Campania's past, while the stunning Amalfi Coast, with more than nine hundred treacherous hairpin turns, leads you to experience history, explore the towns, and delight in the magnificent terraced hillside scenery of Positano, Vietri, and Ravello.

Serene Ravello is a favorite with me; this hauntingly beautiful town southwest of Benevento is perched on a 350-foot-high cliff overlooking the sea and the Amalfi Coast. It is a relaxing and soulful respite from the highly charged activity of Naples. Its sumptuous flower gardens soothe the senses. It is a peaceful place for losing all track of time, as I discovered while having lunch at the elegant Villa Maria, one of Ravello's most highly regarded restaurants. Seated outside under a grape arbor, listening to classical music and gazing at the mountains before me while awaiting lunch, I felt I could have stayed forever. This is the magic of the Campania region.

Piramidi di Melanzane alla Nonna Galasso
(Grandma Galasso's Eggplant Pyramids)

Serves 6 to 8

Extra-virgin olive oil

1 medium-size eggplant, cut into ¼-inch-thick round slices

1 small zucchini, cut into ⅛-inch-thick round slices

1 tablespoon dried oregano

3 small plum tomatoes, cut into thin round slices

¼ pound fresh mozzarella cheese, shredded

Did you know that there is no need to salt smaller-size eggplant since they contain fewer seeds and less water and are not bitter like their larger cousins?

It would be fair to say that eggplant plays a large role in Neapolitan cuisine. As a child I loathed having to eat it in the many ways that my nonna Galasso cooked it. She would probably clap her hands if she could see how much I utilize it today and how much I have grown to like it! I make this quick antipasto when my garden is bursting with royal purple eggplant, redder-than-red tomatoes, and forest green zucchini. The combination is delightful in this stackable antipasto. The idea is to make each layer of vegetables progressively smaller, like a pyramid.

Preheat the oven to 375°F.

Lightly brush a baking sheet with olive oil. Arrange the eggplant slices in rows on the sheet. Brush the slices lightly with olive oil. Top each slice with a zucchini round and brush them with olive oil. Sprinkle the oregano over the tops of the zucchini. Place a tomato slice over each zucchini round and brush the top with olive oil. Sprinkle a little salt over the top of each tomato.

Bake for 25 minutes. Sprinkle the cheese over the tomatoes and continue to bake for an additional 5 minutes, or until the cheese has just melted. Serve hot.

Variation: Use the broiler to melt the cheese-topped rounds instead of baking them.

Pizza Rustica con Olive
(Country-Style Pizza with Olives)

Makes 1 pizza or 8 servings

This savory two-crusted rustic pizza oozing with scallions and two kinds of olives is in answer to a request from viewer Donna Sakowski, who remembered her Italian grandmother making it. What follows is my interpretation. I like to serve it warm and cut into squares as an antipasto accompanied by wine. It also makes a wonderful luncheon item with a salad of arugula, radicchio, and romaine lettuces.

Prepare the dough as directed on page 149.

Heat the 2 tablespoons olive oil in a sauté pan and when it is hot stir in the scallions. Sauté them until they become soft but not brown. Stir in the olives and jalapeño pepper. Add the salt, pepper, and oregano and sauté for 2 or 3 minutes. Transfer the mixture to a bowl and set aside.

Lightly grease or spray a baking sheet with olive oil and set aside.

Divide the dough in half and work with one piece at a time. Roll the dough out into a 14×12-inch rectangle. Transfer the dough to the baking sheet and lightly brush it with 1 tablespoon of olive oil. Spread the olive mixture evenly over the dough to within ½ inch of the edges.

Roll out the second piece of dough and place it over the filling. Seal the edges of the dough by folding the edges of the top dough over the edges of the bottom dough. Brush the top of the dough with the beaten egg. Sprinkle the sesame seeds evenly over the top, then sprinkle the cheese over the sesame seeds. Make an X in the center of the top with a scissors. Cover and let rise 20 minutes.

DOUGH

1 recipe Basic Dough (page 149)

FILLING

2 tablespoons olive oil plus additional for greasing baking sheet and dough

2 bunches (8 ounces) scallions, washed and trimmed and cut into ¼-inch slices

4 ounces (about 16) colossal Cerignola olives, pitted and chopped

1 cup Niçoise or Gaeta olives, pitted and chopped

1 tablespoon diced jalapeño pepper

¼ teaspoon fine sea salt

Grinding of black pepper

1 teaspoon dried oregano

1 egg, slightly beaten

1 tablespoon sesame seeds

2 tablespoons grated Pecorino cheese

Campania

Preheat the oven to 375°F.

Bake the pizza for 35 to 40 minutes, or until the dough is nicely browned on the top and bottom. Remove the pizza with a wide metal spatula to a cooking rack. Cut into 2-inch squares while warm and serve.

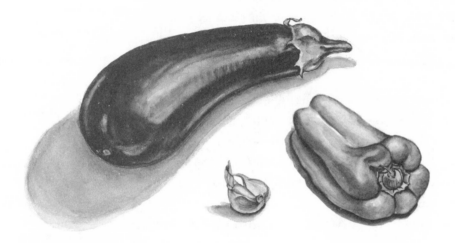

Pizza con Gorgonzola e Pomodori Secchi
(Gorgonzola and Sun-Dried Tomato Pizza)

Makes 2 pizze

Those who dismiss blue-veined Gorgonzola cheese as too pungent and smelly have not eaten this cheese at its best. Made since the Middle Ages in the town for which it is named, Gorgonzola can be piccante *(sharp) or* dolce *(sweet). The sharper version is firmer in consistency and a straw color. It is made from combining two curds. Gorgonzola dolce is creamy white in texture and color, spreadable, and made from one curd. See Mail Order Sources (page 347) for further information. This pizza with Gorgonzola dolce and sun-dried tomatoes has become one of my husband's favorites. It is a culinary marriage of the region of Lombardia's famous cheese combined with the intense flavor of Campania's dried plum tomatoes in olive oil. Just these two ingredients blanketed over an airy pizza dough made from flour, yeast, and potato water results in a masterpiece. Start thinking about making this pizza the next time you boil potatoes. Save the water used to boil the potatoes and ½ cup of the mashed potatoes to make the dough. The taste and texture of this dough is so wonderful that it will become a favorite in your house as well. Baking this pizza on a baking stone results in a crispier crust. The baking stone should be preheated for at least 30 minutes before baking.*

PIZZA DOUGH

1½ pounds all-purpose potatoes, washed, peeled, and cut into 1-inch-thick pieces

2 cups reserved potato-cooking water

1 package active dry yeast

½ cup reserved mashed potatoes

1 teaspoon salt

1 teaspoon olive oil

5 to 5¼ cups unbleached all-purpose flour

TOPPING

½ pound Gorgonzola dolce cheese, rind removed, cut into small pieces

1 cup sun-dried tomatoes in olive oil, drained and cut into small pieces

Place the potatoes in a saucepan, cover them with water, and bring to a boil. Cook the potatoes until fork-tender; drain them and reserve 2 cups of the cooking water and allow to cool to lukewarm.

Mash the potatoes, reserving ½ cup for the dough and using the remaining potatoes as a side dish.

Pour the 2 cups reserved potato water into a large bowl or an electric mixer fitted with a dough hook. Stir in the yeast and allow

Campania

149

the mixture to "proof" for 10 minutes, or get chalky looking with small bubbles on the surface. Mix in the reserved mashed potatoes, salt, and olive oil.

Stir or mix in 1 cup of the flour at a time, mixing well after each addition. Use only enough flour to create a ball of dough that winds around the dough hook if using an electric mixer or comes away from the sides of a bowl if doing this by hand. The dough should be slightly tacky. Resist the temptation to add too much flour.

Transfer the dough to a lightly greased bowl. Cover the bowl tightly with plastic wrap and allow the dough to rise in a warm but not hot place (about 70°F) until it has doubled in size.

Punch the dough down with your fist and transfer it to a work surface lightly dusted with flour. Knead the dough for 3 or 4 minutes. Divide the dough in half. Work with one piece at a time and roll the dough into a 12- or 13-inch circle. Transfer the dough to a pizza pan or a parchment-lined peel if baking the pizza on a baking stone.

Preheat the oven to 375°F if baking the pizza on pizza pans, or preheat the oven to 425°F if using baking stones and do this 30 minutes prior to baking. (If you only have one stone, bake one pizza at a time.)

Distribute half of the cheese over the surface of the pizza and sprinkle on half of the tomatoes.

Repeat the steps with the second piece of dough. Cover the pizze with clean towels and allow them to again rise for about 25 minutes.

If using a baking stone slide the pizza from the peel with the parchment paper and bake until the underneath crust is golden brown and the edges of the pizza have started to brown, about 30 minutes. Remove the pizza from the oven with the peel and allow to cool for a few minutes. Cut the pizza with a scissors and serve hot.

Bake the second pizza on the stone as above.

If using pizza pans, bake one on the bottom rack and one on the middle rack, alternating the positions halfway through the cooking process. This should take about 30 to 35 minutes altogether.

Remove the pizze from the oven, cut them, and serve as above.

Note: If you want to bake only one pizza, use only half the topping ingredients called for and freeze the remaining dough in a heavy-duty plastic bag for up to 6 months.

Pizza di Scarola
(Escarole Pizza)

Serves 8

PIZZA DOUGH

1 teaspoon active dry yeast

1½ cups warm water
(110°–115°F)

4 cups (approximately)
unbleached all-purpose
flour

1 teaspoon salt

1 teaspoon olive oil

1 egg, lightly beaten

Coarse salt for sprinkling

FILLING

¼ cup raisins

1½ pounds escarole, washed
and leaves separated

¼ cup extra-virgin olive oil

1 small onion, peeled and
diced

2 teaspoons capers in brine,
diced

2 tablespoons pine nuts

¼ teaspoon salt

Grinding of black pepper

Pizza di scarola is one of those traditional Neapolitan pies served every Christmas Eve just before going to midnight mass. It is a good example of making something out of nothing, for which the Neapolitans are famous. A few olives, an onion, pine nuts, raisins, and bitter greens such as escarole become a succulent filling for a basic pizza dough. (Anchovies are also a popular ingredient, but I prefer the filling without them.) This is not pizza in the open-faced tradition; instead, the filling is encased in the dough and formed into a turnover, giving it a more elegant look. Serve it as an antipasto or a light lunch.

In a large bowl or in an electric mixer dissolve the yeast in the water and let it sit for 5 minutes. Begin adding the flour 1 cup at a time, allowing each addition to be mixed in thoroughly. Add the salt and olive oil after the second cup of flour. You may not need to use all the flour, just enough to allow the dough to move away from the sides of the bowl and form a ball.

Place the dough in a lightly greased bowl and cover it tightly with plastic wrap. Allow the dough to rise in a warm (70°F), but not hot, place for 3 hours. This slow rising will help to develop the dough's taste and texture.

While the dough is rising, make the filling. Put the raisins in a small bowl and cover them with hot water. Allow the raisins to plump up for about 10 minutes. Drain the raisins, coarsely chop them, and set aside.

Bring a large pot of water to the boil, add the escarole, and cook it, uncovered, for about 5 minutes. Drain the escarole in a colander and squeeze as much water as possible out of the leaves. On a cutting board, coarsely chop the leaves and set aside.

In a sauté pan heat the olive oil, stir in the onions, and sauté them until softened. Stir in the escarole and capers, and cook the mixture for 3 or 4 minutes. Stir in the pine nuts and continue cooking for 1 minute. Stir in the raisins, salt, and pepper. Transfer the mixture to a bowl and allow to cool to room temperature.

Punch down the dough and transfer it to a lightly floured work surface. Roll the dough out into a 14-inch circle. Spread the escarole filling evenly over half of the dough. Fold the remaining half of the dough over the filling to make a turnover. Pinch the edges closed, then seal it by pressing all around with the tines of a fork.

Place the pizza on a lightly greased baking sheet; cover it, and allow it to rise for 30 minutes. Just before baking, brush the top of the dough with the beaten egg and sprinkle the salt over the egg wash.

Preheat the oven to 400°F.

Make a few gashes with a clean razor or scissors in the top crust.

Bake for 35 to 40 minutes on the middle oven rack until the pizza is golden brown.

Transfer the pizza to a cutting board and allow it to cool for 10 minutes. Cut the pizza into thick slices and serve warm.

Did you know that escarole is also delicious as a salad green?

Riso del Mezzogiorno al Mario
(Mario's Mezzogiorno Rice)

Serves 4

3 tablespoons extra-virgin olive oil

1 small hot red pepper, minced

1 large red sweet pepper, seeded and cut into strips

3 anchovies in salt, rinsed

6 oil-cured green olives, pitted

6 oil-cured black olives, pitted

3 cloves garlic, minced

1 tablespoon capers in brine, rinsed

1 tablespoon butter

⅔ cup sliced mushrooms

1 cup heavy cream

1 cup Arborio rice

Fellow chef Mario Ragni, who makes his home in Umbria, loves to experiment with regional flavors. Here he combines the lively flavors of the Mezzogiorno (southern Italy) with traditional northern ingredients of butter and cream to create an earthy sauce for boiled Arborio rice, which is used for making risotto. This short-grain, starchy rice can be found on grocery store shelves or in Italian specialty stores or can be ordered by mail (see page 347).

Heat the olive oil in a sauté pan, then add the hot pepper, sweet pepper strips, anchovies, and green and black olives. Sauté, stirring occasionally, until the pepper strips begin to soften. Stir in the garlic and capers and cook together until the peppers are very soft. Cool the mixture slightly, then transfer it to a food processor. Pulse to make a smooth puree. Transfer the sauce to a bowl, cover, and set aside.

Melt the butter in the same sauté pan and stir in the mushrooms. Sauté them until they no longer give off any water but are not brown. Stir in the heavy cream and the reserved pepper sauce. Keep the sauce warm and covered while the rice is cooking.

Cook the rice in 3 cups of water until it is al dente and has absorbed most of the water. Drain the rice in a colander and add it to the warm sauce. Stir to blend the mixture thoroughly. Serve immediately.

Campania

154

Frittata di Zucchine
(Zucchini Omelet)

Serves 6

Neapolitans love their vegetables, and they should. The region of Campania is blessed with the right mix of elements: brilliant sun, warm climate, and fertile volcanic soil for growing fabulous vegetables. The tradition of vegetable cooking has been preserved well in my family. One of the best known dishes, eaten on Fridays, was Nonna Galasso's frittata di zucchine, which in dialect was known as cacuzza. Light and airy, this frittata is great to team with a simple salad and a glass of wine.

¼ cup extra-virgin olive oil

1 small zucchini, washed, dried, and thinly sliced into rounds

1 clove garlic, minced

6 large eggs, lightly beaten

Salt to taste

Grinding of black pepper

⅓ cup grated Parmigiano-Reggiano or Pecorino Romano cheese

Heat the olive oil in a nonstick 10- or 12-inch sauté pan. Add the zucchini and garlic and stir the mixture gently in the oil for 2 or 3 minutes. Lower the heat to medium low, cover the pan, and continue cooking just until the zucchini begins to look soft. Stir the salt and pepper into the eggs and slowly pour the mixture over the zucchini. Sprinkle the top with the cheese, cover the pan, and continue cooking just until the eggs have set.

Transfer the frittata to a serving dish and cut into wedges to serve—or serve directly from the sauté pan.

Campania

On the Road to Napoli

$\mathcal{T}$he invitation to sample the wines of the Villa Matilde *azienda* outside Naples and have lunch with Salvatore Avallone, one of the owners, was gladly accepted, and Guy and I, along with a few friends, drove to the azienda from Castelgondolfo by way of the autostrada. The scenery along the way was like a set of beautiful postcards. Wherever one looked there was a sensual treat, from the bald and bold-faced Massico mountain range, a remnant of volcanic activity, to the flocks of sheep grazing so high on hilltops that they looked like white pin dots, to the valley farmland neatly delineated and bulging with new broccoli crops, to the vineyards stretching beyond any visible boundaries.

Salvatore greeted us with a firm handshake; he is a gracious man with dark hair, gentle eyes, and a mild manner. Upon meeting him one can sense his dedication to his family's wine-making business. In my travels to Italy I have been to many wineries, listened to detailed explanations of the harvesting, fermenting, aging, and bottling process of wine making, and it still astounds me what sheer dedication and a great deal of luck it takes to make good wine. I have come to appreciate the work of the oenologist, whose job it is to create great wine.

Salvatore is eager to show us the vineyards. As we drive along the dirt road with vines along either side—mile after mile of grapevines, some of old Greek stock—I have a sudden urge to sample a few grapes known as Alianico; the tightly packed clusters look almost black, not purple. The taste is excellent; the grapes are juicy and sugary.

We have arrived during the harvest, what the Italians call the *vendemmia,* and the workers are in the field having a lunch break under some olive trees. Nearby some of the fieldhands have set up a makeshift bocce game and just the sight of it triggers memories of watching the men in my old neighborhood play this game when I was a child. No women allowed. I make a mental note to really try to get the hang of it.

After the tour, Salvatore invites us to sample the wines and have lunch in the azienda's cozy country-style *ristorante.* We enjoy some typical Neapolitan dishes including *un assaggio,* a tasting of assorted antipasti including double-crusted pizza with cauliflower; *bruschetta,* toasted slices of coarse bread topped with chopped tomatoes, oregano, and olive oil; and *pane farcito,* bread stuffed with nuts, olives, and peppers. The *primo piatto* (first course) of small rigatoni was served with a tomato sauce made with pancetta, pork, wild fennel, onion, and olive oil. The *secondo piatto* was *bracciole,* a rolled stuffed beef like Nonna Galasso used to make, and then a marinated potato salad in olive oil, mint, and oregano. These last two dishes brought back warm, nostalgic memories of Nonna's Neapolitan cooking.

All of the food was of course accompanied by the appropriate wines from the estate. As is the custom, Italians enjoy several small courses that make up the meal, and this means time—lots of time—at the table. I looked at my watch and realized that we had been eating and conversing for well over two hours!

Knowing that we still needed to drive into Naples, we were anxious to thank our host and be on our way. Guy was doing all the driving, so he asked Salvatore what was the best way to get to Naples. "Ah," he said. "I am going to Naples now myself, so follow me."

That seemed like a good plan—until we left the sanctity of the winery and began following Salvatore on the superstrada. Now the words "follow me" took on a whole new connotation. No car chase in a James Bond movie could come close to capturing the harrowing ride we were about to have. Salvatore drove like a Neapolitan! That meant *fast,* at a speed of 140 kilometers per hour, faster by far than we were used to, but Guy, determined not to lose sight of our guide, managed to stay within range and followed Salvatore's route exactly. With both hands welded to the steering wheel, he wove in and out of traffic, sometimes crossing over into oncoming traffic, which meant several huge trucks heading right toward us. He disregarded all traffic lights, grazed by numerous cars, zipped through darkened tunnels, and seemed to keep a cool head. My entire body was stiff, my hands clenched, my eyes watching every car's move, with sheer panic overcoming me. That wonderful lunch we had just consumed was lodged right in my throat, where it would remain for the rest of the day. I am sure that Salvatore never once thought that we were *not* behind him; to him such driving was normal. As we neared the exit for Napoli, he motioned us on to our destination with a gallant wave of his hand out the window, and from that moment we understood how to navigate the streets of Naples . . . we simply suspended any notion of traffic rules.

Peperoni Imbottiti
(Stuffed Peppers)

Serves 4

The word imbottire *means "to stuff," as in these wonderful roasted and baked sweet bell peppers housing a flavorful filling of bread crumbs, anchovies, capers, and olives. Next to tomatoes, peppers are probably a Neapolitan cook's best friend, and this is only one of the myriad ways they are prepared. Serve these as a main course or as an antipasto.*

4 large sweet bell peppers of assorted colors

¼ pound (about 8 large), Cerignola olives in brine, pitted

¼ cup capers in salt, rinsed

6 whole basil leaves, stemmed

4 or 5 sprigs Italian parsley, stemmed

¼ cup extra-virgin olive oil plus 1 tablespoon for drizzling over the peppers

1 large clove garlic, minced

3 anchovies in olive oil, drained

½ cup bread crumbs

Grinding of coarse black pepper

Roast the peppers whole on an outdoor grill or under an oven broiler on a broiler pan, turning them occasionally until they are blackened all over. Transfer the peppers to a paper bag and allow them to steam until cool. Peel away the skin and remove and discard the stems. Carefully open the peppers up along one side and wipe out the seeds with paper towels. Try to keep the peppers in one long, continuous piece to make it easier to stuff. Set the peppers aside.

In a food processor, mince together the olives, capers, basil, and parsley. Transfer the mixture to a small bowl and set aside.

In a sauté pan heat ¼ cup of the olive oil until hot. Stir in the garlic and sauté until the garlic softens. Add the anchovies and stir until the anchovies dissolve. Add the minced olive mixture and cook over medium heat for 2 minutes. Stir in the bread crumbs and continue to cook until the ingredients are well blended. Stir in the pepper. Allow the mixture to cool so it is easier to handle.

Preheat the oven to 350°F.

Open up each pepper so it is one flat piece. Divide the stuffing mixture among the peppers, packing them tightly. Beginning at

Campania

159

the short end, roll up each pepper like a jelly roll and place them all in a baking dish. Drizzle the remaining tablespoon of oil over the top of the peppers. Cover the dish with aluminum foil and bake for 25 to 30 minutes, or until they are hot. Remove the foil and serve the peppers immediately.

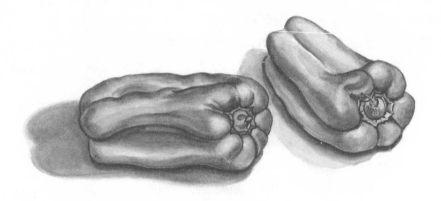

Spaghetti alle Cozze
(Spaghetti and Mussels)

Serves 6

*Sit in any ristorante in Naples and on the menu will be various tantalizing seafood and fish dishes like clams and spaghetti (*spaghetti al vongole*) and mussels and spaghetti (*spaghetti alle cozze*). As with any shellfish, be sure that there are no cracks in the shells and discard any clams or mussels that do not open in the cooking process. In this recipe, a simple white wine sauce compliments the sweetness of the mussels.*

1 pound spaghetti

1 tablespoon salt

¼ cup reserved cooking water

3½ pounds mussels, debearded and well scrubbed

¾ cup dry white wine

½ cup olive oil

3 cloves garlic, thinly sliced

½ teaspoon dried red pepper flakes

¼ teaspoon sea salt

Grinding of black pepper

3 tablespoons finely minced parsley leaves

In a pasta pot bring 4 to 6 quarts of water to a rapid boil. Stir in 1 tablespoon of salt and the spaghetti. Cover the pot and bring the water back to the boil, then uncover the pot, and cook the spaghetti until it is al dente, firm but not mushy. Drain the pasta, reserving ¼ cup of the water, and set it aside.

While the spaghetti is cooking, make the mussel sauce.

Put the mussels in a large sauté pan that can later accommodate the cooked spaghetti. Pour in the wine, cover the pan, and bring the wine to a boil. Lower the heat to medium and cook, covered, until all the mussels open. If any do not open, discard them. Remove the mussels from the pan with a slotted spoon and transfer them to a bowl. Strain the liquid in the pan through a cheesecloth-lined strainer over a bowl and reserve.

Remove the mussels from their shells and place them in a bowl. Discard the shells. Wipe out the sauté pan and then heat the olive oil. Stir in the garlic and sauté it until the garlic is golden brown. Remove the garlic and discard it. Stir in the red pepper flakes and cook for 1 minute. Add the wine, salt, pepper, and the reserved

Campania

161

cooking water. Raise the heat to high and allow the mixture to boil, uncovered, for about 2 minutes. Add the mussels and the parsley and heat for 1 minute. Stir in the spaghetti and toss the mixture rapidly until heated through.

Serve immediately in soup bowls.

Calamaretti in Brodo al Pomodoro Piccante

(Baby Squid in Spicy Tomato Broth)

Serves 6

You either love them or hate them, but calamari (squid) have long been part of the Italian culinary scene. The name calamaro is from the Latin calamus and refers to the midnight-black inky liquid that squid excrete when approached by prey. This ink is also used to make a classic ink sauce for pasta. How to cook calamari without it turning into chewy rubber bands has always been the bane of home cooks. Here are a few tips: Buy them small, no longer than 4 to 6 inches in length if you are going to sauté or deep-fry them; buy a larger size for stuffing and baking. Buy fresh if possible; squid bodies should look plump and white, not yellow. In this recipe, small squid are simmered with tomatoes and served with capers and olives in a slightly spicy tomato broth. I prefer the San Marzano variety of tomatoes.

Put the tomatoes through a food mill or a sieve set over a large bowl to remove the seeds. Set the juice aside.

Heat 1 tablespoon of the oil in a 2-quart sauce pan and stir in the scallions. Cook them until they soften and turn a dark green color. Transfer the scallions to a dish and set aside to use as a garnish.

Add the remaining oil to the pan and cook the shallots until they begin to soften. Stir in the garlic and continue cooking until the garlic is soft. Raise the heat to high and pour in the wine. Cook, stirring occasionally, for about 3 minutes. Lower the heat to medium. Stir in the squid and red pepper flakes and cook them for 2 or 3 minutes, stirring frequently.

Slowly pour in 4 cups of the reserved tomato juice. Keep the remainder for another use. Stir the ingredients well, cover the pan,

2 (32-ounce cans) whole plum tomatoes

¼ cup olive oil

1 small bunch scallions, green tops only, cut into 1-inch pieces

5 large shallots, peeled and minced

3 cloves garlic, minced

½ cup dry white wine

2 pounds small-size cleaned squid plus tentacles

½ teaspoon red pepper flakes

½ cup coarsely chopped and pitted oil-cured black olives or Gaeta olives

¼ cup capers in salt, rinsed

1 teaspoon salt

Grinding of coarse black pepper

½ teaspoon celery salt

2 tablespoons freshly squeezed lemon juice

Campania

and simmer for 10 minutes. Uncover the pan and continue cooking for about 12 minutes, or until the squid are tender. Five minutes before the squid are done, stir in the olives, capers, salt, pepper, celery salt, and lemon juice.

Ladle the squid and some of the broth into individual soup bowls. Sprinkle the reserved scallions over each and serve immediately.

Variation: Instead of shallots, substitute leeks.

Scarola e Fagioli
(Escarole and Beans)

Serves 6

½ cup dried cannellini or white northern beans

1½ pounds escarole, leaves separated, well washed and cut into ½-inch wide strips

¼ cup extra-virgin olive oil

1 large clove garlic, cut into slivers

½ teaspoon dried red pepper flakes

Grinding of coarse black pepper

½ teaspoon salt

This is one of those cucina povera *(poor food) dishes that my mother remembers eating as a child and which she prepared often. It is nothing more than greens (escarole) and beans, but it makes a nutritious vegetable or main vegetarian course. Escarole is notoriously full of dirt, so be sure to clean the leaves well in several changes of water. In this recipe the escarole is not boiled, which is the conventional way to cook it, but wilted in a covered pot. Soak the cannellini or white northern beans the day before to soften them and reduce the cooking time. If you want to used canned beans, be sure to rinse them well to remove the excess salt.*

Put the beans in a bowl, cover them with water, and allow them to sit overnight. When ready to cook, drain the beans and transfer them to a pot. Cover the beans with 2 cups of water and cook them over medium-high heat until tender. This will take about 30 minutes. Do not allow the beans to get mushy; as soon as they are fork tender, drain them and set them aside.

Place the escarole strips in a soup pot with only the water clinging to them. Cover the pot and wilt the strips; this will take about 5 minutes. Drain the escarole, and squeeze as much water as possible out of it. Coarsely chop the strips and set aside.

Heat the oil in a sauté pan and cook the garlic until it softens and begins to turn brown. Remove the garlic and discard it. Add the escarole and red pepper flakes to the pan and cook, stirring frequently, for 3 or 4 minutes. Stir in the cannellini beans, pepper and salt, and mix the ingredients well. Transfer to a dish and serve hot.

Variation: Mix in 1 cup prepared tomato sauce with the cannellini beans.

Campania

Melanzane alla Parmigiana di Zia Anna

(Aunt Anna's Eggplant Parmigiana Casserole)

Serves 8

½ cup unbleached all-purpose flour

½ teaspoon salt

Grinding of black pepper

2 medium-size eggplants, stemmed, peeled, and cut into thin slices

3 large eggs, slightly beaten

½ cup canola or peanut oil

2½ cups tomato sauce

⅔ cup grated Parmigiano-Reggiano cheese

In my first cookbook, Ciao Italia, *there is not one recipe for eggplant alla Parmigiana. The reason was that I thought everyone knew how to make it. It was not until I did a segment on a version of eggplant alla Parmigiana that I realized I had been doing an injustice to my readers. This recipe was made on the series by the mayor of Providence, Rhode Island, Buddy Cianci. Buddy uses his great aunt Anna's recipe, which creates a very light-tasting, nongreasy eggplant that is even good served cold between slices of coarse bread as a wonderful sandwich. There is great debate among cooks as to whether to fry the eggplant in olive oil or vegetable oil. I prefer vegetable oil, which produces a lighter-tasting dish.*

Put the flour, salt, and pepper in a heavy-duty paper bag. Close the bag and shake the ingredients to blend them. Add the eggplant slices a few at a time to the bag, then close the bag and shake to coat the slices. Transfer the slices to a dish.

Spread a thin layer of tomato sauce over the bottom of a 9×12-inch casserole dish and set aside.

Preheat the oven to 350°F.

Heat the oil in a large sauté pan. While it is heating, coat the slices of eggplant in the beaten egg on both sides. Fry the slices in the oil until they are golden brown on each side. As they brown, transfer them to a baking sheet lined with paper towels.

Place a layer of the slices in the baking dish, slightly overlapping them. Spoon on a thin layer of tomato sauce and one-third of the grated cheese. Continue making layers until all the eggplant is used. Finish off the top layer with tomato sauce.

Campania

Cover the dish tightly with aluminum foil and bake it for 35 to 40 minutes. Remove the dish and allow it to sit for 15 minutes before cutting it. Serve hot.

Note: This is even better made a day ahead of time. Cut it when cold for neat, even pieces.

Variation: To make a Sicilian version of this recipe, use Caciocavallo cheese, pine nuts, and raisins between the eggplant layers.

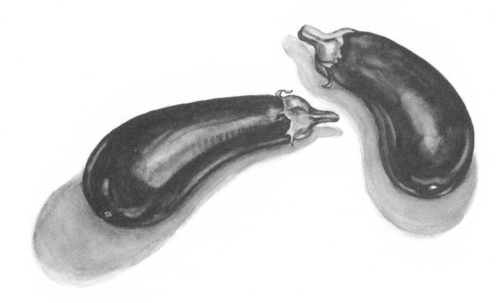

Pollo Scarpariello
(Shoemaker-Style Chicken)

Serves 3 to 4

3 pounds bone-in chicken pieces, cut into small pieces

1 cup freshly squeezed lemon juice

Grated zest of 2 large lemons

1½ teaspoons salt

Grinding of black pepper

½ cup flour

1 tablespoon extra-virgin olive oil

1 tablespoon butter

3 large cloves garlic, peeled and finely minced

½ cup minced parsley leaves

Pollo scarpariello, or shoemaker-style chicken, is a country-style Neapolitan favorite with many variations. With just a few choice ingredients and seasonings the taste is sensational. Small bone-in chicken pieces provide the best flavor, and freshly squeezed lemon juice is a must. Marinate the chicken at least one day before cooking in a heavy-duty zipper-lock bag, shaking it occasionally to ensure it gets evenly seasoned. The secret to the crispy golden crust is to use a good-quality heavy sauté pan; the chicken is browned on high heat to seal in the juices.

Wash and dry the chicken pieces and set aside.

In a plastic zipper-lock bag combine ½ cup of the lemon juice, the zest, salt, and pepper. Add the chicken pieces, close the bag, and shake to distribute the ingredients around the chicken pieces. Refrigerate overnight.

Remove the chicken from the marinade and dry the pieces well with paper towels. Discard the marinade. Pour the flour into a large paper bag, add the chicken pieces, close the bag tightly, and shake the bag to coat the chicken pieces with flour. Remove the chicken pieces to a dish and set aside.

In a heavy-duty sauté pan large enough to hold all the pieces in a single layer, heat the olive oil and butter until hot. Add the chicken pieces, skin-side down, and brown them well over high heat. This will take about 10 minutes. Lower the heat to medium and continue to cook the chicken, uncovered, for about 20 minutes, or until the chicken is fork-tender. Remove the chicken to a warm platter.

Stir the garlic into the drippings and cook it over medium heat until soft. Pour in the remaining lemon juice, add the parsley, and stir and cook for 1 minute, scraping up any browned bits remaining in the pan. Pour the juice over the chicken pieces, season with additional salt and pepper, if desired, and serve immediately.

You'll get more juice from lemons if they are at room temperature, not refrigerated. Roll them around before squeezing.

Pollo alla Cacciatora
(Hunter-Style Chicken)

Serves 8

4 pounds chicken, cut up

1 teaspoon sea salt

½ teaspoon coarsely ground black pepper

6 tablespoons olive oil

1 large onion, peeled and chopped

3 cloves garlic, peeled and minced

1 bay leaf

2 (28-ounce) cans whole tomatoes

2 bell peppers (1 red and 1 yellow), cored, seeded, and cut into strips

½ pound button mushrooms, sliced

On one of the remote shoots for the "Going Home for Good Italian Food" series, I visited my mother, who made one of my very favorite dishes, pollo alla cacciatora *(or hunter-style chicken), a country-style dish in which chicken pieces are simmered together with tomatoes and sweet bell peppers. No one knows why this dish is called hunter-style, except perhaps that in the Renaissance those who could afford to enjoy poultry were the well-to-do, who also enjoyed the sport of hunting. This dish developed in central Italy and has many variations. I often receive letters from viewers asking for the recipe. Use free-range chickens which are grain-fed and chemical free; they cost a little more but are readily available in grocery stores. And if possible, use a heavy cast-iron skillet, for even browning and cooking.*

Wash and dry the chicken pieces. Rub the pieces with the salt and pepper and set them aside.

In a large heavy-duty skillet, heat the olive oil and cook the onions until they are soft but not browned. Stir in the garlic and continue cooking until the garlic softens. Add the chicken pieces and brown them evenly on all sides. Add the bay leaf. Add the tomatoes, squeezing them slightly with your hands, and also add any tomato juice. Lower the heat to a simmer, cover the pot, and cook the chicken for ½ hour. Uncover the pot, stir in the peppers, cover the pot, and cook until the peppers are soft and the chicken is fork-tender. Stir in the mushrooms, cover the pot, and cook for about 5 minutes, or just until the mushrooms are soft.

Serve immediately with good crusty bread, or with rice or potatoes.

Campania

The Art of Getting By

*B*efore I visited Naples, everything I knew about it came from what my Neapolitan nonna, Anna Galasso, had told me. People were poor, living conditions were hard, food was scarce, there was a lot of crime, and it was hard to find work. These factors and others brought her to America around 1900, when she was in her early twenties.

When I finally went to Naples, I found a city of contrasts. My first encounter was framed by the elegant hotels along Via Partenope, one of the main streets along the shore (*lungomare*) offering gorgeous views of the sea, and of large ships slowly passing by on their way to nearby Capri, Ischia, and other ports. The panoramic sweep included the sleeping giant, Mount Vesuvius, looming not too far in the distance. Closer to shore fishermen lowered and raised their nets as their vividly colored boats bobbed gently in the water.

Jutting out to sea across from Via Partenope was the foreboding-looking Castel Dell'Ovo (Castle of the Egg). This ancient fortress, the oldest castle in Naples, provides a dramatic backdrop where brides like to have their photos taken, and it is a favorite place for lovers to cozy up on the rocky ledges that flank the water's edge. It is also a spot for the *polizia stradale* (traffic police) to hover and, on a moment's notice, stop motorists for a check of their licenses, while paying no attention at all to the hundreds of vehicles whizzing by without any concern for traffic lights or pedestrians.

Not far from Via Partenope is the expansive Piazza del Plebiscito with the impressive and opulent Palazzo Reale, a seventeenth-century royal palace built for the Spanish viceroys who ruled Naples. Opposite the palace is an architectural wonder, the nineteenth-century church of San Francesco di Paola, which architecturally bears a striking resemblance to the Pantheon in Rome. The space between these two monumental structures was originally intended for ceremonies and military parades, and today is a "communal living room" for Neapolitans of all ages to congregate with their families and friends. Here they gossip, sit on mopeds, eat gelato, read the paper, people-watch, and stroll arm-in-arm with no particular destination in mind. When I am in these settings it is an opportunity to see people for who they really are, and the Neapolitans exhibit a zest for life found nowhere else in Italy. They live life on the edge, unabashed and with gusto. They test fate at every turn, as evidenced in the way they drive, argue, and turn negative situations to their advantage.

To experience the real and everyday Naples a visit to the old neighborhoods is a must, whether it is the Spanish quarter (Quartieri Spagnoli), or Spaccanapoli, which means "split Naples." If you are observant in these places you can get an idea of how Neapolitans live and cope. These living and working neighborhoods are defined by narrow crowded streets shaded by buildings that appear to close in on themselves. Row after row of laundry strung from building to building block out the sunshine, but make a statement about how to cope in confined spaces. Scores of people crowd the walkways on their way to shop or work; children play soccer in spaces no bigger than a closet, and some men pass the time of day amid the chaos by claiming a small section of the sidewalk and enclosing themselves in a makeshift tent to play a game of cards.

There are shops of every description on these streets, from butchers to bakers to tripe sellers, and open-air market areas where fish from the tiniest of fresh sardines to huge tuna and swordfish are cut, sold, and wrapped in large paper cones. In the produce market every imaginable fruit or vegetable is available, including carrots, celery, onions, and herbs already tied together like a bouquet garni ready to add to the soup pot, an indication that today's Neapolitan women do not have the time to spend in the kitchen that their nonnas did.

A walk down the famous Via San Gregorio Armeno reveals a colorful street made famous by the *presepio* trade, the handcrafted nativity figures made by local artists from terra-cotta and dressed elegantly in the costumes of old Naples. I stopped to look for figures in some of the jam-packed shops. I soon learned by observing what one of the elements of Neapolitan success was . . . the ability to argue. If you want to pay a fair price for a presepio—or anything—knowing how to strike a good deal and the art of persuasion are key.

Today's presepio reflects more than the manger scene of the Christ Child, shepherds, and the Three Kings; there are figures of present-day politicians, Sophia Loren, the *pizzaiola* (pizza maker), the prosciutto-maker, the wet nurse, and scenes of life in old Naples, as well as the perennial favorite, Pucinella, the masked clown in baggy white pants, pointed hat, and ruffled shirt. He is the classic and complex character symbol of Naples, a symbol of fortune and fate, of laughter and tears, of good and evil, of conflict and resolve, of intrigue and innuendo, and who, above all, embodies *l'arte di arrangiarisi*—the art of living by one's wits.

Coping and ingenuity go hand in hand in this crowded, boisterous city of contrasts. No matter what fate has in store for a Neapolitan, he or she will find a way to deal with it, whether it is the music grinder who positions himself strategically on the street, playing for your entertainment while his hat becomes a receptacle for money, or the puppeteer who pulls all the right strings to amuse you and shame you into recognizing that his talents are not for free, or the trinket peddler who stands on a corner all day long, repetitiously demonstrating how a battery-operated toy works. Even in restaurants you may be serenaded by a wandering musician who will expect you to show your satisfaction with a slip of a few lire.

In Naples, the game is life lived to the best of one's ability, and for that we must all have a little bit of Pucinella within.

Sartù

(Neapolitan Rice, Pork, and Vegetable Mold)

Serves 8 to 10

3 tablespoons butter (for greasing mold)

1 cup toasted bread crumbs

FILLING

1 pound ground pork

¼ cup fresh bread crumbs

1½ teaspoons fine sea salt

2 tablespoons grated Pecorino cheese

1 egg

1 tablespoon extra-virgin olive oil

2 tablespoons butter

½ cup diced onion

8 ounces button mushrooms, wiped and sliced into thirds

1 cup fresh or frozen peas

Grinding of fresh black pepper

It was in Sorrento that I was first introduced to sartù, *an impressive-looking rice mold with a meat and vegetable filling, but Naples lays claim to the dish. Today* sartù *has many adaptations and has been simplified from the richer versions of the past, which contained chicken livers, sausages, cheeses, and assorted vegetables. The most important thing to remember when making* sartù *is to prepare the mold well by coating it with butter and bread crumbs, and then chilling it thoroughly in the refrigerator. The preparation, which can be done in stages, begins with making a risotto in which Arborio rice, a short-grain, starchy rice, is cooked slowly with the addition of hot broth. The entire dish can be stored in the refrigerator for several hours or even overnight before baking. Use a 10-cup ring mold or charlotte mold for best results.*

Generously butter the mold and coat it with the bread crumbs, pressing the bread crumbs into the mold if necessary. Cover and chill the mold for several hours, or overnight if desired.

To prepare the filling, in a bowl combine the pork, bread crumbs, 1 teaspoon salt, cheese, and egg. Mix gently with your hands to combine. With wet hands form small meatballs the size of gum balls.

Heat the olive oil in a sauté pan, and when it is hot brown the meatballs, in batches if necessary, until they are golden brown. With a slotted spoon remove the meatballs to a bowl and set aside. (At this point the meatballs can be refrigerated for 2 days in advance of assembling the dish.)

In the same sauté pan melt the 2 tablespoons butter, stir in the onions, and cook them until they begin to wilt. Stir in the mushrooms and cook until the mushrooms exude their juices and they begin to brown. Stir in the peas and cook for 1 minute. Add the remaining ½ teaspoon salt and a grinding of black pepper. Combine the mixture with the meatballs.

To prepare the rice mixture, melt the 3 tablespoons butter in a heavy-clad 3-quart saucepan, add the rice, and cook it over medium heat, stirring constantly, until all the grains of rice are coated in the butter. Slowly pour in the broth, 1 cup at a time, and continue to stir and let the rice absorb each addition of liquid before adding more. You may not need all the broth. The rice should be still firm but cooked through. Stir in the grated cheese and remove the saucepan from the heat. Let the rice cool slightly, then stir in the parsley and eggs.

Preheat the oven to 325°F.

Remove the mold from the refrigerator. Line the bottom of the mold and the sides with about two-thirds of the rice mixture. Make sure there are no bare spots. Spoon the meatball mixture into the rice-lined mold. Cover the top with the remaining rice, patting it tightly and making sure the edges are sealed with rice.

Cover the mold with aluminum foil and bake it for 30 minutes. Remove the aluminum foil and bake for another 10 minutes. Remove the mold from the oven and let stand for about 5 minutes. Have a serving dish or platter ready. Place the dish on top of the mold. Use potholders to hold onto the mold and gently turn the mold over and out onto the serving dish. Do not remove the mold immediately. Let it sit for a few minutes, then shake the mold to make sure that the rice has been released. Lift the mold off and serve the *sartù* immediately.

RICE MIXTURE

3 tablespoons butter

2 cups Arborio rice

4 to 5 cups hot beef, chicken, or vegetable broth

¾ cup grated Pecorino cheese

2 tablespoons chopped fresh parsley leaves

2 eggs

Campania

175

Biscottini d'Anice di Mamma

(Mom's Little Anise Cookies)

Makes at least 10 dozen 1-inch cookies

2 sticks unsalted butter, at
   room temperature

2 cups sugar

6 large eggs, at room
   temperature

2 tablespoons vanilla extract

1 tablespoon anise extract

½ cup heavy cream

Grated zest of 1 large orange

Grated zest of 1 large lemon

9 cups unbleached all-
   purpose flour

2½ tablespoons baking
   powder

¼ teaspoon salt

GLAZE

4 cups confectioners' sugar

¼ to ½ cup milk, light
   cream, or half-and-half

I always loved the way the whole house smelled of licorice after my mother made these amazing anise-flavored cookies. They were and still are one of her standby proven recipes. She made them for any occasion, from weddings to casual visits with friends. The cookies can be frozen in layers for up to four months. I use a heavy-duty stand mixer to make the dough. If this is not possible, divide the ingredients and make two batches. After baking, the cookies are tossed in a thin confectioners' glaze to give them a shiny coating.

In a mixer cream the butter and sugar together until light and fluffy-looking. Beat the eggs in 1 at a time. Beat in the vanilla and anise extracts, the cream, and the orange and lemon zests.

On a sheet of wax paper sift together the flour, baking powder, and salt. On low speed, gradually add the flour mixture a little at a time to the sugar mixture. Beat on medium speed until well blended.

Cover the bowl and chill the dough for 2 hours to make it easier to handle.

Preheat the oven to 350°F.

With your hands roll small pieces of the dough into 1-inch-diameter balls. Place the balls 1 inch apart on ungreased baking sheets. Bake for 14 to 17 minutes, or until the cookies are firm to the touch.

To make the glaze, in a large bowl mix the confectioners' sugar with enough of the liquid to create a thin glaze. Cover the bowl and set aside.

Campania

Remove cookies to a cooling rack, but do not let them cool completely. While still warm, toss them by hand a dozen at a time into the confectioners' glaze, allowing the excess glaze to drip off. Place the glazed cookies on a cooling rack with sheets of wax paper underneath the rack to catch the drippings. Allow the cookies to dry completely.

To freeze, arrange the cookies in single layers in heavy-duty plastic containers, separating each layer with a sheet of wax paper.

Pastiera
(Neapolitan Ricotta and Rice Pie)

Makes one 10½-inch pie

PASTA FROLLA (PASTRY DOUGH)

2 cups unbleached all-purpose flour

1 cup cake flour

1½ teaspoons salt

2 tablespoons sugar

1 stick cold unsalted butter, cut into bits

1 extra-large egg, slightly beaten, plus 1 egg yolk

5 to 6 tablespoons ice water

2 tablespoons turbinado or raw sugar

FILLING

1 cup long-grain rice

2 cups whole milk

3-inch piece of vanilla bean, slit lengthwise

1 pound ricotta cheese, well drained

3 large eggs

¼ cup freshly squeezed orange juice

2 tablespoons grated orange zest

Easter pie (pastiera) is found all over Italy, but its origins are Neapolitan. Tender pasta frolla *pastry pies filled with fresh ricotta cheese and rice, sweetened with sugar, were made in batches, wrapped in clear cellophane, and given away as Easter gifts. Many variations of this classic have survived; some use wheatberries or orzo (tiny pasta) in place of rice, but my favorite still remains the one from home, made with long-grain rice. For the* pasta frolla, *I mix all-purpose flour with cake flour for a more delicate pie crust texture. If you have a kitchen scale, weigh the flour for accuracy. If you do not have a scale, lightly spoon the flour into a dry weight measuring cup, and level it at the top with a butter knife.*

Lightly spray a 10½×1-inch tart pan with removable bottom with butter spray. Set aside.

To prepare the dough, mix the all-purpose and cake flours, salt, and sugar in a food processor or bowl. Add the butter to the flour mixture and pulse to blend if using a food processor, or use a pastry blender or fork to blend the ingredients by hand. Add the whole egg and enough ice water to make a dough that is soft and not dry. Do not overmix or the dough will be tough. Gather the dough into a ball and wrap it tightly in plastic wrap. Chill the dough for 30 minutes.

To prepare the filling, pour the rice and milk into a 1-quart saucepan, scrape the seeds from the vanilla bean into the saucepan with a small knife, cover, and bring the rice to a boil. Lower the heat to medium-low and continue cooking the rice until all the

Campania

178

water is absorbed. This will take about 10 minutes. Let the rice cool.

In a large bowl, beat the ricotta cheese, eggs, orange juice and zest, and sugar until smooth. Stir in the vanilla extract and cinnamon. Fold in the cooled rice. Set the mixture aside.

Preheat the oven to 375°F.

Divide the dough in half. Roll each half on a lightly floured surface into a 14-inch circle. Line the tart shell with one rolled-out half and trim the edges even with the top sides of the tart pan.

Fill the tart shell with the ricotta and rice filling. There will be a little of the filling left over. This can be baked separately in a small ovenproof dish or in small ramekins.

Carefully roll the second sheet of dough loosely over the rolling pin and unroll it over the top of the filled tart. Trim off the excess dough, making sure the edges are sealed. Use the leftover dough to make a decorative pattern on top of the tart. I use a small rabbit cutter to make cutouts for the top.

Brush the tart with the egg yolk and sprinkle the turbinado sugar evenly over the top.

Bake in the middle of the oven for 40 to 50 minutes or until the top is golden brown and a skewer comes out clean when inserted into the center of the tart.

Cool the tart on a rack, then carefully remove the sides of the tart pan and place the tart on a decorative serving dish. Cut into wedges to serve.

1 cup sugar

1 tablespoon vanilla extract

1½ teaspoons cinnamon

Did you know that the Monday after Easter is called Pasquetta, Little Easter, in Italy and is a holiday almost as big as Easter? It is a day for Italians to relax in the countryside. Often a *pastiera* is brought along and enjoyed as picnic food.

Note: Instead of orange juice and orange zest, candied fruits and raisins can also be used.

Variation: The rice can also be cooked in 2 cups of water instead of milk.

Campania

179

Torta al Limone
(Lemon Curd Cake)

Serves 8 to 10

LEMON CURD
(makes 1¾ cups)

½ cup freshly squeezed lemon juice (about 4 large lemons)

1 tablespoon grated lemon zest

1 cup plus 2 tablespoons sugar

3 tablespoons unsalted butter, cut into bits

⅛ teaspoon salt

4 jumbo eggs, lightly beaten

½ cup whipping cream

CAKE

1½ cups cake flour

1½ cups sugar

6 large eggs, separated and at room temperature

½ cup cold water

1 teaspoon vanilla extract

¾ teaspoon cream of tartar

2 tablespoons limoncello liqueur

Torta al Limone (Lemon Curd Cake) is not for the faint of heart. This beautiful and light summertime cake takes its inspiration from limoncello, a lemon liqueur from the Amalfi Coast that is made by steeping lemons in pure alcohol and sugar. It is served all over Italy in frosty glasses. I like to use limoncello as a flavoring for this layered sponge cake filled with a dense lemon curd, which I have lightened in taste by combining with whipped cream to create a mousse consistency. The lemon curd should be made a day ahead and will keep for up to a week in the refrigerator.

To make the lemon curd, in the top of a double boiler combine the lemon juice, zest, sugar, butter, and salt. Cook together over medium heat until the butter melts and the sugar no longer feels gritty in the bottom of the pan. Slowly pour in the eggs, continually mixing them, and cook over medium heat until the mixture thickens and coats the back of a spoon.

Transfer the curd to a small bowl. Cover the bowl tightly with plastic wrap and refrigerate for several hours or overnight until ready to use. When ready to fill the cake, whip the cream until stiff, then fold it into the lemon curd.

Preheat the oven to 325°F.

To make the cake, sift the flour three times and set aside.

In a large bowl of an electric mixer beat the sugar with the egg yolks until they are thick and pale yellow in color. Gradually beat in the water, then the vanilla. With a spatula fold in the sifted flour 2 tablespoons at a time. Set aside.

In another bowl, with clean beaters, beat the egg whites with the cream of tartar until soft and shiny, but not dry, peaks form. Fold the whites into the egg yolk mixture and pour the batter into an ungreased 10-inch tube pan.

Bake for 40 minutes, or until a wooden skewer inserted into the middle of the cake comes out clean. Invert the cake pan over the neck of a wine or soft drink bottle and let the cake cool completely. The inversion will prevent the cake from sinking as it cools.

To fill the cake, cut it into three layers using a serrated knife. Place one layer on a cake dish. Spritz the layer with some of the limoncello liqueur. Spread half of the lemon curd filling evenly over the cake layer. Place the second layer over the filling and spritz the second layer with the liqueur. Spread the remaining lemon curd evenly over the cake. Top with the last layer of cake.

Whip the remaining cream in a bowl with the sugar until stiff. Frost the cake with the whipped cream. Place the lemon wedges in a decorative pattern on top of the cake.

Refrigerate the cake for at least 2 hours before serving. To serve, use a serrated knife to cut the cake into wedges.

FROSTING

1½ cups whipping cream

2 tablespoons sugar

1 lemon, cut into wedges

Did you know that there is a difference between heavy cream and whipping cream? Whipping cream contains stabilizers that allow it to hold its whipped state. Use it as a frosting or garnish on desserts.

Campania

Pastry of the Nobles

Years before I ever set foot in Italy I read about *sfogliatelle,* those multilayered, clamshell-shaped pastries made from flaky puff-pastry dough and filled with creamy ricotta cheese, semolina, and flecks of candied orange peel. I was determined to have them when I made my first trip to Sorrento. Nothing else mattered. When I arrived, my first stop was a *pasticceria* (pastry shop) where I bought *sfogliatelle* still warm from the oven. It was so flaky that it shattered all over me when I bit into the thin-as-paper, crispy layers of dough. As I tasted the velvety filling oozing out the sides, I could not help but lick my fingers, barely resisting the temptation to have one more.

The word *sfoglia* means flaky, or thin layers. There are two types of sfogliatelle, *sfogliatelle ricce* and *sfogliatelle frolle.* What they have in common is the filling. What makes them different is the pastry dough. *Ricce* are made with flour and *strutto* or lard, while the *frolle* are made with flour and butter. The dough made with lard results in crisp baked layers, while the *pasta frolla* dough made with butter yields a softer type of pastry. There are also variations on the filling. At the Santa Rosa pastry shop on Via Bologna, Amarena cherry jam is piped along the opening of the sfogliatelle after they are baked.

Sfogliatelle are rarely made by home bakers because of the laborious process and the importance of using the finest lard, which used to be rendered by hand. Sfogliatelle are part of the grand tradition of Neapolitan pastries along with rice pie (*pastiera,* page 178) and *babà,* and in my opinion represent some of the best sweets in all of Italy. No historical source can pinpoint when sfogliatelle were invented, but most surmise that these time-consuming delicacies were the work of monastery kitchens. In fact, the monastery of Santa Rosa on the

Amalfi Coast takes credit for inventing sfogliatelle. Nevertheless, over time other monasteries and cloistered orders stole or copied the recipe, and began making and selling sfogliatelle to noble families as a way to raise much-needed revenues. Noble households could well afford the expensive ingredients of ricotta cheese, sugar, fine flour, and flavorings that went into creating these pastries and bought them not only as treats for themselves, but as a way to impress important guests. That is why they are often referred to as *sfogliatelle della nobilità* (pastry of the nobles).

What we do know for sure is that in 1818 an innkeeper by the name of Pasquale Pintauro turned his establishment, which is situated today on Naples's Via Toledo, into a well-known pastry shop. He began making and selling sfogliatelle, *zeppole,* and other traditional Neapolitan desserts. Not content to stop there, he also set up shop on the street with an oven and a counter so customers could see how the pastries were made. There he sold them *"caure caure"* (warm). They are still sold warm today from small carts on street corners, at nearby bars, and in pastry shops. In the morning as Neapolitans are hustling to work they stop for a cappuccino and sfogliatelle ricce or frolle to get them through the morning.

On pages 184 and 186 are recipes for both versions of sfogliatelle and the filling recipe is on page 187. Read the recipes thoroughly before beginning the process and give yourself plenty of time. Your efforts will be well rewarded.

Sfogliatelle Ricce
(Rich Flaky Pastry)

Makes 16

2 baking sheets lined with
  parchment paper

2 sheets prepared puff
  pastry, thawed and kept
  covered and refrigerated

4 tablespoons best-quality
  lard or unsalted butter,
  melted and cooled

My first book, Ciao Italia, *contains the recipes for* sfogliatelle ricce *(rich) and* sfogliatelle frolle *(tender). Since the best sfogliatelle ricce are made with high quality lard that is nearly impossible to find today, and because of the health risks associated with fat, I suggest using already prepared, high-quality puff pastry. There are several good brands on the market. As discussed in "Pastry of the Nobles" on page 182, most sfogliatelle is now commercially made, but if you want to make them, here are two versions of the dough, one with commercially prepared puff pastry and the other with* pasta frolla. *Be sure that the puff pastry remains as cold as possible. Chill it for several hours before rolling it out, which is best done on a cold marble board that has been refrigerated for several hours. The filling can be made ahead of time and refrigerated until needed. The recipes that follow will yield about 16 sfogliatelle, but I have also made them in miniature size, which are perfect for a dessert tray when serving a large crowd.*

Line two baking sheets with parchment paper and set aside. Roll each puff pastry sheet into a 16×22-inch rectangle on a cold marble board, if possible. Otherwise use a lightly floured work surface. Brush the sheet evenly with the lard or butter. This will create those flaky layers when the dough bakes. Starting at the shortest end nearest to you, roll the dough up tightly like a jelly roll. Cut the roll into 2-inch pieces. If you want to make miniature size pieces, cut the dough into 1-inch pieces.

Form the dough into shells. This is the tricky part. Think of a clam shell. Use your thumbs to push the dough away from the center to form a shell or V shape.

Fill each shell with about 2½ tablespoons of the filling (see page 187); for miniature shapes use about 1 tablespoon of the filling. Place the sfogliatelle on the parchment-lined baking sheets, spacing them 1 inch apart. Refrigerate them for 1 hour.

When ready to bake, preheat the oven to 425°F.

Bake the sfogliatelle on the middle rack, one sheet at a time, about 20 to 25 minutes, until they are evenly browned. Cool them slightly on the baking sheet, then remove them with a spatula to a cooling rack.

To serve, sprinkle the sfogliatelle while slightly warm with confectioners' sugar and a line of ground cinnamon running down the center.

Variation: Make the sfogliatelle and freeze them unbaked on the baking trays until they are hard. Wrap each sfogliatelle in plastic wrap and transfer them to a heavy-duty zipper-lock plastic bag. Freeze. Take out as many as needed and bake them frozen as directed above for about 20 minutes.

Sfogliatelle Frolle
(Tender Flaky Pastry)

Makes 16

1½ cups unbleached all-
   purpose flour

½ cup pastry flour

⅛ teaspoon salt

¾ cup (1½ sticks) cold
   unsalted butter, cut into
   bits

½ cup ice-cold water

½ cup good quality lard,
   melted and cooled
   (see instructions page 184)

In this adaptation for sfogliatelle frolle *(tender sfogliatelle), unbleached flour and pastry flour are used to create a dough that is softer in texture than the* sfogliatelle ricce *version on page 184. Be sure to measure the flour correctly, as described on page 178, otherwise the dough may be too tough. Cold is the secret word in making the dough. Cold butter, cold water. This technique will help keep the dough flaky so that the layers will separate as they bake.*

Combine the flours and salt in a bowl or whirl them together in a food processor. With a fork or pastry blender, work the butter into the flour until pieces are the size of rice grains. Add the water gradually until a moist, rough ball of dough is formed. You may not need all the water. Gather up the dough into a ball and wrap it in plastic wrap. Refrigerate the dough for at least 2 hours.

If using the food processor, add the butter to the flour mixture and pulse until the butter is the size of rice grains. Slowly add the water through the feed tube until a rough ball of dough starts to form. Do not overwork the dough or the gluten in the flour will toughen the dough. Gather up the dough and form it into a ball and wrap as above.

Divide the dough in half, and roll and form it as directed for sfogliatelle ricce on page 184. Continue process until the shells are ready for filling.

Ripieno per Sfogliatelle
(Flaky Pastry Filling)

This is the classic filling for sfogliatelle. *To achieve a creamy and thick filling, be sure that the ricotta cheese is well drained and that the ingredients are well beaten. For a variation that is very popular in Naples, add a little Amarena cherry jam (see mail order sources, page 347) at the opening of the sfogliatelle after they are cooled. A good quality store-bought cherry jam can also be used. Make the filling up to 2 days ahead of time and refrigerate it until you are ready to fill the sfogliatelle.*

1 cup whole milk

¼ cup semolina flour

1 cup whole-milk ricotta cheese, well drained

1 large egg, beaten

¼ cup sugar

½ teaspoon vanilla extract

1 tablespoon grated orange zest

¼ cup finely diced candied citron or candied fruits

Bring the milk to a boil in a saucepan over medium-high heat. Stir in the semolina flour. Continue stirring to keep the mixture smooth and cook for 3 to 4 minutes, or until the mixture is the thickness of cooked cream of wheat. Pour the mixture into a bowl. Beat the cheese in with a hand mixer until the mixture is well blended. Beat in the egg, sugar, and vanilla. Stir in the orange zest and the citron or candied fruits.

Fill the sfogliatelle dough as directed on page 184 or refrigerate the filling, covered, until ready to use.

Antipasti

Maccu (Raw Fava Bean Spread)

Panelle (Chickpea Fritters)

Antipasto di Pecorino ed'Olio di Oliva (Pecorino Cheese and Olive Oil Antipasto)

Sandwich Siciliano con Formaggio e Sarde (Sicilian Sardine and Cheese Sandwich)

Stimpiratu (Jellied Chicken Wings)

Primi Piatti

Baccalà in Bianco (Codfish Stew)

Pescespada con Spaghetti, Salsa di Pomodori ed'Olive (Swordfish with Spaghetti, Tomato Sauce, and Olives)

Pasta con Salsa di Zucchine con Ricotta (Pasta with Zucchini and Ricotta Cheese Sauce)

Contorni

Cuori di Carciofi e Patate al Forno (Oven-Baked Artichoke Heart and Potato Casserole)

Carciofi Ripieni con Quattro Formaggi (Artichokes Stuffed with Four Cheeses)

Insalate

Insalata di Zucchine, Peperoni Rossi e Ricotta Salata (Zucchini, Red
  Pepper, and Ricotta Salad)
Insalata Fredda di Baccalà e Cavolfiore (Cold Codfish and Cauliflower
  Salad)
Insalata di Carciofi (Artichoke Salad)
Insalata Ennese (Belgian Endive, Pomegranate, and Orange Salad)
Insalata di Fagiolini, Patate, Piselli e Cipolla (Green Beans, Potatoes,
  Peas, and Onion Salad)

Dolci

Semifreddo di Monte San Giuliano
Gelato di Mandarini (Mandarin Orange Ice Cream)
Biscottini al Vino (Little Wine Cookies)
Salsa di Melagrana (Pomegranate Sauce)
Latte Fritto (Fried Milk)

Sicily is heat, prickly pears, colorful painted fishing boats, fishing nets, gelato, hand-painted tiles, mountains, tuna, artichokes, fava beans, shepherds, almond trees, Greek temples, unbearable traffic, markets, fried food, swordfish, scirocco winds, mosaics, palm trees, oranges, cassata cake, cannoli, pageants, pupi di zucchero, puppets, wild fennel, ricotta cheese, Pecorino cheese, Marsala wine, salt pans, monasteries, hand-painted carts, miniature donkeys, grapes, Mount Etna, Holy Week mysteries, incense, vineyards, bougainvillea, sea chants, the malocchio.

———————

*W*hen I announced to the crew that we were going to film in Sicily, they were very excited by the idea. I wanted to expose our television audience to the real Sicily—a breathtaking chunk of land bathed in Mediterranean sunlight, with spectacular rugged mountains, hillsides, a patchwork quilt of colors, and serene and sloping valleys, all surrounded by a sea that has nourished and ravished it for centuries. And I wanted our audience to meet the real Sicilian people, hardworking and proud of their heritage. I wanted to dispel the tarnished image of Sicily as a place overrun by mafia barons, an image that has been unfairly and all too commonly foisted on the public by Hollywood.

On an unusually cold April day the television crew and I arrived at Punta Raisi airport in Palermo, packed our gear into a van, and began our journey of discovery. Our center of operations was the province of Caltanisetta, the very heart of Sicily, and our home would be a farmhouse in the wine production area of Regaleali near the small town of Vallelunga. For me the visit was twofold, since my paternal grandparents both came from this province, and it was a chance for me to reconnect with my roots.

As we lost our way over patched roads, we admired brilliant green foliage and fields of dense yellow flowers that seemed to form a tightly woven carpet. One of the main spring crops, fava beans, was ripe for the picking, and sheep and shepherds were everywhere, reminding me that Sicily is still very much an agrarian society. The Madonie Mountains looked spectacular with snow-covered peaks, which at night cast giant shadows against a pink and purple sky. It is said that Saint Rosalia, the patron saint of Palermo, is buried in a grotto at the top of Mount Pellegrino; her bones were discovered by a farmer in the twelfth century. Saint Rosalia is revered in Palermo because she delivered the city from a devastating plague, and the Palermitani have never forgotten this miracle. Every July 13, a special festival called the Festino is dedicated to her for her miraculous intercession.

One of our first filming locations was the city of Agrigento, site of some of the best-preserved Greek temples in the world. If you want to understand the history of Sicily you must go to Agrigento because the Greeks contributed so much to Sicilian culture. They taught the Sicilians how to make wine, grow olives, and use spelt, an ancient grain for baking bread, pasta, and even pastry dough. But the Greeks would not be the only foreign influence that Sicily would host against its will. The Arabs arrived in the ninth century and landed at Marsala on the western coast. They brought, among other things, sugarcane, rice, cinnamon, and saffron. They introduced the process of making ice cream, chickpeas, pastries, fruit-flavored ices, and nougat made from honey and sesame seeds. These foods gave Sicily an affection for sweets. To this day it is said that Sicilians have a sweet tooth, and a visit to any *pasticerria* (pastry shop) or *gelateria* (ice cream shop) will confirm this observation.

With the Norman invasion led by Roger II in 1063, Arab influence waned. One of the masterpieces of Roger's reign was the construction in the twelfth century of the cathedral at Cefalu on Sicily's north coast. In the cathedral, an exquisite Byzantine mosaic of Cristo Pantocratore illustrates the melding of cultures. Christ gives his benediction with his right hand; in his left hand he holds a book open to pages written in Greek and Latin.

The struggle for control of Sicily continued with the French and then the Spaniards. The Spaniards brought new ingredients to Sicily, including *pan di spagna* (Spanish bread), which is a sponge cake used to make the traditional and elaborate *cassata* cake that is filled with sweetened ricotta cheese. The Spaniards also brought pumpkin, tomatoes, cocoa, corn, potatoes, beans, and turkey. The French brought elaborate cooking preparations and introduced the *monzù,* French-trained chefs, to Sicily.

As I traveled around the interior of Sicily, I began to have a better understanding of how and why some of the classic dishes of the island came to be. Pecorino cheese and ricotta cheese must be made every day when the sheep are brought in for milking; no wonder the Sicilians love to eat fresh clumps of ricotta cheese with spaghetti and tomato sauce, or have it for dessert with orange marmalade spooned over the top. Fields and fields of fava beans are used as fodder but are also turned into soup and made into a thick paste for coarse bread; pine nuts are ground for pesto, combined with vegetables, used in stuffings and desserts. Oranges are so plentiful that they are left to rot on the ground. Not long ago, the government actually bulldozed acres and acres of orange trees because the fruit was not marketable. I remember my father telling me that when my grandparents came in steerage to Ellis Island, they carried bread, olives, cheese, and a bagful of oranges, and this is what they lived on during the ocean crossing. The orange became a symbol of hardship for my grandparents, as it was for many Sicilians.

Sicilian food is lively with vivid colors. It is inventive too, like the combination of sweet and sour ingredients—sugar and vinegar mixed with herbs and garlic—to create something the Sicilians call *agrodolce.* This is one of the defining flavors of Sicilian cooking, and it infiltrates everything from marinated fish dishes to salads and vegetables such as eggplant and lots of main-course dishes as well.

To visit Sicily is to experience it on many different levels, with many different realities, namely those that are historical, superstitious, religious, and practical. There is much that is mysterious about this largest island in the Mediterranean, and many rituals that we cannot understand because they have been intertwined for so long, the result of so many cultures coming together. We can only appreciate Sicily from afar.

Estratto
(Tomato Extract)

2 twelve-ounce jars

Over the years many viewers have written to me about their Italian heritage; some have even asked me to help them find their relatives in Italy, and many have inquired about old recipes now lost. One in particular is the request for real tomato paste, extract, or concentrate. In Italian this is called estratto, estrattu, or in dialect, 'strattu and is one the most labor-intensive products turned out by the Sicilians in the summer months. Estratto is a very concentrated, thick, dark red tomato pulp that is used to thicken tomato sauces and is added to stews and soups. It is also called conserva. *To make it not only requires the most wonderful meaty plum tomatoes, but also the intense summer heat and the patience of Job, since the pulp must be stirred for hours by hand to evaporate liquid.*

The tomatoes are picked at the height of ripeness, then cut into quarters and put into plastic baskets, where they are squeezed to release their juices. The tomatoes are cooked only with salt until they are soft. They are then pureed, resulting in a thick pulp that is spread on wooden boards and set out in the sun. The pulp is stirred by hand until the water begins to evaporate. At night the boards are brought in and taken back outside the next day, and the process is repeated. In about two days' time, the pulp becomes very thick and eventually turns into a solid mass. Each day the estratto *is kneaded with oiled hands. Finally the concentrated pulp is put into jars and covered with a layer of olive oil. Sicilian cooks scoop spoonfuls of* estratto *into soups, stews, and sauces; just a little is needed because the flavor is so concentrated.*

I have not seen estratto *anywhere in Italian markets in the United States. A good imported tomato paste is the closest thing you will find, and I recommend buying the ones in tube form. Or try making this version of a*

14 unblemished plum tomatoes, washed and dried

3 cups red wine vinegar

8 fresh basil leaves

2 tablespoons capers in brine, drained

2 tablespoons whole black peppercorns

2 teaspoons fine sea salt

2 tablespoons grated Parmigiano-Reggiano cheese

2 to 2½ cups extra-virgin olive oil

2 sterilized 12-ounce jars

Sicily

195

concentrated tomato pulp that can be used as a sauce for pasta, on pizza, and stirred into soups and stews. Using a dehydrator will give you the best results.

Need a quick sauce for a chunky-style pasta such as rigatoni or zitti? Simply puree 6 ounces (half a jar) of these tomatoes in a food processor until a paste-like consistency is obtained. Toss with 12 ounces of cooked hot pasta.

Core and cut the tomatoes in half, lengthwise. Place them cut side down in a dehydrator and dry according to the manufacturer's instructions; or place the tomatoes cut side down on wire racks set on baking sheets and dry them in a 225°F oven until they are the consistency of dried apricots. Do not dry them until they are brittle; they should be bendable. This oven process may take longer than a dehydrator depending on the size of the tomatoes, but plan on at least a day to do this in the oven.

Bring the wine vinegar to a boil in a large noncorrosive pot. Add the tomatoes and blanch them for 1 minute. Remove the tomatoes with a slotted spoon and drain them.

Begin layering the tomatoes in the sterilized jars, adding half the basil, capers, peppercorns, salt, and cheese to each jar. Slowly pour the oil into the jars, pressing down on the tomatoes slightly as you pour. Make sure the tomatoes are completely submerged under the oil or they will be exposed to air and potential bacteria. Cap the jars and place them in a cool spot overnight.

The next day check the level of the oil and if any tomatoes are sticking out of it, add more oil to cover them. Check the jars two or three more times to see if the tomatoes have absorbed the oil. Add more oil as needed.

Store the jars in a cool place for 6 weeks before using. This will "cure" them. Refrigerate the jars; when ready to use bring the jars to room temperature.

Maccu
(Raw Fava Bean Spread)

Serves 4 to 6

In Sicilian dialect the word is maccu. *In Ligurian dialect the word is* marro, *but no matter what the dialect word is, this spreadable paste made from fresh fava beans is delicious. It is best to use young fava beans since they will be much creamier than older and bigger beans. If larger beans are the only kind available, they will need to be cooked first in boiling water before proceeding with the recipe. Boil until the outer skin of the bean easily slips off, and the beans are soft enough to be mashed between the fingers. Fava beans are also available frozen. See the mail order sources on page 347.*

3 pounds fresh fava beans, shelled (about 3 cups)

2 cloves garlic, peeled

¼ to ½ cup extra-virgin olive oil

¼ cup grated Pecorino cheese

Grinding of black pepper

12 small slices bread, toasted

In a food processor, grind the fava beans to a pulp with the garlic cloves. Slowly pour enough olive oil through the feed tube with the motor running until a smooth but not too runny paste forms. The fava beans should have the consistency of mashed potatoes.

Transfer the mixture to a bowl and stir in the cheese. Spread a small amount on top of the toasted bread slices and drizzle each one with a little extra-virgin olive oil and pepper to taste. Serve the toasts immediately. Extra paste can be stored in a jar in the refrigerator for up to 5 days.

Did you know that fava beans love to grow in cool weather and will germinate in soil as cold as 40 degrees? See the mail order list on page 347 for seed sources.

Panelle
(Chickpea Fritters)

Makes 32 fritters

2½ cups (8 ounces) chickpea flour

1 teaspoon baking powder

1 teaspoon fine sea salt

1 teaspoon coarsely ground black pepper

3 cups water

3 tablespoons finely minced fresh parsley or oregano (optional)

4 to 6 cups vegetable oil

Did you know that chickpeas are one of the world's oldest foods and considered a "poor food" by historians, who have dated their use to prehistoric times? Chickpeas are packed with protein and can be served in a variety of ways, from soups to marinated salads.

Walking through the streets of the kinetic city of Palermo is an experience for all the senses. Your eyes are drawn at once to a melting pot of architectural styles from Byzantine to Baroque. Beautiful ornate fountains are everywhere, and the hordes of people and dizzying traffic make for fever-pitch activity. Your nose tells you that something good is cooking just around the corner—delicious street food sold from little carts. Buy a panino (sandwich) stuffed with lamb intestines, or iris (bread filled with sheep's-milk ricotta cheese and chocolate), or my favorite, panelle, which are golden, fried fritters made from ground chickpea flour, water, and herbs. On December 13, Sicilians celebrate the feast of St. Lucy, patron of eyesight, by eating panelle. You will never be able to eat just one. Panelle are easy to make and a great antipasto idea for a party. See the mail order sources (page 347) for chickpea flour if you cannot find it in your area.

In a heavy-duty saucepan or copper pot mix the flour, baking powder, salt, and pepper together off the heat. Slowly stir in the water and blend in with a heavy-duty whisk, being careful to avoid lumps from forming. Stir in the parsley or oregano, if using.

Cook the mixture over medium heat, whisking constantly until it thickens and begins to move away from the sides of the pan. Remove the pan from the heat.

Using a rubber spatula, divide and spread the mixture thinly among four 9-inch plates, making sure to cover the plate completely to the rim. Set the plates aside to cool for 2 to 3 minutes. Run a butter knife around the outside of each plate. Carefully pull the panelle away from the dish. Stack the panelle on top of each other and cut them in half lengthwise, then into quarters. Cut each quarter in half. There should be 32 panelle.

In a deep fryer heat the vegetable oil to 375°F. Fry the panelle until they are nicely browned. Drain them on brown paper and serve immediately.

Variation: Another way to form the panelle *is to spread the cooked mixture out onto an oiled cookie sheet or cutting board. Let the mixture cool and then cut into rectangles. Or fill an empty tin can with the bottom removed with the mixture and let it cool. Push the mixture out with your hand. Cut the dough into rounds and fry. These are best eaten hot.*

Note: To make ahead, form and cut the panelle *and freeze them, uncooked, in single layers on a cookie sheet. When they are frozen, remove the* panelle *to plastic bags and seal well. Defrost as needed and fry.*

The Vucciria

It takes a visit to Palermo's lively food markets to begin to understand the intricate nature of Sicilian cooking. There are four major markets: Ballarò, near the train station; Capo, near the Teatro Massimo; Borgo Vecchio, in Corso Scina near the waterfront, and my favorite, the showy Vucciria, near the Quattro Canti. Unchanged for centuries, these markets coexist with the hustle of modern-day Palermo whizzing by in all directions. They are visual culinary encyclopedias of Sicily's foods, past and present.

The Vucciria is the most ebullient of the markets, where everything for sale is openly displayed in wooden barrels and crates, a custom that has been in place since the ancient Arabs ruled Sicily in the ninth century. Teetering towers of fruits, vegetables, and olives are dazzling in the bright Sicilian sun. Tomatoes saturated with color and taste, sweet and hot peppers so shiny they slip from your hands, uncommon-looking squash, crates of wild, feathery fennel, and numerous other varieties of produce bring squeals of admiration.

In the fish quarter, huge cauldrons of boiling oil are ready to cook up *fritto misto,* a mixture of fresh fish and seafood, including octopus, squid, shrimp, and clams. Swordfish, which run in the Straits of Messina, are a hallmark of Sicilian cooking. They are displayed atop thrones of ice, sword pointing triumphantly skyward. At the stalls selling fresh tuna, the fishmonger delights in telling everyone about the hefty price the fish will bring on the Japanese market. If you like sea urchins, the roe of this spiny delicacy is popular as a sauce over spaghetti. Fresh, silver-colored sardines, a staple in the Sicilian kitchen, are abundant. The classic way to prepare them in Palermo is with thick spaghetti called *bucatini,* plus pine nuts, raisins, wild fennel, and saffron. This seemingly unlikely combination encapsulates on a plate the foreign influences of the Arabs and Spaniards on Sicilian cooking.

Just meandering between the tight-fitting stalls is enough to induce hunger pains, and when that happens I head straight for the *friggitoria* (fry shop), where typical "street foods" are sold—*arancine* (rice balls), *croquette di patate* (potato croquettes), and *iris* (fried puffs of yeast dough filled with sheep's-milk ricotta cheese, sugar, and chocolate). Another favorite street food is *panelle* (chickpea fritters that can only be described as high-class potato chips, except that they are made from chickpea flour, an Arab contribution to Sicilian food)—see the recipe on page 198. Originally, street food was considered food for the poor and included the innards of fish and meat. And because at one time the citizens of Palermo were forbidden to have ovens for baking and cooking due to a scarcity of wood and coal, it became a tradition to buy foods that were already prepared.

Antipasto di Pecorino ed'Olio di Oliva
(Pecorino Cheese and Olive Oil Antipasto)

Serves 4

½ pound aged Pecorino cheese, cut into ½-inch cubes

¼ cup extra-virgin olive oil

Grinding of coarse black pepper

1 tablespoon dried oregano

¼ cup pitted and diced black oil-cured olives

If you have aged Pecorino cheese in the refrigerator, this antipasto can be made in no time. Pecorino is made exclusively from sheep's milk; it is salted and aged. Some varieties are studded with green or black peppercorns. You may be familiar with Pecorino Romano, which simply means sheep's-milk cheese from the region of Lazio, which includes Rome, but Pecorino is also a specialty cheese of other regions of Italy, including Tuscany, Sicily, and Sardinia. In this antipasto, the cheese is cubed and marinated in extra-virgin olive oil with oregano. No additional salt is used in the recipe because the cheese is salty enough. A variation is to add oil-cured black olives. Serve it with slices of crusty bread.

Did you know that hard cheese will grate much more easily if allowed to come to room temperature first?

In a bowl combine the cheese, olive oil, pepper, and oregano and toss with a spoon to coat the cheese well. Stir in the olives. Cover the bowl and allow the cheese to marinate for at least 2 hours at room temperature before serving as part of an antipasto with good crusty bread.

Variation: Diced red sweet peppers and thin slivers of fennel also make a nice combination.

Sandwich Siciliano con Formaggio e Sarde
(Sicilian Sardine and Cheese Sandwich)

Serves 4

"Please e-mail me a quick idea for a Sicilian-type sandwich." I get this kind of request all the time. Here is a very authentic Sicilian sandwich that was made for me at Al Forno panificio in Vallelunga. Use a good thin baguette with a sesame seed crust, if possible. This is one of those instances where fish and cheese together do complement each other.

1 (12- or 14-inch-long) sesame seed baguette, cut in half lengthwise

⅓ cup extra-virgin olive oil

⅓ cup grated Pecorino cheese

¼ to ½ teaspoon coarsely ground black pepper

6 or 7 salted sardines, cut into small pieces

Drizzle the olive oil evenly over one half of the bread. Set aside.

In a small bowl combine the cheese and the pepper. Sprinkle the mixture evenly over the olive oil. Top the cheese mixture with the sardines.

Place the second half of the baguette on top of the sardines. Use a sharp knife and cut the baguette into 4 equal pieces.

Sicily

Sampling Sicily's Bounty

One year I escorted a group of viewers to Sicily to give them an overview of Sicilian food. As with most of my trips to Palermo and western Sicily, we began at the Vucciria, after which we worked our way out of the city into the countryside, stopping at small artisanal farms where the *formaggiaio* (cheese monger) made sheep's-milk (Pecorino) and ricotta cheese twice a day. Cheese making and wine production are two of the principal food industries in Sicily; most of the cheese made is for local consumption, while most of the wine is for export.

The process of making cheese, both fresh and aged, begins with heating milk and adding rennet so that the milk will coagulate into curds. Watching this process was complicated for the group of viewers to grasp, but for the cheese monger it was a mechanical, second-nature operation known from childhood. He moved through each step of the process with lightning speed, and in no time he was offering our group fresh, warm ricotta cheese made from the whey. It is at places like the farm and the cheese house where one begins to see the rhythm of life in agricultural Sicily and to comprehend what Sicilian food is all about.

Bread, wine, and almond paste (*pasta reale*) are artisanal in nature too. For centuries, durum flour, hard wheat, has been coveted for making bread and pasta. The ancient Romans recognized the agricultural wealth of Sicily and utilized its resources to sustain and maintain the Roman army. Even the stems of wheat were utilized in the kitchen, where *maccaruna di casa* (homemade macaroni) was wound around the stems and left to dry.

Almonds have been cultivated in Sicily since the Greeks arrived;

there are over eighteen varieties of almond trees, which must be planted close together if they are to bear fruit. Today almond trees blanket Sicily; their pink and white blossoms brighten the landscape in February, and out of the abundant harvest came the art of marzipan, cleverly fashioning a paste of finely ground almonds, sugar, and egg whites into realistic-looking fruits, vegetables, and whimsical creatures.

Most people think of Marsala wine when asked to describe Sicilian wines. But there are others, including the white Nozze d'Oro from Regaleali and decent table wine from Palermo and Trapani known as Corvo, both white and red.

Our group was able to tour the Marsala wineries on the west coast. It came as a great surprise for them to learn that it was an Englishman, John Woodhouse, who developed the method for making fortified wine from alcohol, cooked must, and sweet wine. Marsala can be dry or sweet, and it is indispensable in my kitchen for making veal Marsala and *zabaglione,* an eggy-rich custard that is best eaten warm.

Stimpiratu
(Jellied Chicken Wings)

Serves 10 to 12

1 pound large green olives in brine, rinsed

½ cup capers in brine, rinsed

4 pounds chicken wings

½ cup olive oil

1½ cups red wine vinegar

Small pieces coarse bread, cut into ½-inch-thick slices

The recipe for this unusual Sicilian antipasto of cold chicken wings with capers and olives was sent to me by Beth Yeaton, a Ciao Italia *viewer. It comes from her Sicilian Nonna D'Orto, who learned it from her mother-in-law. The dish is served with homemade crusty bread to soak up the jellied juices of the chicken.*

Crack the olives and remove and discard the pits. Place the olives in a pot with the capers. Cover with water and boil the ingredients for 3 or 4 minutes. Drain well and set aside.

Cut off the tip section of the chicken wings and discard them or save them for stock. Cut the remaining wing pieces at the joint to separate the sections. Rinse and drain the pieces well.

In a sauté pan, heat the wings for a few minutes, to dry them. Add the olive oil to the pan and stir to combine the oil with the wings. Cover the pan and continue cooking over medium heat for 30 minutes. Stir in the olives and capers and cook for an additional 10 minutes. Stir in the vinegar and cook, uncovered, for 10 to 15 minutes. Transfer the ingredients to a bowl. Cover and chill for several hours or overnight.

Serve the wings cold with slices of coarse bread.

Baccalà in Bianco
(Codfish Stew)

Serves 4 to 6

Gloucester, Massachusetts, is a fishing community and home to nearly 32,000 Sicilians who settled there to make their living from the sea much as they had done in their native Sicily. The life of a fisherman is physically exhausting and very dangerous, as evidenced by the community's monuments dedicated to fishermen. For an introductory segment on fresh codfish for one of my programs, I traveled to Gloucester to cook with Angela Orlando Sanfilippo, president and CEO of the Fishermen's Wives Association. Angela was born in Porticello, Sicily, and is an expert on all kinds of fish and seafood cookery. She is a national spokesperson and activist for reform and fairness in the fishing industry. One of her most requested recipes is baccalà in bianco *(fresh codfish stew). She begins with a* soffritto, *a sauté of onions and potatoes that becomes the base for a stew in which water is the only liquid. Pine nuts and raisins, two typical ingredients of many Sicilian dishes, are added when the stew is served. When I sampled the dish, I knew it would become a favorite. The broth was light, the fish meaty and delicate, and the seasonings perfect. The dish can also be made with dried and rehydrated codfish, but the taste will be very different.*

½ cup olive oil

1 large white onion, thinly sliced

½ cup minced Italian parsley leaves

4 large potatoes, peeled and cut into chunks

3 cups hot water

3 pounds fresh cod fillets, cut into chunks with skin attached

¼ cup pine nuts

¼ cup raisins

Fine salt to taste

Grinding of coarse black pepper

In a soup pot heat the olive oil, stir in the onions, and cook over medium heat until they are wilted down but not browned. Stir in the parsley and potatoes and cook, stirring occasionally, until the onions are golden brown. Add the water and stir the ingredients. Place the codfish chunks on top of the mixture and sprinkle on the pine nuts and raisins. Cover the pot and allow to cook for 15 minutes. Uncover the pot, stir the ingredients carefully, and season to taste with salt and pepper.

Ladle the fish into soup bowls and serve immediately.

Pescespada con Spaghetti, Salsa di Pomodori ed' Olive

(Swordfish with Spaghetti, Tomato Sauce, and Olives)

Serves 4 to 6

1 tablespoon olive oil

1 pound swordfish, in one piece

1 pound spaghetti

1½ tablespoons salt

2 cups prepared tomato sauce, preferably homemade

¼ cup reserved cooking water

16 black oil-cured olives, pitted and coarsely chopped

This recipe for swordfish with spaghetti and tomato sauce is one that I enjoyed in Mondello, a Sicilian seaside community near Palermo. It is easy to put together if you have homemade tomato sauce on hand. Whenever I serve it to company, the response is "I never thought to cook swordfish with tomato sauce and spaghetti." Be sure to use fresh swordfish and do not overcook it.

Heat the olive oil until it begins to smoke, then lower the heat to medium and cook the swordfish, turning it once. It is cooked when a fork is easily inserted into the fish.

Transfer the fish to a cutting board and allow it to cool for 10 minutes. With a knife remove the skin and discard it. Cut the fish into ½-inch cubes. Set aside.

Cook the spaghetti in 4 to 6 quarts of rapidly boiling water with 1 tablespoon of the salt. The spaghetti is done when there is no white flour remaining in the center of a strand. It should be firm—al dente—but cooked throughout.

While the spaghetti is cooking, heat the tomato sauce in a saucepan and keep it warm.

Drain the spaghetti, reserving ¼ cup of the cooking water. Return the spaghetti to the cooking pot with the reserved water and the tomato sauce. Mix quickly over low heat. Add the swordfish pieces and stir gently for 1 minute. Stir in the olives and the remaining salt.

Transfer the mixture to a serving platter and serve at once. A few whole olives and a sprig of fresh basil make a nice garnish.

Did you know that 1 pound of pasta requires 4 to 6 quarts of boiling water, to which 1 tablespoon of salt has been added, to cook properly?

Sicily

Sicilian Scenes

$\mathcal{I}$t is always a pleasure and a treat to be on location shooting remote footage for *Ciao Italia*. These short vignettes introduce the themes of each show and give me a chance to meet fascinating people who are knowledgeable about Italy and Italian food—people from whom we can all learn something new. Some of the most amazing and hospitable people the crew and I have met in our ten years of travel were not professional chefs, food writers, or food store owners; they were the residents of the province of Caltanissetta in central Sicily.

I will never forget our visit to the weekly market in the little town of Vallelunga. Sheep and shepherds dominate the landscape for miles in this secluded space, which has not been affected by even a ripple of the technological age. Driving through the town to scout out the best shoot locations, I saw many one-room homes with dirt floors, hidden only from the outside world by flimsy curtains covering the doorways. Goats and other animals shared the sparse living quarters, and the *mula,* or she-donkey, was still the primary mode of transportation over the rough terrain.

Market day is a big deal for the citizens of Vallelunga, a bringing-together of residents from miles around, and traveling vendors from all over Sicily. The vendors set up near the main street of the town and offer everything from pots and pans to the freshest locally made cheeses. The street is transformed into one large grocery-store aisle.

Our camera was set up to follow me through the market, and as we discussed the movement and angle of the shot, a pool of women of assorted ages began to congregate near me, asking questions as to what we were doing. I had to listen closely to their dialect, which was not easy for me to understand. I responded in my elementary Italian that no, we were not from California here to shoot a movie about their town. When I told them we were here to capture the flavor of Sicilian life, the lines on their worn faces relaxed and an element of trust shone through. It was an honor for them, they said, to think that we were interested in what they were all about. These proud and hardworking people led me to each vendor's stall; the egg man showed me the freshest eggs, the candy man offered me the sweetest candy, the fishmonger explained why he had the tastiest fish, and so on.

One of the more poignant moments occurred when I told them that my grandparents came from the nearby town of Santa Caterina Villarmosa. *"Un miracolo,"* they said, and at the mention of the town's name, one woman grabbed my face between her hands and kissed me on both cheeks. That gesture meant everything; it said that I was connected to them and this place. That depth of feeling was captured on video for all the world to see and gave our viewing audience a unique look at real Sicilian life. For me there was no greater thrill.

Pasta con Salsa di Zucchine con Ricotta
(Pasta with Zucchini and Ricotta Cheese Sauce)

Serves 4 to 6

The first time I had zucchine con ricotta I was staying on a farm in Sicily where the cheese is made each day. Ricotta cheese is made from re-cooking the leftover whey, and it is a pretty wonderful by-product. Few things can compare to the taste of just made sheep's-milk ricotta, warm and moist, creamy white and dripping in its own whey. Since Sicilians produce so much ricotta, imaginative cooks there have come up with lots of ways to serve it. I use it in this recipe as a sauce for pasta; teamed with small, tender disks of sliced zucchini, it is a delicate dish. I have embellished it somewhat by adding Gorgonzola dolce cheese (see page 149) and a little heavy cream for a truly regal repast.

1½ cups ricotta cheese, well drained

¼ pound Gorgonzola dolce cheese, cut into pieces

¼ cup heavy cream or half-and-half

¼ teaspoon freshly grated nutmeg

2 tablespoons extra-virgin olive oil

1 medium onion, peeled and diced

2 small zucchini, washed and sliced into ¼-inch-thick rounds

½ teaspoon fine sea salt

¼ teaspoon fresh ground black pepper

1 pound penne or rigatoni

1 tablespoon salt

¼ cup reserved pasta cooking water

In a bowl mix together the ricotta and Gorgonzola cheeses, heavy cream or half-and-half, and nutmeg and set aside.

In a large, deep 14-inch sauté pan heat the olive oil, add the onion and sauté it, stirring occasionally, until the onion has wilted. Stir in the zucchini and continue cooking it until it softens and begins to brown. Stir in the salt and pepper. Continue cooking for about 5 minutes, or until the zucchini is nicely browned on both sides. Stir the cheese mixture gently into the zucchini, cover the pan, and keep the sauce warm over low heat while the pasta cooks.

Cook the pasta in 4 to 6 quarts of rapidly boiling water, adding 1 tablespoon of salt to the water just before adding the pasta. Cook the pasta until it is al dente, still firm but cooked throughout. To test for doneness, break a strand of pasta—if the center is still white, this is an indication of raw flour; continue to cook the pasta until no trace of white flour remains.

Sicily

211

Drain the pasta, reserving ¼ cup of the cooking water.

Add the pasta to the sauté pan with the zucchini and cheese mixture; stir in the reserved cooking water and combine the ingredients over medium-low heat until hot. Transfer the pasta and zucchini to a platter and serve immediately.

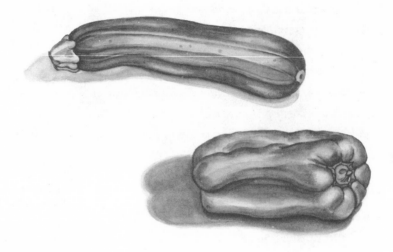

Cuori di Carciofi e Patate al Forno
(Oven-Baked Artichoke Heart and Potato Casserole)

Serves 6

Vegetables are such an important part of the Italian diet that I devote two episodes each season to what is growing in the vegetable garden. The year that we filmed in Sicily the crew and I visited local markets as well as home gardens. And it was clear that vegetables make up a big part of the Sicilian diet. Eggplant and artichokes are particular favorites. I have a particular fondness for artichoke hearts baked with layers of potatoes; the dish is similar to scalloped potatoes. Instead of struggling to remove the chokes from the artichokes before cooking them, cook them intact; the choke will then effortlessly come out with a spoon.

4 artichokes, medium-sized (2 pounds)

4 cups chicken broth or water

1 bay leaf

2 baking potatoes (1½ pounds), peeled and cut into ⅛-inch slices

1 teaspoon fine sea salt

¼ teaspoon white pepper

2½ cups whole milk, light cream, or heavy cream

6 tablespoons grated Pecorino cheese

Cut the stem ends of the artichokes, and remove the lower outer two layers of artichoke leaves and discard them. Cut ½ inch off the artichoke tops and discard them.

Place the artichokes upright in a pan just large enough to hold them snugly. Pour in enough of the chicken broth or water to cover them. Add the bay leaf. Bring the artichokes to a boil, then lower the heat and cook them, covered, until you can easily pull away an artichoke leaf. Drain the artichokes and allow them to cool. Discard the bay leaf.

Remove the remaining large outer leaves. (Save them to nibble on as a snack.) With a spoon carefully remove the hairy chokes and discard them. You are now left with the artichoke hearts. Cut the hearts into ¼-inch slices and set them aside.

Toss the potatoes in a bowl with the salt and pepper.

Preheat the oven to 350°F. Lightly butter a 14×2½-inch-deep casserole or au gratin baking dish. Make a layer of potatoes in the dish, overlapping the potatoes slightly. Place half of the artichoke slices over the potatoes, then make another layer of potatoes and artichoke hearts, ending with a final layer of potatoes.

Slowly pour the milk or cream over the potatoes. Cover the dish with a sheet of aluminum foil and bake for 45 minutes. Uncover the dish, sprinkle on the cheese, and bake for an additional 15 minutes, or until the cheese has browned slightly. Serve immediately.

Carciofi Ripieni con Quattro Formaggi
(Artichokes Stuffed with Four Cheeses)

Serves 4

*C*ynara scolymus *is the botanical name for artichokes. According to Greek mythology, Zeus, ruler of all the gods, the heavens, and earth had an insatiable burning love for Cynara, a beautiful young maiden who refused his affection, and because of this rejection, Zeus turned her into an artichoke! This is where the notion that artichokes are an aphrodisiac comes from. Artichokes* (carciofi) *are one of the first signs of spring in Italian markets. They can range in color from dark green to purple-green. There are over eighty varieties grown in the world, and Italy is the largest producer, yielding two thirds of the world crop. In the United States only the globe artichoke is available. Unfortunately, many people are reluctant to cook artichokes, thinking that the preparation is too involved, too messy, too thorny, and too time-consuming. But the little extra time that it takes is worth the effort. In this recipe the artichokes are boiled whole, then the leaves are spread apart and stuffed with a mixture of four cheeses and baked with fresh tomato sauce.*

4 globe artichokes, weighing 8 ounces each

Juice of 2 large lemons

1½ teaspoons salt

2 cups ricotta cheese

½ cup grated Asiago cheese

¼ cup grated Parmigiano-Reggiano cheese

¼ cup grated Pecorino cheese

Grinding of black pepper

1 tablespoon minced fresh parsley leaves

¼ teaspoon oregano

Olive oil for greasing baking pan

1 cup prepared tomato sauce, preferably homemade

Wash and dry the artichokes. With a knife cut off and discard about ¼ inch of the top of the artichoke and trim the stem end even with the base of the artichoke so that it stands flat. With your hands pull away the tough outer leaves of the artichoke, usually the first two layers. With a scissors trim the thorn ends off the remaining artichoke leaves and discard them.

Roll the artichokes under the palm of your hand on a work surface to loosen the leaves. Spread the center leaves of the artichoke out with your hands and use a melon baller to scoop out the hairy center choke and the lighter yellow leaves. Discard the choke and yellow leaves.

Place the artichokes in a saucepan large enough to hold them snugly side by side. Cover the artichokes with fresh cold water. Add the lemon juice and 1 teaspoon of the salt. Bring the water to a boil and cook the artichokes for about 8 minutes, uncovered. Remove the artichokes with a slotted spoon and allow them to cool.

Preheat the oven to 350°F.

In a bowl mix the cheeses, the remaining salt, pepper, parsley, and oregano. Gently spoon a little of the cheese mixture between the layers of leaves of the artichokes. Fill the center cavity with some of the cheese. Do not pack too much of the cheese mixture in the artichokes or they will expand and collapse in the oven.

Place the artichokes in a lightly greased casserole dish. Pour the tomato sauce over the artichokes. Cover the dish with aluminum foil and bake for 20 to 30 minutes, or until hot. Serve immediately.

Did you know that using an aluminum pot to boil artichokes will turn them gray in appearance? Be sure to use a stainless-steel or a copper pot to avoid this.

Insalata di Zucchine, Peperoni Rossi e Ricotta Salata

(Zucchini, Red Pepper, and Ricotta Salad)

Serves 4

Fresh sheep's-milk ricotta cheese is also made into ricotta salata *(salted ricotta) by salting and aging fresh ricotta cheese. As it ages it becomes firm and gratable. Sicilians like to use it over* bucatini, *a thick spaghetti-like pasta hollowed out like a long tube, and it is just right sprinkled over this marinated zucchini, red pepper, and mint salad. Make the salad a day ahead to allow the flavors to mingle. Look for ricotta salata in Italian grocery stores or in your supermarket dairy section. See the mail order section (page 347) for other sources. A good substitute is feta cheese, which will need to be crumbled instead of grated.*

⅓ cup extra-virgin olive oil

3 tablespoons red wine vinegar

2 tablespoons minced fresh mint

¼ teaspoon fine sea salt

¼ pound ricotta salata, grated

3 small zucchini, cut into thin strips

1 large sweet red pepper, cored, seeded, and cut into thin strips

Grinding of coarse black pepper

Combine the olive oil, vinegar, mint, and salt in a jar and shake well. Set aside.

In a salad bowl combine the ricotta salata, zucchini, and red pepper. Pour the dressing over the top and toss well. Top with a grinding of black pepper. To serve the salad later, cover with a piece of plastic wrap and allow it to marinate for several hours at room temperature. If making the salad a day ahead, refrigerate it and bring it to room temperature the following day.

Did you know that the ancient Romans chewed on fresh mint leaves after meals to refresh and clean their mouths?

Sicily

Insalata Fredda di Baccalà e Cavolfiore
(Cold Codfish and Cauliflower Salad)

Serves 6

2 pounds dried salted cod

1 head cauliflower, trimmed and cut into small florets

2 cups water for cooking the cod

5 tablespoons extra-virgin olive oil

Juice of 1 large lemon

2 tablespoons cider vinegar

½ teaspoon fine sea salt

¼ teaspoon coarsely ground black pepper

¼ cup Sicilian green olives in brine, pitted and coarsely chopped

⅓ cup minced fresh Italian parsley leaves

*My husband's mother, Antoinette Esposito, was fond of this cold codfish (*baccalà*) salad with cauliflower, which she served during Lent and occasionally on Friday nights. You can find dried salted cod on display in Italian grocery stores and in some Asian markets. Grocery stores also carry salted cod in wooden boxes. Since the codfish will need to be rehydrated, start the process two days ahead. Remember to change the soaking water frequently or allow sufficient time for tap water to slowly drip on the fish and refresh it completely. This is a wonderful and filling salad for a hot summer day. Serve it with crusty bread.*

Place the codfish in the kitchen sink and allow tap water to drip on it for a day to rehydrate it. Or immerse it in a pan of water and change the water several times during the day(s) until the fish is refreshed and plump. During the process, rinse the fish four or five times under cold water to rid it of the salt.

Fill a 2-quart saucepan with 2 cups of water. Place a steamer basket in the pot and pile the florets on the basket. Cover the pan and bring the water to a boil. Lower the heat, and steam-cook the florets until they are tender but not mushy. This will take about 5 to 6 minutes. Or cook the florets in 2 quarts of boiling water until tender if you do not have a steamer basket. Drain the florets in a colander and transfer them to a large bowl to cool.

Transfer the codfish to a sauté pan, add 2 cups water, 2 tablespoons of the olive oil, and the lemon juice. Cover the pan and cook the fish over medium-low heat for about 15 minutes, or until the fish easily flakes when pierced with a fork. Drain the codfish with a slotted spoon and transfer it to the bowl with the florets.

Mix the remaining olive oil with the vinegar, salt, and pepper and pour it over the fish and cauliflower mixture. Add the olives and parsley and toss gently. Serve at room temperature.

Insalata di Carciofi
(Artichoke Salad)

Serves 4

¾ cup extra-virgin olive oil

2½ tablespoons red wine vinegar

¼ cup spicy mustard

2 cloves garlic, peeled and crushed

¼ cup diced onion

2 tablespoons minced Italian parsley

Fine sea salt to taste

Coarsely ground black pepper to taste

8 small artichokes, about 2 inches in diameter, or 4 globe artichokes

¼ cup lemon juice

½ teaspoon fine sea salt for boiling the artichokes

Did you know that artichokes are difficult to pair with wine? They leave a sweet and dry aftertaste in the mouth that masks the flavor of wine.

The Italian regions of Puglia and Sicily produce artichokes that are so tender they can be eaten raw. Sicilians are fond of roasting them over glowing embers at Easter time, when artichokes make an abundant appearance in the markets. Larger varieties, such as the globe artichoke, require the removal of the hairy fibers and choke from the interior as well as the tough exterior leaves. Small California artichokes are perfect for this Sicilian-style salad with spicy vinaigrette. How do you tell when an artichoke is perfectly cooked? When you can easily remove one of the outer leaves.

Combine the olive oil, vinegar, mustard, garlic, onion, parsley, salt, and pepper in a jar. Cap the jar and shake the ingredients well to combine them. Set aside.

Wash the artichokes, remove any tough outer leaves, usually the bottom two layers, and discard the leaves. Spread the center of the artichoke open with your fingers and scrape out the hairy choke with a spoon. Place the artichokes upright in a nonreactive saucepan just large enough to hold them firmly in place. Fill the pan with water to just cover the tops of the artichokes. Add the lemon juice and salt.

Cover the pan and bring the water to a boil. Reduce the heat to medium-high and cook the artichokes until they are tender, about 10 to 12 minutes for small artichokes, 20 to 25 minutes for the larger ones. Drain the artichokes and cool.

With a knife cut the artichokes in half and arrange on each of 4 salad plates. Pour some of the dressing over each half and serve immediately.

Breaking Sicilian Bread

In my bread book *What You Knead* I referred to the Italian phrase *buono come il pane,* meaning "as good as bread." These are close-to-the-chest words used by Italians to describe someone who is thought of very highly, as bread is thought of very highly. I have often reflected on how appropriate the analogy of good bread to a good person is because historically bread in its simplest and coarsest form has been the sustaining and nurturing foundation of much of the world population's food chain. Bread has meant the difference between starvation and survival; it has been the bargaining chip in wars between nations; it has meant power to the powerful, and in the case of ancient Rome, it was the coveted food that gave strength to the Roman armies—thanks to the vast wheatfields of Sicily.

In Italian homes it would be unthinkable to be without *pane.* It is an essential part of every meal. It is so important that Italian restaurants impose a cover charge on a basket of bread when it is brought to your table.

One of my fondest memories of making bread was in Sicily with a bread baker by the name of Carmelo Di Martino, an unassuming and polite farmhand who had been making bread from the age of nine. With deep, piercing blue eyes and silver-gray hair, he bore an uncanny resemblance to Paul Newman. He was short of stature, but his hands were large and weathered, evidence of arduous work.

One day, the television crew and I arrived to film Carmelo and me making bread in an old-fashioned *madia,* a large trough on iron legs that stood about three feet high. The building where Carmelo worked and lived was a rustic and drafty farmhouse with not much lighting. The kitchen was sparsely furnished, and I wondered what was in the green and brown ceramic pot that Carmelo reached for once the camera and lights were set up and we were ready to start taping. Then I saw him scoop out a mass of dough that he called the *cresciuta;* this was dough saved from the previous day's baking and used to give extra strength to new dough. Each time Carmelo made new dough, he broke off a portion and placed it in the cresciuta pot so he would have it to add to the next day's baking. It reminded me of starter dough, which is essentially what cresciuta is.

I watched as he poured the semolina flour from a huge paper sack into the madia. Then he drove his fist into the center of the flour and created a crater or *fontana* (well) into which he added the cresciuta and boiling hot water. I was amazed when he took several cakes of fresh yeast, crumbled them quickly between his hands, and dissolved them into the hot water. I thought for sure that would kill the yeast but Carmelo shook his head, gave a quick laugh, and said not to worry. This is the procedure he had been following since childhood. There was no reason to doubt him.

He began to work the mass of flour, water, and yeast with his hands, adding water as he mixed. There was no formula, no recipe, there was only intuition and years of manipulating dough on a daily basis. Carmelo created a fairly wet dough. I asked if I could help with the kneading. Little did I know what a workout this would be. Bent over the trough, I mimicked Carmelo's actions, using my knuckles to punch down and knead the dough instead of the palm of my hands. After about twenty minutes or so my back began to hurt and my knuckles were sore, but I was not about to quit. As we worked, Carmelo and I talked about the importance of bread in his life. He told me that he made an average of 90 loaves each month, rising at 4:00 A.M. to start the process. The first loaf always went to the landowner of the farm; the rest were stored for future use or sold.

When we finished kneading, the dough was golden yellow and silky soft. I had beads of perspiration covering my forehead, but

Carmelo had nary a hair out of place. He quickly broke off a chunk of the smooth dough and placed it in the cresciuta pot; then he lopped off larger pieces and rolled them into voluptuous-looking rounds. He sprinkled the tops with sesame seeds and placed each one on a heavy wool blanket; then he covered the loaves with another blanket and told me that now the loaves must sleep for three hours.

But the job of making bread had just begun. Now we had to prepare the wood-burning oven to bake the loaves. Carmelo gathered up a large group of twisted grapevines and olive tree twigs and shoved them into the oven. He lit a fire under them and they began to crack and hiss. Eventually the temperature rose to over 600 degrees and turned the vines and twigs into white ash. Carmelo swept out the ashes and began to position the loaves in the back of the oven, eight at a time, with a long wooden peel. He moved the loaves around on the oven floor, for even browning, as easily as a seasoned hockey player moves a puck on the ice.

We stopped tape to wait for the loaves to bake, then resumed the story of Sicilian bread as Carmelo took each loaf out of the oven. They were brown, crusty, and beautiful with a tight, golden yellow crumb. Carmelo's face beamed with satisfaction, the satisfaction of knowing that today, like every other day in his life since the age of nine, he had made perfect bread. He offered me a piece and without missing a beat looked into the camera and said, "*È buono,*" and it was.

Insalata Ennese

(Belgian Endive, Pomegranate, and Orange Salad)

Serves 4

½ pound (about 4 small) Belgian endive, washed

1 rib celery, washed and cut into thin slices

6 Cerigonola olives in brine, pitted and cut into slices

2 blood or navel oranges, peeled and cut into segments

1 tablespoon capers in salt, rinsed and diced (optional)

½ cup pomegranate seeds

DRESSING

2 tablespoons freshly squeezed lemon juice

¼ teaspoon fine sea salt

1½ teaspoons sugar

3 tablespoons extra-virgin olive oil

Looking at the surrounding pristine countryside of Sicily from the belvedere in Enna gives one a sense of why this city was envied for its invincible location high atop a mountain perch. On Enna's street corners are peddlers with cartfuls of broccolo *(cauliflower) for purchase. Long as a baseball bat,* zucchine lunge *(long zucchini) is available too, as are creamy white, tight heads of Belgian endive. The Ennese make a wonderful salad using endive, pomegranate seeds, and blood orange segments. The pomegranates and oranges are very refreshing with a sweet-tart flavor. Since pomegranates are not available year-round, I buy them in season, extract the seeds, and freeze them. That way I can enjoy the salad all year long; it is particularly attractive at Christmastime. If you cannot find blood oranges, use navel oranges instead.*

Cut the endive in half lengthwise, then cut each half in half and separate the leaves from the stem. Place the leaves in a salad bowl and add the celery, olives, oranges, and capers (if used).

To prepare the dressing, in a bowl whisk the lemon juice, salt, and sugar together. Slowly pour the olive oil into the lemon mixture, whisking until the mixture thickens a bit and is smooth.

Pour the dressing over the salad and toss. Sprinkle on the pomegranate seeds and serve.

Insalata di Fagiolini, Patate, Piselli e Cipolla

(Green Beans, Potatoes, Peas, and Onion Salad)

Serves 6 to 8

One of the most exciting cooking adventures I have had in Sicily was watching chef Mario Lo Menzo create some of the dishes of the aristocracy. Mario was the head chef for many years to a Sicilian winemaker, and as such made many elaborate dishes that would not be familiar to most Sicilians. When French cooking became influential in Sicily, many chefs, including Mario, adapted elements of French cooking into their own. Because of this, Mario is what is known as a monzù *("sir," from the French* monsieur*). Some of the dishes he turned out were rich with butter and cream, like his chicken in champagne sauce, but I prefer Mario's more rustic cooking, like this wonderful salad of green beans, potatoes, peas, and mint. I have taken a little liberty with this recipe; instead of raw onion in the salad, the onion is "cooked" in white wine vinegar until all the vinegar has evaporated, imparting a wonderful flavor. This salad is a great choice for any time of year and should be made early in the day so it has time to fully marinate.*

1 yellow onion (4 ounces), peeled and thinly sliced into rings

½ cup white wine vinegar or distilled white vinegar

½ cup extra-virgin olive oil

⅓ cup packed minced mint (¾-ounce package)

1½ teaspoons fine sea salt

¼ teaspoon fresh ground green peppercorns

¾ pound green beans, ends trimmed

2 red-skin potatoes, washed and cut into 1-inch cubes

¾ cup fresh or frozen peas

In a sauté pan over medium heat, steep the onions in the vinegar until all the vinegar has evaporated. Transfer the onions to a shallow salad bowl or platter.

Pour the olive oil into the bowl or platter, add the mint, salt, and pepper. Toss the onions in the olive oil mixture and set aside.

Bring 2 quarts of water to a boil and cook the green beans for 5 minutes, or until a knife is easily inserted into them. Do not overcook them; they should not be mushy. With a slotted spoon transfer the beans to a colander, and rinse them immediately under cold water to stop the cooking process. Reserve the cooking water. Dry

Did you know that vinegar was one of the ancient food preservatives used by the Romans? The others were olive oil, salt, and honey.

Sicily

the beans on paper towels and transfer them to the bowl with the onions and olive oil.

Cook the potatoes in the same water you used to cook the beans. This should take about 5 minutes, or just until a knife is easily inserted into them. One minute before the potatoes are done, add the peas to the pot. Drain the potatoes and peas in a colander, then transfer them to the salad bowl with the beans.

Gently mix all the ingredients together; add additional salt and pepper to taste. Allow the salad to marinate, covered, at room temperature for several hours prior to serving.

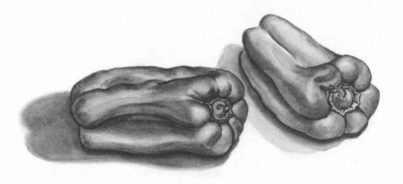

Cuori di Carciofi e Patate al Forno
(Oven-Baked Artichoke Heart and
Potato Casserole), page 213

Semifreddo di Monte San Giuliano, page 227

Focaccia di Cipolle, Patate e Semi di Zucca
(Onion, Potato, and Pumpkin Seed Focaccia), page 250

Spezzatelle (Dandelion Soufflé), page 283

Pane di Fichi Secchi ed'Anice
(Dried Fig and Anise Bread), page 301

Sformato di Pane Stratificato
(Molded Tomato Bread Salad), page 345

Insalata d'Aragosta dal Corsaro
(Lobster Salad Corsaro Style), page 344

Conchiglie con Finocchio (Pasta Shells with Fennel), page 329

Semifreddo di Monte San Giuliano

Serves 8 to 10

*Erice is etched forever in my memory; this almost mystical city, 751 me-
ters high atop Monte San Giuliano on the western coast of Sicily, seems per-
petually bathed in nebulous mist. The drive up the hairpin mountainside to
the center snakes by breathtaking vistas of neatly laid out valleys for as far
as the eye can see. Monte San Giuliano is named in honor of Saint Giuliano, who inspired the Norman count, Roger, in a dream to rise up against the
Arab colonizers of Sicily. In mythology, Erice was associated with the cult
of Aphrodite, the goddess of love. Its narrow streets are fitted with neatly
cut, squared stone and the endearing stone houses have wonderful flowered
courtyards that have retained their medieval characteristics. Erice is known
for its arts and crafts. One of these is* pasta reale, *meaning "royal paste,"
and is a dough made from almonds, egg whites, and sugar, fashioned by
hand into realistic-looking fruits, vegetables, flowers, and whimsical items.*

*The pastries made in Erice are sought after as well, and originally were
the work of cloistered nuns. The* pupi Siciliani *(Sicilian puppets) have long
been part of Erice's and other parts of Sicily's cultural heritage. On Sunday
evenings puppet shows are staged; they were originally meant to distract
people from their cares and tell a continuous story, with one part being told
each Sunday evening. It was in Erice that I had a wonderful meal beginning
with marinated eggplant in olive oil and mint, fresh sardines, tomatoes and
mozzarella cheese, green olives, and* broccoli, *which is fried green cauliflower. This was followed by couscous and an elaborately made fish soup,
and the finale to the meal was a* semifreddo *(partially frozen) dessert made
with cream, eggs, sugar, and caramelized almonds. I loved it so much that I
did not hesitate to ask the chef for the recipe. When making the dessert you
will have some of the almond mixture left over. It can be stored in jars in the
refrigerator for months and used in cakes or on top of ice cream, or enjoyed*

**2 cups (8 ounces) whole
 natural almonds**

2 cups sugar

2½ cups whipping cream

5 large eggs, separated

Did you know that Sicily is ablaze
with almond trees in February,
yielding both bitter and sweet
almonds that are used in many
Sicilian desserts and even in
caponata, a Sicilian sweet-and-
sour eggplant relish?

Sicily

as is for a great snack. I recommend that you make the almond mixture, known as croccante *in Italian, a day or two ahead.*

Line a 10×4×3-inch loaf pan with plastic wrap, allowing the excess to hang over the edges. Line a 7×3½×2½-inch loaf or similar pan with plastic wrap, and allow the excess to hang over the edges. Set the pans aside.

Spray a cutting board or a marble slab with butter or cooking spray and set aside.

In a 1-quart heavy-duty saucepan combine the almonds and 1¼ cups of the sugar. Cook the mixture, stirring constantly, over medium-high heat until the sugar begins to melt and coat the almonds. This will take about 10 minutes to do. Do not allow the almonds to burn, so take care to turn down the heat if necessary. The almonds should look shiny and well coated.

Immediately pour the almond mixture out onto the cutting board or marble slab, and working very quickly smooth it out with the back of a wooden spoon. Allow the mixture to cool and harden. When hard, use an 8- to 10-inch chef's knife to cut the almonds into small, coarse pieces. You will need to push down very hard with the knife to cut the almond mixture. Set aside.

In a large bowl beat the cream with ¼ cup of the remaining sugar until stiff. Set aside.

In another bowl beat the egg yolks with the remaining ½ cup of sugar until the eggs are lemon-colored and the sugar is well blended. Set aside. With clean beaters beat the egg whites in a separate large bowl until soft peaks form that are shiny and fluffy. With a rubber spatula fold the egg white mixture into the egg yolk mixture until well blended, then fold the whipped cream into the egg mixture until well blended. This is now the semifreddo, ready to freeze.

Spread ½ cup of the almonds in the base of the 10×4×3-inch loaf pan. Spread 2 heaping cupfuls of the semifreddo over the almonds, then sprinkle another ½ cup of the almonds over the mixture. Make two more layers of semifreddo and almonds, ending with the semifreddo. Fold the overlapping pieces of plastic wrap over the top of the pan and gently push on it to smooth the ingredients. Cover the pan completely with plastic wrap, then a sheet of aluminum foil, and freeze.

Use the remaining semifreddo mixture to fill the smaller pan in the same manner.

When ready to use, unwrap the aluminum foil and open up the plastic wrap on top of the pan. Place a serving dish over the top of the pan and invert the semifreddo onto the dish. Gently pull away and discard the plastic wrap. Allow the semifreddo to stand at room temperature for a few minutes. Cut it into slices and serve immediately. Save the smaller pan of semifreddo for future use.

Gelato di Mandarini
(Mandarin Orange Ice Cream)

Makes 2½ quarts

11 small mandarin or
  clementine oranges

2 cups water

4¼ cups sugar

¼ teaspoon salt

2 cups half-and-half

2 cups heavy cream

5 extra large egg yolks

No zuppa inglese, tiramisù, torta di ricotta, *or rich* cannoli *will ever take the place of* gelato *(ice cream) as my favorite dessert. Like so many others, I am truly addicted to this cool and creamy treat that was first introduced into Italy by the Arabs and perfected by the Sicilians. Gelato is made with egg yolks, sugar, cream, and flavorings. Once you master the technique of making gelato, the variations on the theme are endless. This recipe for* gelato di mandarini *combines the sweet delicate juice of tiny mandarin or clementine oranges, but if these are unavailable, navel oranges will do. A nice presentation idea is to fill the orange shells with the gelato, freeze them, then cut them into wedges for serving with fresh fruit, biscotti, or cakes. A lemon reamer or juicer yields the most juice and keeps the shells smooth-looking.*

Cut 10 of the oranges in half and squeeze the juice to make 1¾ cups. With your hands or a small spoon, remove the white pith and membrane from 8 of the orange shells; wrap them in plastic wrap and refrigerate until ready to fill. Grate the zest of the remaining oranges and set it aside.

In a 3-quart saucepan combine 2 cups water and the sugar. Cook over medium-high heat, stirring occasionally, until the mixture comes to a boil. Boil gently, stirring constantly, until the mixture is syrupy looking, about 8 minutes. Remove the saucepan from the heat, stir in the orange juice, zest, and salt, and set it aside.

Heat the half-and-half in a separate saucepan to just below scalding (175°F). Set it aside and keep it warm.

Combine the half-and-half, heavy cream, egg yolks, and syrup mixture in a large heatproof bowl. Fill a 4- or 6-quart pot one-third full of water. Place the bowl on top of the pot, making sure that the water in the pot does not touch the bottom of the bowl or the egg yolks will curdle during cooking. Cook over medium heat until the mixture thickens slightly and coats a spoon.

Remove the bowl from the top of the pot, cool slightly, then cover with plastic wrap and refrigerate the mixture overnight to allow it to thicken.

Make the gelato in an ice cream maker, following the manufacturer's directions. Homemade ice cream will not be as hard as store-bought when ready, but rather the consistency of frozen yogurt.

Fill the orange shells with ice cream, smoothing the top. Wrap each filled shell in plastic wrap and freeze until the ice cream is hard. When ready to serve, unwrap the shells and, with a sharp knife, cut each shell in half and serve as an accompaniment to cookies, cakes, or fruit.

Transfer the extra ice cream to plastic containers and freeze for up to 4 months.

Biscottini al Vino
(Little Wine Cookies)

Makes about 6 dozen cookies

1 cup sugar

1 cup vegetable oil

1 cup dry red wine such as
  Corvo Red

4½ cups unbleached all-
  purpose flour

2 teaspoons baking powder

1 egg plus 1 tablespoon
  water mixed together for
  egg wash

The whole house smells wonderful when wine cookies are baking, and they bring back lots of nostalgic memories for me. This was one of the cookies that all the Italian ladies in the neighborhood made, using homemade wine derived from Concord grapes. They were made for dunking in wine, so they were always on hand when company called. It is best to chill the dough for at least 2 hours before forming it into small bagel-shaped cookies. These are great keepers as well as great dunkers. The subtle lavender color is pretty, too.

In an electric mixer on medium speed blend together the sugar, vegetable oil, and wine.

Sift the flour and baking powder together, then add them to the sugar mixture and blend the ingredients together at medium speed, until a soft dough is obtained. The dough should not be sticky, but soft and smooth.

Transfer the dough to a bowl. Cover the bowl tightly with plastic wrap and refrigerate for at least 2 hours, or overnight. Once chilled, the dough is very easy to work with.

Preheat the oven to 350°F.

To form the cookies, break off small pieces and roll them under the palm of your hand to form a 4-inch rope that is ½ inch thick. Bring the ends together and pinch them tightly, forming a circle that looks like a miniature bagel. Place the cookies ½ inch apart on ungreased baking sheets and brush the top of each cookie with the egg wash.

Bake the cookies for 17 to 20 minutes, or until the tops are firm to the touch and the bottoms are golden brown. Remove the cookies to a cooling rack and cool completely. Store the unused cookies in airtight containers.

Salsa di Melagrana
(Pomegranate Sauce)

Makes 2 cups

6 large pomegranates
3 tablespoons cornstarch
½ cup sugar

I have an unremitting passion for pomegranates. In Sicily the juice is extracted from the ruby red, tightly packed seeds to make a refreshing tart drink or a slushy ice called a granita. *I like to break open the skin, fish out the seeds, and just eat them as is. Sometimes I use them in citrus salads, another common practice in Sicily, and sometimes I make a sauce for ice cream or for the* Semifreddo di Monte San Giuliano *(page 227). The sauce can be made several days ahead of time and refrigerated. It will need to be thinned down with a little water and heated slightly before using. Extracting the juice is a messy job, so wear old clothes. You will need a juicer for this recipe.*

Cut the pomegranates in half and extract the juice using a juicer. You should have about 2 cups of juice. Set it aside.

In a saucepan off the heat combine the cornstarch and the sugar. Make sure there are no lumps in the cornstarch. Slowly pour the pomegranate juice into the cornstarch and sugar mixture and mix with a wooden spoon to thoroughly combine the ingredients.

Cook the mixture over medium heat, stirring constantly. The sauce will become shiny looking and darker in color as it thickens. The consistency should be like that of honey. Transfer the sauce to a container when cool. Use it immediately as a topping for ice cream or fruit, or refrigerate it for later use.

Note: Cornstarch can be very lumpy; before using it in recipes, use a spoon and a fine-mesh sieve to smooth it out.

Latte Fritto
(Fried Milk)

Makes 2½ dozen 2½-inch squares

Latte fritto *(fried milk). The name intrigues me and I have enjoyed it in Sicily, but research shows the origin of this dessert is the region of Liguria. Its consistency is similar to a velvety pudding with a crunchy bread-crumb coating that provides a nice textural contrast. The milk mixture is cooked, then cooled and cut into pieces and fried. This makes a perfect party offering when small squares are cut. Or cut the pieces larger for serving 8 to 10. This is also a refreshing dessert choice served with a simple fruit sauce, such as the Pomegranate Sauce (page 234).*

2 large eggs

2 cups plain fine bread crumbs

4 cups whole milk

⅔ cup sugar

Grated zest of 1 large lemon

1½ cups unbleached all-purpose flour

¼ cup vegetable oil

In a shallow bowl lightly beat the eggs with a fork and set aside.

Place the bread crumbs in another shallow bowl and set aside.

Bring the milk to a boil in a 2-quart saucepan. Add the sugar and stir to dissolve it. Stir in the lemon zest. Whisk in the flour slowly, a little at a time. Continue to whisk over medium-high heat until the mixture thickens, about 2 to 3 minutes. Take care not to burn the milk.

Pour the mixture onto a 12×10-inch baking sheet and spread it to a ½ to ¾ inch thickness with a rubber spatula. Butter a piece of wax paper and gently place it over the surface. Chill the mixture for 1 hour to make it easier to cut.

With a knife cut the mixture into 2½-inch squares. Coat each square with the beaten egg, and then carefully coat each one with bread crumbs. Place the coated squares on a baking sheet as you finish them.

In a sauté pan heat the vegetable oil, and when it is hot fry the squares in batches until they are golden brown on each side. Drain the squares on brown paper. These are best served warm.

Variation: Use a round 3-inch fluted cookie cutter to get 14 rounds. There will be waste when using a round cutter and the scraps will not be easy to reroll unless they are chilled first.

Part Two

Bringing

Italy

Home

Ciao, Mary Ann, Do You Have...?

Antipasti

Focaccia di Oliva, Rosmarino e Pancetta (Olive, Rosemary, and
    Pancetta Focaccia)

Focaccia di Cipolle, Patate e Semi di Zucca (Onion, Potato, and
    Pumpkin Seed Focaccia)

Primi Piatti

Pasta Fatta in Casa (Homemade Pasta)

Salsa di Pomodori (Tomato Sauce)

Salsa di Pomodori di Antonio Stella (Anthony Stella's Tomato Sauce)

Pesto di Rucola (Arugula Pesto Sauce)

Gnocchi di Patate di Antonio Stella (Anthony Stella's Potato Gnocchi)

Zuppa di Polpettine (Baked Meatball Soup)

Zuppa di Manzo e Verdure con Polenta (Beef Vegetable Soup with
    Polenta)

Zuppa di Minestrone (Minestrone Soup)

Secondi Piatti

Ossobuco con Pomodori e Vino Rosso (Veal Shank with Tomatoes and
    Red Wine)

Orecchiette in Salsa di Pomodori con Agnello (Lamb Shanks in Tomato
    Sauce with Orecchiette)

Fusilli con Salsa di Porri (Twisted Pasta with Leek Sauce)

Salsiccia con Penne e Salsa di Pomodori (Sausage with Penne and
    Tomato Sauce)

Timballo alla Teramamo (Crêpes with Spinach and Veal Teramamo
   Style)
Spezzatelle (Dandelion Soufflé)
Vitellone al Forno (Oven-Cooked Veal)
Stufato di Vitellone con Erbe e Vino (Veal Stew with Herbs and Wine)
Scaloppine al Limone e Salsa di Capperi (Veal Cutlets with Lemon and
   Caper Sauce)
Pollo al Vino (Chicken in Wine)
Farrotto (Farro Cooked in the Style of Farrotto)
Farrotto con Merluzzo (Farro with Codfish)

Dolci

Pane di Fichi Secchi ed'Anice (Dried Fig and Anise Bread)
Panettone (Christmas Bread)
Panettone Emporio Rulli (Gary Rulli's Panettone)
Biscotti ai Pinoli (Pine Nut Cookies)
Ossi di Morto (Cookies of the Dead)
Pizzelle Colorate (Colored Pizzelle)
Tortine di Pesche (Little Peach Cakes)
Cuppelle (Molded Wafer Cookies)

Dear Mary Ann:

Thank you for sharing your beautiful memories . . . You brought tears to my eyes. . . . God bless you! Thanks for taking the time to inform and entertain . . . I'm delighted to see your show on PBS. . . . Food is made with love, and you prove that on your show. . . . I learn lots from you. Keep up the good work. . . . You make cooking look like so much fun. . . . Our family has enjoyed many of your fine recipes. . . . I'll keep watching you! . . . My mother finds much joy in watching you. . . . Ciao Italia *is so much more than cooking. . . . Your Mom's Whiskey Cake has given our family a new birthday tradition. . . . Thank you for letting me share my love of food with you. . . . I hope this show is on for the next 100 years. . . . You taught me how to make Caponata! . . . You inspire me to be a little more creative. . . . My mother and I love your program. . . . My son recites your program ending: "Until I see you nella cucina again". . . . I have learned so much from you over the years. . . . Thank you for this excellent cooking and teaching show. . . . I am dreaming about this recipe. . . . You remind me so very much of my late beloved mother. . . . You've got a great, no-nonsense, yet loving approach. . . . No gimmicks, no gadgets, no hype. I love it. . . . You are the only cook my mother watches. . . . Your program is a complete delight. . . . Thank you for the fond memories of my heritage. . . . Your recipe for apple cake made my two uncles cry with happiness. . . . Thank you for all the treasures. . . . We love Italian food. . . . Loved the show! . . . We love you.*

*T*his chapter contains some of the most-asked-for recipes by our television audience, a few of which have appeared in my earlier books. It seems that everyone always wants to stay close to the foods of their youth, so you will find, among others, Chicken in Wine (*Pollo al Vino*), Pine Nut Cookies (*Biscotti al Pignoli*), Easter Pie (*Pastiera*), and Homemade Pasta (*Pasta Fatta in Casa*).

*Ciao, Mary Ann,
Do You Have . . . ?*

Many of these recipes are from the regions of Italy that I have presented on the series; they come from both professional and self-trained chefs who have been guests in my television kitchen. Some are from well-known personalities and home cooks, like children's author and illustrator Tomie de Paola, who shared a leek sauce recipe (page 276) that is perfect for the squiggly pasta called fusilli. Revered and well-respected New York cooking teacher Anna Nurse contributed her Pugliese Lamb Shanks in Tomato Sauce (page 274), which is perfect served with orecchiette (little ear-shaped pasta). Chef Anthony Stella of Ristorante Osteria shared his family's favorite Abruzzese Timballo (page 280) from the town of Ofena in the region of Abruzzi.

Some of the recipes have been contributed by *Ciao Italia* viewers, like Grace Gallucci, who made her family's *Spezzatelle* (page 283) on one of our programs; this dish is a delicious and little-known Dandelion Soufflé from Foggia, in the region of Puglia showing the French influence in that area.

You will find new twists on old favorite recipes too. For instance, when a viewer asked, "What can I do with pumpkin seeds?" I suggested a wonderful focaccia dough embedded with toasted pumpkin seeds and topped with carmelized onions and paper-thin slices of potatoes (page 250). Creating new recipes is a challenge that I enjoy, and I will admit that I am not perfect in the kitchen. There is the occasional thumbs-down experimental recipe, but for the most part, just loving to cook and being open to new ideas pays off. And that is the central message of our series—have fun, be curious, ask questions, and enjoy.

Flour Power

One of the frequently asked questions that I get about *Ciao Italia* is "What is your favorite thing to make?" Bread and pasta is my standard answer. Ironically these are two foods that people tell me they have the most trouble with. On the television series I have demonstrated many recipes on how to make bread and pasta using the traditional Italian *fontana* method, which is a fountain of flour constructed directly on a work surface. The liquid ingredients are poured into the center and the flour is worked into the liquid by hand, starting on the inside of the flour wall and working clockwise until enough of the flour has been pulled in to create a ball of dough. But I have also demonstrated how to make pasta and bread in a food processor or mixer, since this is easier for some people to do.

In this book you will find recipes for making both homemade pasta dough and bread dough, but before you decide to make them, I would like you to take the time to read the following information, which may help eliminate some of your fears about working with doughs.

Flour is a very complex thing. Use the wrong flour in a recipe and the results can be disastrous. There are many types of flour; in this book I have used King Arthur unbleached all-purpose flour for most of the recipes. This is a flour with a protein content of around 11 percent; it is an all-purpose hard-wheat flour with enough gluten strength to allow for easy kneading of dough for bread and pasta.

Cake flour, on the other hand, would not be suitable for making bread or pasta because it is a low-protein flour, around 5 or 6 percent, depending on the brand. For cakes and pastry, you want to avoid gluten development, which would make cake texture tough and pastry dough too hard. In some cases, a high-protein flour can be used for cakes such as pound cakes, fruitcakes, or other dense-type varieties. But for sponge cakes, such as the Torta al Limone on page 180, angel food cakes, and the like, where a tender crumb is the objective, use a cake flour. How do you know what percentage of protein a flour will have? Look on the bag of flour that you are purchasing for this information.

Keep in mind that in Italy flours are measured by weight, not volume. To do this invest in a kitchen scale. But if you do not have a scale, then get into the habit of using the "sprinkle and sweep" method of measuring flour that is described in my bread book, *What You Knead* (William Morrow Publishers Inc., 1997).

Use metal or plastic measures for measuring dry ingredients such as flour, and use glass measures for measuring liquids. To measure flour by the sprinkle-and-sweep method, lightly spoon the flour into a measuring cup with a spoon until the flour is over the rim of the measuring cup. With a butter knife sweep off the excess flour so that it is even with the rim. Now you have a true cup of flour and it can weigh anywhere from 3.5 to 4 ounces, depending on the flour. The exact method of measuring flour is by weight, so if you are serious about baking I suggest you invest in a good kitchen scale. If you keep these simple steps in mind, then you will avoid using too much flour in a recipe, and when making pasta or bread, you will find the dough a delight to work with.

As a rule I buy flour by the 50-pound bag because I go through it very quickly, but if you find that a 5-pound bag of flour lasts forever, then I suggest that you keep it in the refrigerator once it is opened to keep it fresh and avoid it becoming rancid. Flour can also be frozen; just remember to bring it out and allow it to come to room temperature before you use it for mixing with yeast.

Ciao, Mary Ann,
Do You Have . . . ?

Impasto Base

(Basic Yeast Dough)

Makes about 2 pounds dough

1 package active dry yeast

2 cups warm water

1 tablespoon wheat gluten
with vitamin C

5 to 5½ cups unbleached all-
purpose flour

1 teaspoon fine sea salt

This basic all-purpose yeast dough is a snap to make and very versatile for pizza, bread, rolls, focaccia, and breadsticks. Using wheat gluten with vitamin C when making the dough will greatly increase its rising capacity, and will give breads and pizzas a longer shelf life and a softer crumb texture. You can find wheat gluten next to flour in the baking aisle, or through the mail order sources (page 347). You can also make the recipe without using wheat gluten.

In a large bowl or in the bowl of an electric mixer fitted with a dough hook, dissolve the yeast in ½ cup of the water and allow it to get foamy and chalky-looking. Pour in the remaining water. Stir in the wheat gluten (if using) and begin mixing in the flour 1 cup at a time, allowing the flour to absorb the water. Stir in the salt with the third addition of flour. Mix with your hands or use the dough hook on the mixer to make a ball of dough that is not sticky. Do not use more flour than you need—use just enough to hold the dough together in a rough ball—or the dough will be difficult to knead.

When the dough is smooth transfer it to a lightly greased bowl. Cover the bowl tightly with plastic wrap and let it rise until doubled in bulk, about 1 hour. When ready to use, punch down the dough with your fist and form it into bread loaves, pizza crusts, rolls, breadsticks, or focaccia.

Note: If you want to make the dough ahead of time, punch it down after the first rising, put the dough in an oil-sprayed plastic bag, and refrigerate it. When ready to use, transfer the dough to a bowl, cover the bowl with plastic wrap, and allow it to rise until almost doubled. This may take about one hour. Punch down the dough and proceed with the recipe. I do not recommend freezing the dough for too long as it loses some of its punch.

Note: Hodgson Mill makes wheat gluten with Vitamin C, available in the baking aisle of supermarkets.

Focaccia di Oliva, Rosmarino e Pancetta
(Olive, Rosemary, and Pancetta Focaccia)

Makes one 12- or 13-inch round

¼ pound pancetta or other bacon, diced

1½ cups warm water

1 teaspoon active dry yeast

½ teaspoon sugar

1 teaspoon extra-virgin olive oil

3¼ to 4 cups unbleached all-purpose flour

1½ teaspoons fine sea salt

1 tablespoon fresh rosemary needles

14 cured black olives, pitted and cut in half

Viewers are always interested in yeast-dough-inspired foods. One of my favorites is this black olive, rosemary, and pancetta (Italian unsmoked bacon) focaccia that is made with bruised olives to celebrate the olive harvest in Italy. These are olives that have fallen on the ground and are not perfect for making olive oil. The dough is easy to make, either by hand or in a food processor, and stretches easily into shape.

Cook the pancetta or bacon in a sauté pan over medium heat with no additional fat until it becomes crispy. Remove the pancetta with a slotted spoon and drain it on paper towels. Set aside.

Pour ½ cup of the water into a large bowl or the bowl of a food processor; stir in the yeast and the sugar and let the mixture proof until it looks chalky and bubbles begin to appear. This will take about 5 minutes.

Pour the remaining water and the olive oil into the yeast mixture. Pulse it in the food processor or mix by hand. Stir in the flour, 1 cup at a time, and mix or pulse well until a ball of dough begins to form. Stir in the salt with the last addition of flour. You may not need all the flour; use just enough to create a dough that moves away from the side of the food processor and comes together in one piece, or a dough that when mixed in a bowl does not stick to your hands. Resist the temptation to add too much flour, which would make the dough too tough.

Place the dough on a lightly floured surface and stretch it out with your hands into a rough round. Scatter the rosemary needles and the pancetta over the top of the dough. Fold the dough over

Ciao, Mary Ann, Do You Have . . . ?

on itself to enclose the rosemary and pancetta and begin kneading with your hands until the rosemary and pancetta come through the dough. Knead to evenly distribute the ingredients into the dough.

Place the dough in a lightly greased bowl and cover it tightly with plastic wrap. Let the dough rise in a spot no warmer than 70°F for 2 hours, or until doubled in bulk.

Punch down the dough with your hands and turn it out onto a lightly floured surface. Knead the dough for about 3 or 4 minutes, or until it is smooth and soft. Set aside.

Preheat the oven to 375°F.

Lightly grease a pizza pan or place a piece of parchment paper on a wooden peel. If you plan to bake the focaccia on a stone in your oven, preheat it in the oven for 30 minutes before baking the focaccia.

Put the dough on the pizza pan or peel and stretch it with your hands into a rustic-looking 12- or 13-inch round. Press the olives randomly into the top of the focaccia.

Cover the focaccia with a towel and let it rise for 20 minutes. If using a pizza pan, bake the focaccia for 30 to 35 minutes, or until the focaccia is nicely browned. If using a stone, slide the focaccia with the parchment paper onto the stone and bake for 20 to 25 minutes, or until the focaccia is nicely browned.

Remove the focaccia to a cooling rack and let it cool for 3 or 4 minutes. Cut into pieces with a scissors and serve immediately.

Ciao, Mary Ann,
Do You Have . . . ?

Focaccia di Cipolle, Patate e Semi di Zucca
(Onion, Potato and Pumpkin Seed Focaccia)

Makes one 15×1½-inch deep-dish focaccia or two 13½×14-inch focacce

DOUGH

½ cup hulled unsalted pumpkin seeds

1½ cups warm (110°F) potato water

1 package active dry yeast

3 to 3½ cups unbleached all-purpose flour

1 tablespoon wheat gluten, or ½ crushed vitamin C tablet (optional)

1 teaspoon extra-virgin olive oil

1½ teaspoons fine sea salt

TOPPING

1 large Russet potato

6 tablespoons extra-virgin olive oil

1 pound sweet red onions (2 large), peeled and thinly sliced

4 tablespoons sugar

I must give credit to my maternal grandmother, Anna Galasso, for the trick I have used on my series to demonstrate how to make a good, light-tasting yeast dough. Grandma always saved potato water—either the water potatoes had been boiled in or the water that peeled, uncooked potatoes had been held in. In either case, the potatoes release plenty of starch, which yeast just loves to feed on. When I boil potatoes I make sure to drain off the water into containers that I can freeze. That way I always have potato water on hand, to crumble yeast into.

This dough is what is referred to as a straight dough because it uses just water, active dry yeast, unbleached all-purpose flour, salt, and a little olive oil. To give the dough an added boost while rising I add wheat gluten, available in the baking section of most supermarkets. This is optional, and half a crushed chewable vitamin C tablet will have the same effect. When I knead the dough I embed it with toasted pumpkin seeds for a nice look, nutty flavor, and texture. I top it with onions, paper-thin slices of potatoes, and fresh thyme. For an impressive look I use a deep-dish 15½×1½-inch pizza pan, but you can make two free-form focacce about 13½×15½ inches and bake them on preheated baking stones, which give a nice crisp texture to the crust. Or simply use standard pizza pans. This is a great starter for a rustic Italian dinner.

Preheat oven to 325°F.

Spread the pumpkin seeds on a cookie sheet and toast them for 10 minutes. You will hear a popping noise as they toast. Remove the seeds to a dish to cool.

Make the dough in an electric mixer, food processor, or by

hand. Pour ½ cup of the potato water into a mixing bowl. Sprinkle the yeast over the water and stir it with a spoon. Allow the yeast to "proof," or get bubbly. This will take about 5 minutes. Pour in the remaining water. Mix in 1 cup of the flour, following the measuring instructions on page 245 along with the wheat gluten or Vitamin C (see also Note on page 247). Stir in the olive oil and the salt. Continue adding enough of the flour to create a dough that moves away from the sides of the mixing bowl and is not sticking to your hands. The dough should be slightly tacky but not sticky or gooey feeling. Knead the dough a few times on a lightly floured work surface. Round the dough into a ball and place it in a large bowl. Cover the bowl tightly with plastic wrap and allow it to rise until doubled in bulk. Or make the dough a day ahead, and after it has risen, punch it down and place the dough in a vegetable-oil-sprayed plastic bag. Refrigerate the dough. When ready to use, transfer the dough to a bowl; cover it and allow it to come to room temperature and rise.

Meanwhile make the topping. Peel the potato and cut it into paper-thin slices. (If you want to prep them ahead of time, place the slices in a bowl and cover them with cold water to prevent them from discoloring. Be sure to dry the slices before sautéing them.)

Heat 3 tablespoons of the olive oil in a sauté pan set over medium heat. Cook the potatoes, turning them frequently, until they just start to brown around the edges. Remove the potatoes to a paper-towel-lined dish. Add the remaining 3 tablespoons olive oil, stir in the onions, and cook them until the onions begin to soften. Stir the sugar into the onions and continue cooking them for 2 or 3 minutes. They should look soft and glazed. Raise the heat to high and stir in the vinegar. Continue cooking and stirring until all the vinegar has evaporated. Transfer the mixture to a bowl and allow it to cool.

Punch down the dough with your fists and transfer it to a lightly floured work surface. Stretch out the dough with your

⅓ cup balsamic or red wine vinegar

¼ cup fresh thyme leaves

½ teaspoon coarsely ground black pepper

*Ciao, Mary Ann,
Do You Have . . . ?*

251

hands into a rough-looking round. Spread the pumpkin seeds on top of the dough. Fold the dough over the pumpkin seeds, and knead the dough until the seeds are evenly distributed throughout the dough.

To make one deep-dish focaccia, roll the dough into a 15×11½-inch round, and place it in the pan. To make two thinner and smaller focacce, divide the dough in half, and roll each half into roughly a 13½×14-inch round. Place the rounds on each of two baking-parchment-lined peels.

If making the deep-dish focaccia, spread all the potato slices over the top of the dough. Spread the onions evenly over the potatoes, and sprinkle the thyme and pepper over the onions. Cover with a clean dish towel and allow to rise for 20 minutes. If making two smaller ones, divide and spread the potatoes, onions, thyme, and pepper over the top of each focaccia. Cover them with a clean dish towel and allow them to rise for 20 minutes.

Preheat the oven to 400°F if making the deep-dish focaccia or using conventional pizza pans; preheat the baking stones at 450°F for 25 minutes prior to baking the smaller focacce, then lower the temperature to 400°F.

Bake the deep-dish focaccia for 25 to 30 minutes, or until the bottom crust is nicely browned. Use the same baking temperature and time if using conventional pizza pans. Remove the focaccia from the oven and set the pan on a cooling rack.

If using baking stones, slide the focaccia with the parchment paper onto the stone. You may need to bake one at a time if you do not have a double oven and 2 baking stones. Bake for 20 to 25 minutes, or until the bottom crust is nicely browned. To remove the focaccia from the stone, slip the peel underneath the parchment paper and slide the focaccia onto the peel and transfer to a cooling rack.

Cut the focaccia into wedges with a scissors and serve warm.

Pasta Fatta in Casa
(Homemade Pasta)

Makes about 1¼ pounds pasta

This is my standard recipe for making pasta. Make it in a food processor or by hand and use the traditional fontana *method of making dough. Homemade pasta can be made months ahead and stored in aluminum foil, but it must be thoroughly dry and brittle or it will mold. Semolina flour can be found in specialty shops or ordered by mail. I use a fine grind to give a deeper yellow color to the pasta, and for its nutritional value. If unavailable, use all unbleached flour. The dough can be cut into everything from farfalle to fettuccine to lasagne sheets to pappardelle noodles.*

2½ cups unbleached all-purpose flour

½ cup semolina flour

1 teaspoon fine sea salt

4 large eggs

Combine the flours and salt and mound it on a work surface. With your fist make a hole in the center of the mound. This is the *fontana,* or well. Crack the eggs into the center of the well and beat gently with a fork or your fingers to break up the egg yolks. Using one hand and moving in a clockwise fashion, begin bringing the flour from inside the flour wall into the eggs. Use your other hand to keep the outside of the wall together. If the wall breaks, the eggs will seep out. Continue mixing until a ball of dough is created that is not soupy and holds its shape. Push the excess flour aside and knead the dough until a smooth, soft ball is obtained. Don't worry if you do not use all the flour; adding too much flour will result in a tough dough. On the other hand, if the dough is still sticky, add some of the remaining flour a little at a time until the desired consistency is obtained.

Any leftover flour can be used to dust the sheets of dough when they are cut. Knead the dough until smooth; form it into a round,

Ciao, Mary Ann,
Do You Have . . . ?

253

and allow it to rest covered under a bowl for 30 minutes. This will allow the gluten in the dough to relax and make it easier to roll out.

To make the dough in a food processor, insert the metal blade into the food processor. Add the eggs and process until smooth. In a bowl mix the flours and salt together, then add the flour to the eggs a cupful at a time and process until a ball of dough forms and leaves the sides of the processor. If the dough is sticky, add additional flour 1 tablespoon at a time and process; if the dough is too dry, add water 1 tablespoon at a time and process. Remove the dough from the processor once it has achieved the right consistency and knead it on a floured surface for about 5 minutes. Cover as instructed above and allow to rest.

To roll the dough out, cut it in four pieces and work with one piece at a time, keeping the others covered. Use a rolling pin to flatten the dough, then roll it through the rollers of a standard pasta machine; the knob on the side of the pasta machine controls the thinness of the dough. Follow the manufacturer's instructions. To cut the dough, feed the rolled-out sheets through the cutters—either fettuccine or linguine are standard cuts on most hand-crank pasta machine. For wide noodles, roll the dough out with a rolling pin and use a sharp knife to make pappardelle (about 9 inches long and 2½ inches wide) or lasagne sheets. Bowties can be made by cutting the rolled dough into 2-inch squares, then pinching the center to form the bowtie shape.

Note: I dry pasta cuts such as linguine and fettucine over dowel rods that are positioned between two chairs. Pasta is dry when the ends begin to curl. Carefully remove the dowel rods and slide the pasta with your hands onto a large sheet of aluminum foil. Close the foil loosely and store the pasta in a cool spot where nothing will cause it to break. Dowel rods are inexpensive round pieces of wood found in the hardware store and can be cut to whatever length you require.

Salsa di Pomodori
(Tomato Sauce)

Makes 4 cups sauce

It doesn't take long to make a simple tomato sauce. Fresh plum tomatoes are best, and I make a lot of sauce with the tomatoes from my garden and freeze it in heavy duty plastic bags. But you can also used canned plum tomatoes when fresh are not available.

In a saucepan heat the olive oil over medium heat. Sauté the garlic until soft. Add the tomatoes, oregano, and salt. Simmer over low heat for about 15 minutes, until slightly thickened. Remove from the heat and stir in the basil.

For a smoother sauce, puree the tomatoes in a food processor or food mill before adding to the saucepan.

¼ cup olive oil

3 cloves garlic, finely chopped

4 cups (about 8 medium) fresh plum tomatoes, coarsely chopped, or canned plum, usually called San Marzano variety tomatoes

1½ tablespoons chopped fresh oregano or 1 tablespoon dried oregano

2 teaspoons fine sea salt

¼ cup chopped fresh basil

Ciao, Mary Ann,
Do You Have . . . ?

255

Salsa di Pomodori di Antonio Stella
(Anthony Stella's Tomato Sauce)

Makes about 6 cups sauce

1 large onion (8 ounces),
   peeled and cut in half
   through the root end

½ cup extra-virgin olive oil

2 (28-ounce) cans of Hunt's
   whole tomatoes

2 teaspoons brown sugar

1 tablespoon fine sea salt

Chef Anthony Stella surprised me with his method for making tomato sauce. Forget about the traditional fresh garlic and fragrant basil as co-ingredients with juicy plum tomatoes. Instead, onions wrapped in cheesecloth and Hunt's canned whole tomatoes are his choice because he believes that these tomatoes are sweeter and more consistent in flavor than the imported San Marzano types. I was skeptical, but Chef Anthony made a believer out of me when he demonstrated this recipe on our series and confirmed that there is indeed more than one way to make a good tomato sauce. It is important that the sauce cook uncovered, and that the sides of the pot be scraped down frequently; these techniques are the secret to good flavor. This is an all-purpose tomato sauce. Chef Anthony especially loves it on his homemade potato gnocchi (see page 258).

Wrap the onion in cheesecloth and set aside.

Pass the tomatoes through a food mill over a bowl. Discard the seeds.

Heat the olive oil in a saucepan and pour in the tomatoes. Stir to blend the ingredients. Place the onion in the center of the pot. Bring the mixture to a boil, and allow it to simmer, uncovered, for 1½ hours. Several times during the cooking, scrape down the sides of the pot. Stir in the sugar and salt. When it darkens in color and has reduced in volume to become thick, the sauce is ready to use, or to freeze for future use.

*Ciao, Mary Ann,
Do You Have . . . ?*

Pesto di Rucola
(Arugula Pesto Sauce)

Makes 2¼ cups sauce

Instead of tomato sauce for gnocchi, try Chef Anthony Stella's Arugula Pesto. Easy to make in a food processor, this sauce will keep for over a week in the refrigerator or can be frozen. Use a salad spinner to really dry the arugula after it has been cleaned. This will ensure that the leaves will not be too watery when processed.

Put the arugula leaves, garlic, and almonds in the bowl of a food processor fitted with the steel blade. Process until the mixture is coarse. Slowly pour the olive oil through the feed tube with the motor running until a somewhat smooth consistency is obtained. Bits of almonds and flecks of arugula leaves should be visible. Transfer the sauce to a bowl and stir in the lemon juice, salt, pepper, and cheese.

Transfer the mixture to a jar and refrigerate or freeze for future use.

4 tightly packed cups arugula leaves (4 large bunches arugula, stemmed, washed, and dried)

2 large cloves garlic, peeled

¼ cup slivered almonds

½ cup extra-virgin olive oil

Juice of 1 large lemon

½ teaspoon salt

⅛ teaspoon freshly ground black pepper

¼ cup grated Pecorino Romano cheese

Note: I freeze the sauce in ¹/₂-cup portions, in zipper-lock plastic sandwich bags. When I need to defrost some, I place a bag in a small saucepan of boiling water for a few minutes.

Ciao, Mary Ann,
Do You Have . . . ?

Gnocchi di Patate di Antonio Stella
(Anthony Stella's Potato Gnocchi)

Makes 13 dozen

4 pounds (about 5) Idaho baking potatoes

1½ teaspoons salt

9 turns of the pepper mill

½ cup grated Pecorino Romano cheese, plus additional for sprinkling on top, if desired

1 large egg, beaten

2 tablespoons unsalted butter, melted

4 cups (approximately) unbleached all-purpose flour

Chef Anthony Stella says that the secret to making light-tasting potato gnocchi is to refrigerate the potato mixture for several hours before forming them. We made these together for a Ciao Italia segment and when the cameras went down, the crew and I were treated to these with Anthony's Tomato Sauce (page 256). We knew they were good when only silence reigned at the dining room table. Try them and see for yourself.

Preheat the oven to 350°F.

Peel the potatoes and wrap them in aluminum foil. Bake the potatoes for 1½ hours. Transfer the potatoes to a food mill fitted with a large disk and set over a large bowl. Pass the potatoes through the food mill. Or use a potato masher to hand-mash the potatoes. Do not use a food processor as this will break down the potato starch and make the potatoes too glue-like.

Spread the potatoes out on a baking sheet. Cover them with a towel and chill them for several hours in the refrigerator.

Spread the potatoes out onto a lightly floured work surface. Sprinkle the potatoes with the salt, pepper, and grated cheese. Drizzle the potatoes with the egg and butter. Work the ingredients into the potatoes with your hands. Begin adding the flour, a cupful at a time, kneading it into the potatoes with your hands. Continue adding and kneading in enough flour to form a soft but not sticky dough. Adding too much flour will result in heavy-tasting gnocchi.

Divide the dough into eight equal pieces and work with one piece at a time, keeping the rest covered. Roll each piece out into

Ciao, Mary Ann, Do You Have . . . ?

258

an 18×2-inch-thick rope. With a knife cut the rope into ½-inch pieces and transfer them to towel-lined baking sheets.

To serve 4 to 6, bring 4 to 6 quarts of salted water to a boil in a pasta pot. Add 3 dozen gnocchi and boil them. When the gnocchi bob to the surface, scoop them out with a slotted spoon and transfer them to a platter.

Toss the gnocchi with 2 cups of Anthony Stella's Tomato Sauce (page 256) and sprinkle the gnocchi with additional grated Pecorino Romano cheese, if desired.

Serve immediately.

———————————————

Note: Since this makes about 13 dozen gnocchi, freeze what you are not going to use. To do this, and to prevent the gnocchi from sticking together when frozen, arrange them in single layers on a baking sheet. Cover the sheet loosely with aluminum foil and freeze. When the gnocchi are hard, transfer them to heavy-duty plastic bags. They freeze well for up to 6 months. Add them frozen to boiling water when ready to cook.

Zuppa di Polpettine
(Baked Meatball Soup)

Serves 8

⅓ cup milk

½ cup fresh bread crumbs

3 tablespoons grated
  Pecorino cheese

½ teaspoon fine sea salt

Pinch of black pepper

3 tablespoons finely minced
  Italian parsley leaves

⅓ pound each of ground
  sirloin, pork, and veal

1 tablespoon extra-virgin
  olive oil

1 small onion, diced

2 carrots, scraped and cut
  into large dice

2 ribs celery, cut into large
  dice

1 small eggplant, cut into
  large dice

3 potatoes, peeled and cut
  into large dice

5 or 6 whole basil leaves,
  thinly sliced

1 (14½-ounce) can vegetable
  broth

Baked meatball soup has always been a favorite with my children, Beth and Chris, and it is really a meal in a pot. Make it at the first hint of colder weather to come. In one of the early broadcasts of the series I explained that baking the meatballs instead of frying them avoids adding any additional fat. Mixing the meats sparingly will prevent toughening and allow the meatballs to remain tender. A combination of beef, pork, and veal produces great flavor and tender meatballs. Make the soup several days ahead and it will taste even better.

Pour the milk into a bowl and stir in the bread crumbs, grated cheese, salt, pepper, and parsley. With your hands mix in the ground meats until the ingredients are well blended.

Lightly grease a baking sheet and set aside.

Preheat the oven to 350°F.

Wet your hands and make small meatballs about the size of malted milk balls. Place the meatballs on the baking sheet and bake them for about 20 minutes. Remove from the oven and set aside.

While the meatballs are baking, heat the olive oil in a soup pot and sauté the onion, carrots, celery, eggplant, and potatoes together for about 5 minutes, or until the onions have softened. Stir in the basil, vegetable broth, tomatoes, water, salt, pepper, and optional cheese rind. Cover the pot and cook over low heat for 30 minutes. Add the meatballs to the soup 10 minutes before the soup is finished cooking.

In a separate pot boil 3 cups of water and add an additional

½ teaspoon salt and the orzo, and cook until the pasta is al dente. Drain and stir the pasta into the soup.

Adjust the seasoning if desired, remove the cheese rind, and serve immediately.

Tip: Cheese rinds add great flavor to soups, so save those Parmesan and Pecorino rinds in a plastic bag and toss them into the soup pot. Discard the rinds before serving the soup.

1 (14-ounce) can whole tomatoes

3 cups water

Salt and pepper to taste

3-inch-piece cheese rind (optional)

½ cup orzo or other small soup pasta

Did you know that Italian parsley freezes beautifully and will retain its flavor and vibrant green color? Wash and dry the leaves, remove the stems and discard them. With a knife finely mince the leaves. Spoon a quarter of a cup of the parsley onto a sheet of paper toweling. Wrap the parsley tightly in a bundle in the towel and place it in zipper-lock plastic sandwich bags. Freeze several packets in a bag and, when needed, simply take what you need from the bag. You do not need to defrost it— just crumble and use as is.

Ciao, Mary Ann, Do You Have . . . ?

Zuppa di Manzo e Verdure con Polenta
(Beef Vegetable Soup with Polenta)

Makes 3 quarts

FOR THE POLENTA

1 cup stone-ground
   cornmeal

3 cups cold water

FOR THE SOUP

1 tablespoon extra-virgin
   olive oil

1¾ pounds meaty beef shin,
   center cut with bone,
   trimmed of any fat

1 medium yellow onion,
   peeled and quartered

2 cups diced fresh plum
   tomatoes

2 stalks celery, washed and
   quartered

2 large carrots, scraped and
   quartered

2½ tablespoons fine sea salt

Grinding of coarse black
   pepper

12 whole cloves tied in a
   small piece of cheesecloth

1 large bay leaf

*Ciao, Mary Ann,
Do You Have . . . ?*

262

How do you make a good beef vegetable soup? Use meaty bones such as neck bones, steak bones, or shin bones; they lend great flavor to the broth. I like to use center-cut beef shin bone for this homey soup. And I follow the same traditions handed down at home, with one exception: I like to add slices of cooked polenta just before serving. Make the soup a day ahead and refrigerate it. This makes it easy to remove the fat that has collected and congealed on the surface of the soup.

To make the polenta, pour the cornmeal into a 1½-quart saucepan and stir in the water with a wooden spoon. Cook, stirring, over medium heat until the cornmeal starts to thicken and leave the sides of the pan. Cook for about 15 minutes, always stirring in one direction to keep the mixture smooth.

Pour the polenta out onto a cutting board, spread it evenly, and let cool. Cut the polenta into 8 pieces, cover with a piece of wax paper, set aside, and keep warm.

In a large soup pot, heat the olive oil and brown the beef shin slowly on all sides. Add the onion, tomatoes, celery, carrots, salt, pepper, cloves, bay leaf, oregano, basil, and the water. Stir the ingredients with a wooden spoon and bring to a boil. Lower the heat and simmer the soup, covered, for 1½ to 1¾ hours, or until the beef shin is tender when pierced with a knife.

With a slotted spoon remove the beef, bones, carrots, and celery and place on a cutting board. Remove the cloves and discard. Pour the remaining liquid and ingredients through a fine-mesh strainer over a large bowl. Press on the solids to extract the juices, then discard the solids. Pour the liquid into a large bowl and set aside.

Trim the meat from the bones and shred it into small pieces. Add the meat to the liquid in the bowl. Cut the carrots and celery into thin slices and add them to the bowl. Cover the bowl tightly with plastic wrap and refrigerate overnight.

When ready to use, remove the plastic wrap; scoop off the fat that has congealed at the top of the bowl and discard it. Pour the soup back into a soup pot and heat on low until hot.

Place a slice of polenta in each individual soup bowl. Ladle the soup over the polenta and serve immediately.

Refrigerate the remaining soup for up to 5 days or freeze for up to 3 months.

1 teaspoon dried oregano

1 large bunch basil

10 cups hot water

Tip: You can make the polenta ahead of time. Cool, cover, and refrigerate it. When needed, cut it into pieces and place on a lightly greased baking sheet. Heat for 5 to 7 minutes or until hot in a preheated 350°F oven.

Ciao, Mary Ann,
Do You Have . . . ?

Zuppa di Minestrone
(Minestrone Soup)

Makes about 3 quarts

2 tablespoons olive oil

1 medium onion, diced

¼ pound pancetta (or bacon), diced

10 whole black peppercorns

1 large sprig rosemary

2 (28-ounce) cans whole peeled plum tomatoes, coarsely chopped

2 cups water

1 (3-inch) piece cheese rind (optional)

1 bay leaf

½ cup diced eggplant

1 cup sliced carrots

1 (19-ounce) can chickpeas, drained and rinsed

¾ cup ditalini, tubetti, or other small soup pasta, cooked, drained and set aside

1 cup cooked green beans or peas

1 cup cooked chopped broccoli

½ cup chopped fresh basil leaves

Salt to taste

*Ciao, Mary Ann,
Do You Have . . . ?*

264

"Do you have a good recipe for minestrone soup?" This is what a large segment of our television family wants to know. Over the years I have scoured many sources regarding the meaning of the word minestrone *and I always come up with the same definition—a big soup with lots of vegetables swimming in a savory broth. I suspect, from watching this soup being constructed at home, that its bigness came from whatever was on hand at the time, and needed to be used up. Minestrone is a soup of creativity, necessity, or what I call the original "kitchen sink" soup. It is found all over Italy made with a variety of ingredients. A good example is the region of Liguria, where cooks stir in spoonfuls of pesto sauce made from the fragrant small-leafed basil that defines much of their cooking. One thing is for certain: vegetables, dried beans, and pasta will find their way into the minestrone soup pot. Don't be timid. Add those leftover vegetables, snippets of herbs, and bits of cheeses from your refrigerator. Minestrone is tolerant of whatever inspires you to add to it, becoming a meal in itself. Serve it with good crusty bread and a green salad.*

Heat the olive oil in a soup pot, stir in the onions, pancetta, peppercorns, and rosemary and cook slowly until the onions are soft and the pancetta begins to brown. Stir in the tomatoes and water and continue to cook over low heat, uncovered, for 3 or 4 minutes. Stir in the cheese rind, bay leaf, eggplant, carrots, and chickpeas. Cover the pot and simmer the ingredients for 40 minutes. Uncover the pot, stir in the pasta, green beans, and broccoli and cook for 5 minutes longer. Stir in the basil and cook for an additional 5 minutes. Season with salt to taste. Fish out and discard the bay leaf, rosemary, and the cheese rind.

Serve piping hot.

Tips: Raw pasta can be added to the soup if a thicker soup is preferred since the pasta will absorb the liquid, but cooking it separately and adding it later allows for a thick but not chunky consistency.

After pouring out the canned tomatoes, pour the water called for in the recipe into the can and swirl it around to get the remaining tomato juices from the can.

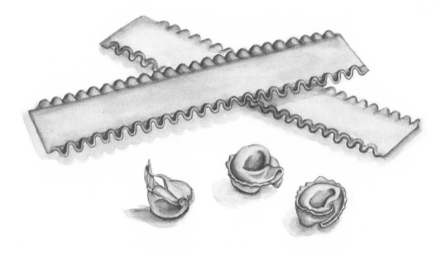

A Typical Day "Nella Cucina"

The alarm clock rouses me at 6 A.M. All night long I have been dreaming about Italian food and now it is time to get ready to go to my television studio kitchen to tape the day's segments, which will become three separate cooking shows. I load up the back of my car with three changes of clothes, all the special cooking equipment that I will need from my home kitchen, as well as just-harvested herbs and vegetables from my garden, and tell myself that it is going to be a long day.

Crew call is at 8 A.M., but the kitchen staff always arrives earlier to begin the day's preparation for the three shows. There are three teams of kitchen workers, and each team is directed by a culinary supervisor. Each team is responsible for one show and that means that for each show there will be backups of ingredients just in case something goes wrong during the taping. And there will be multiples of the finished dishes . . . the ones that magically appear from the oven when you need to show the audience a cooked or baked item that takes longer to prepare than the 26 minutes of real time necessary for the taping.

I greet the kitchen staff and volunteers for the day and we go over the recipes and ingredient trays that will be prepared. There is always a lot of concern and fussing over some foods, like the herbs that go limp under the studio lights, or we worry about whether we have enough of a particular ingredient, or in the case of yeast or pastry dough, whether the doughs will be risen at just the right time or cold enough for me to roll them out at the moment of taping. And someone is always walking around with a mister to spray the plants that we use on the set to make sure that they look as fresh as daisies.

After reviewing the recipes with the staff I head to the makeup area. I have always dreaded makeup, but it is a necessary evil of television, so I submit my face to layers of foundation, blush, mascara, eyeliner, eye shadow, and powder. My eyelashes are so heavy with mascara and my eyes so defined with liner that it makes me look like I have Cleopatra eyes, but I am reassured that this is all going to look just fine on camera. When the makeup session is finished, I head for my spot behind my kitchen counter so that the makeup can be checked on camera. Then I am wired with my microphone and I get a voice level check.

Meanwhile everyone is doing a specific job. The culinary supervisors are chopping, kneading, and sautéing. It is beginning to smell like home cooking in the studio. The dishwasher already has a stack of pots and pans to shine for the show. The set decorator has changed the items in the corner cupboards to reflect the show theme. The herbs we are using in the recipes appear in beautiful pots on my kitchen counter. The stove top is cleaned and shined and the food stylist goes over the presentation dishes and coordinating linens and napkins that will be used in each segment.

Now Kevin Carlson, the director, Paul Lally, the executive producer, and Sally Northrop, the producer, come in for what is referred to as a "walk and talk," where I discuss my actions and where I will be moving to and from on the set so the cameras can follow me. At the suggestion of the director, I walk from the counter to the refrigerator and back, then I am asked to do it again but this time at a slower pace so the cameras can practice a smooth move. We practice a couple of times until the cameraman and I are comfortable with it. Next we discuss the positioning of ingredients and I am reminded to hold the food long enough in my hand for the camera to get a good shot, or I am told to point to the ingredient that I am discussing on the countertop. We make sure that no food labels or the underwriter's label or product name is showing or prominently featured because PBS rules do not allow for such display.

Ciao, Mary Ann,
Do You Have . . . ?

Before the taping begins I ask to see the playback of the introduction that I did for this particular segment. Since the introductory parts of each program (the remotes) are shot weeks before the studio segments, I have to refresh my memory about the content of the piece, what I said and did, and whom I interacted with in the case of a guest appearing on air with me, because I always like to incorporate the information and refer back to the remote in the studio segment.

Now we are ready to do the first show, just one more check of the lighting and a check by the culinary supervisor to see that I have all ingredients and equipment in place. Then I hear Paul Lally say, "Okay, hon, chip a dish." Everything grows quiet and I am alone with my thoughts for a few seconds. Then I see the camera coming toward me and you and I are cooking *nella cucina*.

Everything talked about in the program is done extemporaneously; there is no monitor or script. To be truthful, I could not cook and read off a monitor at the same time. I have to instinctively know what I want to say. I attribute this to my longtime experiences in Italy and years of cooking, so talking and cooking without the benefit of cue cards or scripts is much more natural for me.

I have found, from letters and e-mails and comments from viewers, that talking about the "good old days" and retelling family food experiences strikes a chord with a lot of people. So many people have said that my cooking reminds them of how things were done at home; for many viewers the emotional tie is more important than the entertainment itself.

As I take you through the recipe steps and techniques, a lot of information is going through my mind. Besides the camera in front of me, there is the floor director, squatting out of camera sight and holding time cards with big black numbers that let me know how much time I have left in the program. This always makes me feel like I am in a horse race because there is so much cooking to cover in 26 minutes or so, and the key is not to rush the process, but to strive for an even conversational flow to the segment as if just you and I are cooking together.

It has always been my practice to prepare two or three recipes in each show. This is considered ambitious and I have been told by my producers that maybe I do too much, that maybe I should eliminate some of the recipes. But it is hard to break old habits, especially when it has always been my style at home to be able to cook several things at one time, and I feel the same about my television kitchen. But at home there are no cue cards with time limits, so to cook several dishes is not a problem. On television this creates a huge sequential situation, in which I begin one recipe, and if the ingredients need time to boil, sauté, wilt down, etc., I move to the next recipe, get it started, and then shuffle between the recipes so the viewers have the concept of real time passing. I credit Paul Lally for being able to design these sequential scenes so they make sense to the viewers and allow me the freedom to cook as I do at home.

One question I always get is about bloopers or mistakes in the show tapings. Occasionally we have them. One episode that comes to mind is the show that highlighted how to make a *sformato di spinaci,* a molded spinach dish. This required about four pounds of fresh spinach leaves. As we prepared for the taping, I went over the list of ingredients and cooking equipment that I needed on the set. Everything seemed to be in readiness and we began the taping. No sooner had I cooked the spinach then I heard "tape stop" from the floor director. There was a camera move problem. That fixed, I was asked to start from the beginning. And that was fine until I realized as I was reintroducing the segment that I did not see another huge display of fresh washed spinach on my counter. So I needed to give a signal of some sort to the culinary supervisor so that we would not have to stop the tape again. I started talking about the merits of using fresh spinach as I got other things ready for the recipe, hoping that one of them would realize what I needed. Suddenly I saw one of the culinary

Ciao, Mary Ann,
Do You Have . . . ?

supervisors crawling on the floor on her hands and knees with the colander of spinach, and out of camera range she placed it on the counter where it should have been in the first place. Without missing a beat, I reached for it without the viewer ever knowing that there was a slight problem.

Sometimes the completed program ends up being too short or too long, with an average of 30 seconds to 2 minutes of time to fill. Too long is an easier problem to fix because we can edit out portions, but too short means that you have to get creative and be able to think on the spot. A good example was a shellfish show that I had just completed in which we had showcased mussels. At the conclusion of the taping, the producer, who always walks around with a stopwatch, came in from the control room to tell me that I was a minute or so short and was there anything else I could do. I decided to make a marinated mussel salad and called for the kitchen staff to get me lemon juice, wine vinegar, parsley, garlic, celery, salt, pepper, and some beautiful-looking sweet red peppers. I put this all together and created a mussel salad that filled the remaining time.

The final wrap-up of the program is called the present. The food stylist comes in and creates the beauty shots of the prepared dishes. A lot of thought goes into what color of platter, bowl, or dish will best show off the food; after all, we want to "sell the food" to the viewer. With the right colored tableware, place mats, or tablecloths the food is arrayed and camera-ready. My last action is to recap for the viewer everything we cooked that day and then say good-bye. This can range from 50 seconds to a minute of air time. We practice the ending for time, then we tape it and the lights go down. Everything is cleared away and we begin preparations for the second show immediately. We will repeat the sequence of events two more times before day's end.

By the time we are all ready to go home for the day we will have cooked an average of nine dishes for the show with multiple backups.

The next day we will do it again and continue until we have a full series of shows.

The hardest thing for me to do when I get home from the studio is to face a chorus of voices asking "What's for supper?"

The recipes in this chapter are ones that are asked for over and over again, so I have put them all in one chapter to make it easier to locate them.

Ciao, Mary Ann,
Do You Have . . . ?

Ossobuco con Pomodori e Vino Rosso
(Veal Shank with Tomatoes and Red Wine)

Serves 4

¼ teaspoon white pepper

½ teaspoon fine sea salt

2 pounds veal shank

1 teaspoon extra-virgin olive oil

1 medium yellow onion, peeled and quartered

1 bay leaf

1 cup prepared tomato sauce (see page 256)

½ cup dry red wine

On page 28 you will find a recipe for Ossobuco *as prepared in Vicenza at Ristorante Tre Visi, which utilizes the base flavorings known as* i quattro evangelisti. *Here is a less fussy recipe in which the flavoring ingredients have been streamlined and a prepared tomato sauce is used in place of whole plum tomatoes. This dish can be assembled in 15 minutes and left to cook for a couple of hours in a low-temperature oven. The meat will be so tender that it will just fall off the bone. Keep in mind that the key to flavor and tenderness is slow cooking. Begin the process by browning the veal in an ovenproof sauté pan. This is really a critical step for sealing in the juices and browning the meat evenly. Dry the meat well on both sides with paper towels and put the pieces into a sizzling-hot pan. The pan should be large enough to hold the pieces in a single layer so that everything browns uniformly, and the pan should be of a heavy weight to hold the heat. Make sure the pieces of meat are about the same size as well.*

Preheat the oven to 225°F.

On a plate mix the pepper and salt together. Dry the veal with paper towels, then rub both sides of each piece with the pepper and salt. Set aside.

Heat an ovenproof 12-inch sauté pan over high heat for 2 minutes. Lower the heat to medium-high and pour in the olive oil and swirl it around the pan. Add the veal pieces and brown them on both sides. Tuck the onion quarters in between the veal. Add the bay leaf and turn off the heat.

In a small bowl mix the tomato sauce and red wine together.

Ciao, Mary Ann, Do You Have . . . ?

Pour the mixture evenly over the veal. Cover the pan with a tight-fitting lid and bake for 1¾ to 2 hours, or until the veal is tender enough to fall away from the bone.

Serve immediately with some of the pan juices poured over the top.

Orecchiette in Salsa di Pomodori con Agnello
(Lamb Shanks in Tomato Sauce with Orecchiette)

Serves 4

SAUCE

6 cups canned plum tomatoes (2 28-ounce cans)

½ cup extra-virgin olive oil

1 to 1¼ pounds (about 4) meaty lamb shanks

4 cloves garlic, peeled and cut in half

1 large onion, peeled and chopped

¾ cup dry red wine

¾ cup tomato paste

1 teaspoon fine sea salt

Dried red pepper flakes to taste

5 large fresh basil leaves

1 pound orecchiette, store-bought or homemade

1 tablespoon salt

2 tablespoons reserved pasta cooking water

Grated Pecorino cheese for sprinkling

Ciao, Mary Ann, Do You Have . . . ?

274

A few years ago I spent some time in Puglia, the region at the heel of Italy's boot, and it was there that I met the well-known and well-loved New York cooking teacher Anna Amendolara Nurse. Anna's family came from Bari, so the trip to Puglia put together by Oldways Preservation Trust and the International Olive Oil Council was a special one for her. Anna not only knew Pugliese specialties and the culture surrounding them, she was also very active serving on the board of the James Beard Foundation. As we traveled around Puglia I asked Anna about her favorite Pugliese foods. Orecchiette, a dried pasta made from water and semolina flour and shaped by hand into something resembling little ears, was at the top of her list. The indentations were meant to trap a hearty tomato sauce in which lamb shanks were cooked. Anna uses the sauce to serve orecchiette as a first course, then offers the lamb shanks as a secondo, *or second course. I loved the dish so much that I asked Anna to demonstrate how to make it on one of the episodes of* Ciao Italia. *Here is her beloved and much-requested recipe.*

Puree the tomatoes with their juice in a food processor, blender, or food mill. Transfer the tomatoes to a pot large enough to hold the lamb shanks. Bring the tomatoes to a boil, reduce the heat to simmer, and allow the tomatoes to cook while preparing the lamb shanks.

Heat the olive oil in a sauté pan large enough to hold the lamb shanks. When the oil is hot, add the shanks and brown them evenly on all sides. Transfer the lamb shanks to the pot with the tomatoes. Discard all but ⅓ cup of the oil remaining in the sauté pan.

Add the garlic to the sauté pan and cook over medium-low heat until the garlic is golden brown. With a slotted spoon, remove the garlic and add it to the pot with the tomatoes and lamb shanks. Add the onion to the oil and cook over medium-low heat until the onions are soft, about 15 minutes. Increase the heat to medium, pour in the wine, and allow it to evaporate, about 3 minutes. Stir in the tomato paste with a wooden spoon and scrape up any bits of meat that are stuck to the bottom of the pan.

Add the onion mixture to the tomatoes and lamb; stir in the salt and red pepper flakes; cover the pot and allow the ingredients to simmer gently. Stir occasionally. When the meat is fork-tender but not falling from the bones, remove it to a dish, cover, and keep warm. Stir the basil into the tomato sauce.

Cook the orecchiette in 4 to 6 quarts of rapidly boiling water to which 1 tablespoon of salt has been added. Orecchiette take a little longer to cook than other types of dried pasta because of their concave shape. They are cooked when there is no trace of white flour remaining when cut into; the orecchiette should retain their shape and be al dente, firm but cooked.

Drain the orecchiette, reserving 2 tablespoons of the cooking water. Transfer the orecchiette to a serving dish. Mix 2 cups of the tomato sauce with the 2 tablespoons of water and pour it over the orecchiette. Mix well. Serve the pasta immediately as a first course with a sprinkling of grated Pecorino cheese.

Serve the lamb shanks as a second course.

Ciao, Mary Ann,
Do You Have . . . ?

Fusilli con Salsa di Porri
(Twisted Pasta with Leek Sauce)

Serves 4 to 6

2 pounds leeks, well washed
and trimmed of the dark
green stem

¼ cup extra-virgin olive oil

2 tablespoons unsalted
butter

2 cloves garlic, cut into thin
slivers

½ cup dry vermouth

½ cup chicken broth

1½ to 2 teaspoons fine sea
salt

Grinding of coarse black
pepper

1 pound fusilli

Water for cooking the pasta,
reserving ¼ cup of the
cooking water for the
sauce

1 tablespoon salt

Over the years I have had the privilege of cooking with some very talented chefs and amateur cooks and have invited many of them to appear in my television studio kitchen. One of the most frequent visitors has been the well-known children's illustrator and author Tomie de Paola, whose family is from Calabria. Tomie brings not only a knowledge of Calabrian cooking to my kitchen, he also brings an earthy joy and an adventuresome attitude to preparing good food. In one episode showcasing pasta, we filmed in Tomie's well-appointed kitchen, where he made fusilli with an outstanding creamy leek sauce. The secret is to slow-cook the leeks until they become very liquid and creamy. When I asked Tomie where this recipe came from, he was quick to say that one night when some friends unexpectedly were in town, he invited them to dinner before looking in the refrigerator. Only a handful of leeks graced the shelf, so in a pinch this recipe was created.

Cut the leeks into thin rings. You should have about 4 cups. Set aside.

In a large sauté pan (12×3 inches), heat the olive oil and the butter and stir to blend the two. Stir in the leeks and cook over low heat, stirring occasionally, until the leeks begin to soften. Stir in the garlic, and cook for 2 minutes, pressing on the garlic slivers. Raise the heat to high and stir in the vermouth. Cook over high heat for 2 minutes. Lower the heat and stir in the chicken broth, salt, and pepper. Simmer the sauce for 20 to 30 minutes, or until the leeks have become very creamy. Cover the pan, set aside, and keep warm while the fusilli are cooking.

*Ciao, Mary Ann,
Do You Have . . . ?*

Cook the fusilli in 4 to 6 quarts of rapidly boiling water to which 1 tablespoon of salt has been added. Do not overcook the fusilli; they should retain their shape, and be cooked through, but not mushy. One way to test for doneness is to break a piece of pasta in half and if any trace of flour is evident, the pasta is not cooked.

Drain the fusilli, reserving ¼ cup of the cooking water. Transfer fusilli to the sauté pan with the leek sauce. Stir in the water and mix the fusilli and sauce over medium heat until well blended.

Transfer the fusilli and leek sauce to a shallow platter and serve immediately.

Ciao, Mary Ann,
Do You Have . . . ?

Salsiccia con Penne e Salsa di Pomodori
(Sausage with Penne and Tomato Sauce)

Serves 4

1 pound homemade sausages
or store-bought Italian
sausage

½ cup water

1 large onion, thinly sliced

1 pound penne or other
short-cut pasta

3½ cups prepared tomato
sauce (see page 256)

½ pound mozzarella cheese,
cubed

I learned how to make Italian sausage from my parents, and out of the seven siblings only my brother Robert and I continue this tradition. His sausage is very lean and his spicing is just right. Many people think that they need an expensive meat grinder to make pork sausage. Nothing could be further from the truth. All you need is a sausage funnel and natural hog casings. It actually takes longer to make the sausage in a grinder than by hand, and there is the mess to consider afterward. To make this really simple, ask your butcher to grind a pork butt once on coarse and once on fine grind. Then take it home and follow the instructions in my first book, Ciao Italia, *for Salsiccia Fresca. Whether you use homemade or store-bought sausage, this casserole makes a satisfying winter meal.*

Put the sausage in a sauté pan, add the water, and simmer uncovered until the sausage turns gray. Discard the water and continue cooking the sausage until it begins to brown. Add the onions and continue to cook, stirring occasionally, until the sausage has browned on all sides and the onions are wilted. Transfer the onions to a bowl. Set aside.

Remove the sausage to a cutting board and allow it to cool for 5 minutes. Cut the sausage in ¼-inch rounds and add the sausage to the bowl with the onions. Set aside.

Cook the penne in a pasta pot in 4 to 6 quarts of boiling water with 1 tablespoon of salt until it is al dente. Drain the penne and transfer it to the bowl with the sausage. Mix in 3 cups of the sauce and half of the mozzarella.

Preheat the oven to 350°F.

*Ciao, Mary Ann,
Do You Have . . . ?*

278

Transfer the mixture to a 9×13½-inch baking dish. Pour the remaining sauce over the top and sprinkle with the remaining cheese.

Cover the dish with aluminum foil and bake in the oven until bubbly. Serve immediately.

Ciao, Mary Ann,
Do You Have . . . ?

Timballo alla Teramamo

(Crêpes with Spinach and Veal Teramamo Style)

Serves 8 to 10

FOR THE CRÊPES

Butter, to grease pan

Bread crumbs, to coat pan

3 eggs

¾ cup plus 2 tablespoons milk

¾ cup plus 2 tablespoons seltzer water

1 teaspoon salt

1 cup unbleached all-purpose flour

2 ounces (½ stick) unsalted butter, melted

FOR THE SPINACH

1 onion, peeled and minced

¼ cup extra-virgin olive oil

1½ pounds chopped fresh spinach leaves

½ teaspoon ground nutmeg

¼ teaspoon salt

¼ teaspoon ground black pepper

For the tenth season of Ciao Italia *I decided to visit Italian American neighborhoods across the United States to get an idea of what kinds of Italian comfort foods were still being made at home, since I was getting a lot of viewer requests for them. I was fortunate to meet Chef Anthony Stella, who lives in Wilmington, Delaware, and owns a restaurant called Osteria. Anthony's family is from the Abruzzi region and he still makes gnocchi and Timballo alla Teramamo the way it has been done in that region for decades. This recipe was taught to him by his cousin's wife, Rosalba, who is from Teramo, a large city in the Abruzzi. This timballo sounds like a lot of work to put together, but it can be assembled in stages. A timballo is a molded and baked pasta dish, and variations have been prepared many times on my series. Anthony's timballo is a little different; instead of pasta, crespelle, or crêpes, are layered into the mold. The crêpes can be made ahead and refrigerated for several days or frozen for a month if they are well wrapped. The sauce used in this recipe also appears on page 256.*

Generously grease a 12×10-inch baking dish with butter and sprinkle with bread crumbs. Refrigerate until ready to use.

To prepare the crêpes, in blender or bowl combine the eggs, milk, seltzer, salt, and flour. Cover and allow the batter to rest for 1 hour or refrigerated overnight. When ready to use, bring to room temperature and whisk in the butter.

Spray a 7-inch nonstick fry pan with vegetable spray. Heat the fry pan and pour about ¼ cup of the batter into the pan. Swirl the pan to coat the bottom and cook the crêpe until the edges begin to

Ciao, Mary Ann, Do You Have . . . ?

280

brown and the crêpe is firm to the touch. Invert the pan to remove the crêpes as you make them and allow them to cool on a rack lined with a kitchen towel. Continue making crêpes until all the batter has been used. There should be about 20 crêpes.

To prepare the spinach, in a sauté pan cook the onions in the olive oil until soft. Add the spinach, nutmeg, salt, and pepper and cook until most of the liquid has evaporated. Transfer the spinach to a bowl and let it cool.

Preheat the oven to 350°F.

To prepare the veal, in a bowl mix the meat with the salt, garlic, parsley, the grated Pecorino cheese, eggs, and bread crumbs and spread the mixture out onto a cookie sheet. Bake the veal in the oven for 30 minutes. Cool the meat and cut it into cubes. Set aside.

To prepare the sauce, pass the tomatoes through the fine screen of a food mill or through a sieve. Heat the olive oil in a sauté pan, add the onion halves and tomatoes, and bring the mixture to a rapid boil. Lower the heat and simmer the ingredients until thickened. Season the sauce with the sugar, pepper, and salt. Keep the sauce warm.

To prepare the zucchini, salt them and stand them up in a bowl for 1 hour to extract the excess water. Rinse and dry the zucchini. In a bowl combine the eggs, salt, and flour. Dip the slices in the egg mixture, then in bread crumbs. Fry the zucchini in batches in hot peanut oil (375°F). Drain on paper towels and cut the slices into 1-inch cubes. Set aside.

Combine the eggs and cream before you begin the assembly.

Begin to fill the baking dish by covering the bottom of the dish with a layer of 4 crêpes, overlapping them as you go. Spread a thin layer of spinach over the crêpes, followed by a layer of the veal cubes, zucchini, ¼ cup of the grated Pecorino cheese, ¼ of the mozzarella, and ¼ of the egg and cream mixture. Repeat until you have 4 layers of filling and 5 layers of crêpes. Be sure to press down

FOR THE VEAL

2 pounds ground veal

1 teaspoon salt

1 teaspoon minced garlic

3 tablespoons chopped fresh Italian parsley leaves

¼ cup grated Pecorino cheese

2 large eggs, beaten

1 cup bread crumbs

FOR THE SAUCE

2 (28-ounce) cans whole plum tomatoes

½ cup extra-virgin olive oil

1 onion, peeled and cut in half

1 teaspoon brown sugar

1 teaspoon freshly ground black pepper

1 teaspoon kosher salt

FOR THE ZUCCHINI

5 large zucchini, trimmed and cut lengthwise into ¼-inch slices

3 large eggs, beaten

1 teaspoon salt

1 cup unbleached all-purpose flour

1 cup bread crumbs

Peanut oil for deep frying

Ciao, Mary Ann, Do You Have . . . ?

6 eggs, slightly beaten

½ cup heavy cream

1 cup grated Pecorino
cheese

4 ounces fresh mozzarella
balls, cut into ½-inch
cubes

each layer with your hands before adding the next one. Cover the top of the crêpes with tomato sauce. Reserve the remaining sauce to pass at the table.

Bake the *timballo* for 1 hour. Allow it to cool for 15 minutes before cutting. Serve the *timballo* as is or pass additional tomato sauce.

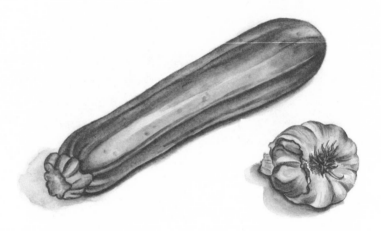

Spezzatelle
(Dandelion Soufflé)

Serves 4 to 6

Passing along the traditions of Italian food to the next generation is very important to me and has been a distinguishing characteristic of Ciao Italia. *It is one of the reasons that I am sharing this little-known recipe for* spezzatelle, *a traditional wild dandelion dish from Foggia, in the region of Puglia, the heel of Italy's boot. Resembling a soufflé after it is baked, spezzatelle shows the French influence in Foggia. The recipe was demonstrated for me by Grace Gallucci, an inspiring cook from Cleveland, Ohio, who learned how to make it from her mother, Giovanina. One of the peculiarities of this dish is the addition of garlic powder and dried onion powder, which, as Grace explains, are used so as not to overpower the taste of spezzatelle or be seen in the dish. This came as a complete surprise to me since the region of Puglia is noted for cooking with* lampasciuoli, *a special type of wild onion. Spring, when wild dandelions are plentiful, is the ideal time to make spezzatelle, but they are also available most of the year in supermarkets.*

2½ pounds (one large bunch) dandelions, stemmed

1 cup reserved dandelion cooking water

3 tablespoons extra-virgin olive oil

¾ pound cubed lamb

1 teaspoon dried onion powder

½ teaspoon dried garlic powder

1 tomato, seeded and chopped

2 tablespoons minced parsley leaves

1 tablespoon minced fresh rosemary

4 large eggs

½ cup crumbled goat cheese

1 cup grated Parmigiano-Reggiano cheese

½ cup shredded mozzarella cheese

1 cup reserved dandelion water, kept hot

Fill a large pot with water and bring it to a boil.

Meanwhile clean the dandelions thoroughly by soaking them in several changes of cold water. Drain them and add them to the pot of boiling water. Cook the dandelions, uncovered, for about 5 minutes. Drain them and set them aside. Reserve 1 cup of the dandelion water and keep it hot.

In an ovenproof 3½-quart saucepan, heat the olive oil and brown the meat. Sprinkle the meat with the onion and garlic powders. Add the tomato, parsley, and rosemary and cook for another 2 minutes. Stir in the dandelions and turn off the heat.

Preheat the oven to 400°F.

Ciao, Mary Ann,
Do You Have . . . ?

In a bowl whisk the eggs together, then whisk in the cheeses, one at a time, until the mixture is well blended and very thick.

Pour the egg and cheese mixture evenly over the top of the meat and dandelions. Bake, uncovered, for 50 minutes, or until the top is nicely browned and puffed.

Remove the spezzatelle from the oven; it will collapse somewhat. With a knife cut it into 4 to 6 wedges. Use a large spoon to lift the wedges out of the pan and serve them in soup bowls. Pour a little of the reserved dandelion broth over the top of each wedge and serve immediately.

Did you know that you can leach out the bitterness of dandelions and other bitter greens by plunging them in ice water after they have been cooked and allowing them to soak for 30 minutes before continuing with the recipe?

One of the great pleasures of being the host of *Ciao Italia* is that I get to meet many fans at cooking events and book signings. Seeing them reaffirms for me that the camera lens is a powerful vehicle that can reach out and intimately touch the human spirit.

In the early production years of *Ciao Italia,* visitors were allowed on the set while we were taping. One day as I was getting ready to do a show, a young couple came in with their son, Nathaniel; he must have been all of seven or eight and had a mop of thick, brown curly hair. His parents began to tell me that he was my biggest fan and that he never missed a show on Saturday, much preferring it to Saturday morning cartoons or any other children's program! I noticed that Nathaniel had a clipboard tucked under his arm to take notes, and he walked around the studio observing everything! He opened and closed refrigerator and oven doors, asked the kitchen staff about the foods that they were prepping, and asked the camera crew how the cameras worked. What really surprised me was how much he could tell me about past shows that I had done, naming the recipes, repeating phrases that I used frequently, even mentioning the names of guests that had appeared with me! He was so acutely aware of everything, so confident and outgoing, that in that moment I felt that he could host the show!

Some of the stories that I have heard from fans at book signings have made me teary-eyed and some have made me laugh. Two Catholic priests, making their way to the table where I was signing copies of my books, leaned over the table and whispered to me that they no longer heard confession for the congregation on Saturday afternoon because they all had to stay home to watch *Ciao Italia* and then decide what to have for dinner! An elderly woman proudly showed me a photo of her poodle sitting in front of her television set watching *Ciao Italia* while commenting, "This dog does not move until your show is over."

And so many husbands complain to me that their wives have forbidden them to change the channel to watch sports events until *Ciao Italia* is over. Even my own husband has not escaped! While making rounds in the hospital one morning, he stopped to see a patient who was engaged in watching *Ciao Italia* and was promptly told to come back later because nothing could interfere with this patient's program! Of course the patient had no idea that her doctor was my husband! On the way to the rest room at a national Home Show, a young gentleman talking on a nearby pay phone started waving to me. In an instant he put down the phone, ran up to me, and said, "You're Mary Ann, right?" Affirming this, he grabbed my arm, led me to the dangling phone, which he picked up, and said, "Honey, I've got Mary Ann Esposito here and she is going to say hi!" His wife and I had a nice conversation and I never got to the rest room before my next appearance.

And there are the more poignant stories as well; a young AIDS patient who was severely depressed after his diagnosis told me that he started watching *Ciao Italia* and started cooking again, which made him feel good about himself; a stroke victim in a wheelchair tried desperately to get the words out to talk to me while tightly holding my hands, and I could sense the effort and determination with which he wanted to say something. It is moments like these that make me realize all that I take for granted. And I cannot count the number of times that people who have lost their parents have said to me that they find joy in watching *Ciao Italia* because it reminds them so much of how their parents cooked and how much of their childhood they could relive through the program. I could write a book just on the personal encounters that I have had, and I have been humbled by many of them.

Paul Lally, the executive producer, was right when he said that *Ciao Italia* was more than a cooking show, and I began to realize it too; *Ciao Italia* is a connection for people, and if it had no other merit, making that connection was all that mattered.

Vitellone al Forno
(Oven-Cooked Veal)

Serves 4

2 tablespoons extra-virgin olive oil

2 tablespoons butter

1 medium red sweet onion, peeled and thinly sliced

1 medium leek, tops removed, washed and thinly sliced

¼ cup balsamic vinegar

½ pound button mushrooms, wiped clean and thinly sliced

2½ pounds veal shoulder chops, wiped dry

5 carrots, scraped and cut into 1-inch pieces

½ teaspoon fine sea salt

Grinding of coarse black pepper

1 cup dry white wine

1 tablespoon finely minced fresh rosemary

The first time I prepared veal on my series I actually got some negative mail from a few viewers, who felt that due to their beliefs about the way that calves are raised, I should not have done the show. Still, many other viewers wanted to know how to cook less expensive cuts of veal. Since Ciao Italia *is about the regional cooking of Italy, I felt that I could not leave out segments that dealt with veal, but it was a long time before I once again decided to cook it on the air, selecting ossobuco (see pages 28 and 272) as the showpiece. Another dish I like to prepare is veal shoulder (the blade cut), which is quite inexpensive, very tasty, and tender if cooked on low heat in the oven. Make this dish ahead; it is even better the next day. It is best to cook this in a 12-inch ovenproof sauté pan, as the procedure begins at the stove top and ends in the oven.*

Heat 1 tablespoon of the olive oil and 1 tablespoon of the butter in an ovenproof sauté pan. Stir in the onions and leeks and cook the mixture over medium heat until the onions and leeks are wilted. Raise the heat to high, stir in the balsamic vinegar, and cook, stirring occasionally, until the vinegar evaporates. Remove the onions and leeks to a dish and set aside.

Add the remaining olive oil and butter to the pan, stir in the mushrooms, and cook them until all their liquid has been given off. Remove the mushrooms to the dish with the leeks and onions.

Preheat the oven to 325°F.

Dry the meat well on both sides with paper towels and add the pieces in a single layer to the pan; brown them well on both sides. Sprinkle the meat with the salt and pepper. Return the onion mixture to the pan and add the carrots. Slowly pour in the wine along the side of the pan. Cover the pan tightly and transfer it to the oven.

Cook for about 1¼ hours, or until the meat is fork-tender. Ten minutes before the dish is done, sprinkle the rosemary over the top of the meat and continue cooking. Cut the meat into serving pieces; transfer the mixture with the juices to a serving platter and serve immediately.

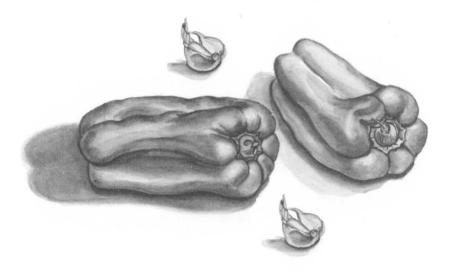

Ciao, Mary Ann,
Do You Have . . . ?

Stufato di Vitellone con Erbe e Vino
(Veal Stew with Herbs and Wine)

Serves 4

3 tablespoons extra-virgin olive oil

1 medium red onion (4 ounces), peeled and thinly sliced

¼ cup red wine vinegar

¼ pound pancetta or bacon, diced

2 pounds boneless veal chuck roast, tied and dried with paper towels

1 teaspoon fine sea salt

¼ teaspoon coarsely ground black pepper

5 sprigs fresh tarragon

5 sprigs fresh summer or winter savory

2 sprigs fresh flat-leaf parsley

2 sprigs fresh rosemary

1 bay leaf

1 cup dry red wine

This recipe showcases the preparation of a tough cut of veal, a boneless chuck roast, which in Italy would come from a calf more than three months old and grazing on pastureland. The chuck cut is from the shoulder. It is very tasty when cooked with pancetta (Italian bacon) and wine. The best way to cook it is very slowly over low heat in a Dutch oven. Be sure that the pot is heavy duty, to retain the heat, and only large enough to hold the meat. I use a 10×3½-inch cast-iron Dutch oven. The veal roast is even better made several days ahead. Pair it with potatoes, polenta, or rice.

Heat 2 tablespoons of the oil in a Dutch oven or heavy-duty pot. Stir in the onions and cook them over medium-low heat until they are very soft. Stir in the wine vinegar, raise the heat to high and allow the vinegar to evaporate. Remove the onions to a dish and set aside.

Add the remaining tablespoon of olive oil to the Dutch oven. Stir in the pancetta and cook it until it begins to brown. Rub the veal roast all over with the salt and pepper, add it to the Dutch oven, and brown it on all sides.

Tie the tarragon, savory, parsley, rosemary, and bay leaf together in a bundle with a piece of kitchen string and place it on top of the roast. Scatter the onions around the roast. Pour in the wine and let it come to a boil, then reduce the heat to simmer and cook the roast, covered, for about 2 hours, or until it is fork-tender.

Remove the roast to a cutting board and let it cool for 20 minutes. With a scissors cut and remove the strings. Discard the

Ciao, Mary Ann, Do You Have . . . ?

290

strings and the bundle of herbs. Use a sharp knife to cut the meat into slices. Return the slices to the Dutch oven. Reheat the meat slowly until hot. Serve the meat with some of the juices poured over the top.

Scaloppine al Limone e Salsa di Capperi

(Veal Cutlets with Lemon and Caper Sauce)

Serves 4

1 pound veal cutlet, cut ⅛ inch thick from the top of the round

¼ cup unbleached all-purpose flour

½ teaspoon fine sea salt

¼ teaspoon ground white pepper

3 tablespoons unsalted butter

⅔ cup dry white wine

⅓ cup freshly squeezed lemon juice

⅓ cup chopped capers in brine, drained

2 tablespoons finely minced Italian parsley leaves

It is an enigma: What sometimes seems like the simplest food preparation is the hardest to execute. Case in point, veal cutlet. I have demonstrated the following recipe for veal cutlets in lemon caper sauce many times, and I still get letters from fans who say that the veal was tough when they made it. Here are the rules I follow for cooking this quick dish. First, get to know a butcher who will cut your veal from the top of the round, a very tender cut. If veal is cut from the leg, it will be tougher. Second, invest in a good, weighted meat pounder. Veal cutlets must have even thickness to ensure consistency in cooking. With the top of the round you will not find it necessary to pound the slices unless they are more than ¼-inch thick. Be sure you are buying very young veal, meaning a milk-fed calf no more than three months old. It pays to ask questions. In this preparation, the veal slices are dredged in seasoned flour and cooked quickly in butter on each side. Capers, white wine, and lemon juice add zest and flavor.

Dry the veal slices with paper toweling and cut them into 5-inch serving-size pieces if they are too long. Set the veal aside.

On a dish combine the flour, ¼ teaspoon of the salt, and the white pepper. Dredge the veal slices in the flour mixture, shaking off the excess flour, and set aside.

In a 12-inch sauté pan, melt the butter over medium-high heat. Cook the veal slices, in batches if necessary, for about 1 minute on each side, or just until the veal turns gray and the edges start to brown. Remove the veal slices as they cook to a dish and keep them covered with a piece of aluminum foil.

Pour the wine into the pan, raise the heat to high, and with a wooden spoon scrape up any browned bits in the pan. Cook for 1 minute, stirring constantly. Pour in the lemon juice and capers and continue stirring and cooking for 1 minute.

Stir in the parsley. Return the veal and any juices that have collected to the pan and cook the veal for an additional 1 minute, turning the slices once so they are coated with the sauce.

Transfer the veal and the sauce to a serving plate and serve at once.

Pollo al Vino
(Chicken in Wine)

Serves 4

3¼ pounds small cut-up
   bone-in chicken,
   preferably free-range

2¾ cups dry white wine

¼ cup white vinegar

3 tablespoons butter

½ pound onions, peeled and
   chopped

1½ teaspoons crushed
   juniper berries

1½ teaspoons fine sea salt

Grinding of fresh black
   pepper

¼ cup balsamic vinegar

I have been stumped trying to duplicate my family's chicken in wine dish for as long as I have been in the kitchen. No one remembers exactly how my Grandmother Saporito achieved that fabulous glazed chicken with the bones permeated with wine flavor. No amount of nostalgic recollecting or toying with ingredients could come close to the taste of hers. She butchered her own chickens and made her own wine, and I believe that accounts for the difference. In another attempt at her recipe, I have created this chicken in wine dish, using free-range chicken, which I feel has better flavor and stands up over the long cooking process. Begin by marinating the chicken pieces in dry white wine for 2 days. Following this step will leave the meat with a rich wine taste after it is cooked . . . but it still does not compare with Grandma's.

Two days before cooking the chicken, place the pieces in a large glass or ceramic baking dish large enough to hold the pieces in a single layer. Pour 1½ cups of the wine and the white vinegar over the chicken, cover tightly with plastic wrap, and refrigerate.

When ready to cook, drain the chicken and dry the pieces well on paper toweling. Set them aside. Discard the wine-vinegar mixture.

In a large sauté pan large enough to hold all the pieces, melt 2 tablespoons of the butter, add the onions, and sauté until they become soft and translucent but not brown. Remove the onions to a dish. Add the remaining tablespoon of butter to the pan and the chicken pieces skin-side down. Brown the chicken quickly on all sides. Return the onions to the pan, sprinkle the chicken with the juniper berries, salt, and pepper. Lower the heat and pour in the remaining 1¼ cups wine. Cover the pan and cook the chicken over low heat for 15 minutes. Uncover the pan and continue cooking over low heat for another 20 minutes, turning the pieces occasionally.

Add the balsamic vinegar, raise the heat to medium, and continue cooking an additional 5 minutes. Serve the chicken with some of the pan juices.

Farrotto

(Farro Cooked in the Style of Farrotto)

Serves 4 to 6

2 leeks (10 ounces), tops and dark green part cut and discarded

2½ pounds cherry tomatoes, stemmed, washed, and drained, yielding 3½ cups cherry tomato juice

4 tablespoons unsalted butter

1 cup farro

There is much discussion over just what farro is. Some say it is an ancient grain known as spelt. Others, like Madeleine Kamman in her book The Making of a Cook, *claim that farro is one of two wild seeds, called emmer, belonging to the genus* Triticum. *I am just happy to cook with it. Some recipes call for boiling the farro with other ingredients, but I treat it like risotto, beginning its journey with a soffrito of delicate leeks. The other key ingredient is fresh cherry tomato juice. I fill bags and bags of cherry tomatoes in the summer from my garden and then freeze them as is. The flavor balance in this dish is exquisite and you are almost tempted to eat it right from the pot. Like risotto, it requires the slow addition and mixing of the liquid until the farro absorbs the juices. When it is ready, the farro should still have a resistance to it but be cooked, not mushy. Farro is available through mail order sources (see page 347).*

Cut the leeks lengthwise in half and place them in a large bowl of water to soak for 5 minutes. Drain the leeks, dry them with paper towels, and slice them into ¼-inch pieces. Set aside.

Puree the cherry tomatoes in batches in a food processor until blended. Pour the puree into a large mesh strainer set over a large bowl and press on the solids with a wooden spoon to release the juices. You will need about 3½ cups of juice. Discard the tomato pulp and skins.

Heat the tomato juice in a small saucepan and keep warm.

Melt the butter in a heavy-clad 1-quart saucepan. Stir in the farro and the leeks. Continue cooking and stirring to coat the ingredients well in the butter. Cook until the leeks soften and become somewhat translucent.

Ciao, Mary Ann, Do You Have . . . ?

Slowly pour in ½ cup of the tomato juice and continue stirring, allowing the farro to absorb all the liquid before adding additional liquid. Continue stirring and adding liquid until the farro is cooked. It should be neither hard nor mushy. Season with salt and pepper. Serve immediately.

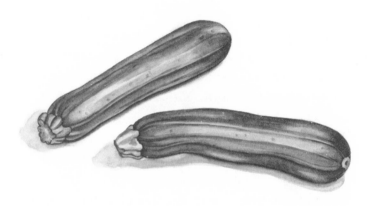

Farrotto con Merluzzo
(Farro with Codfish)

Serves 4 to 6

1 pound skinless codfish

3 cups water

4 tablespoons unsalted
butter

½ cup farro

2 cups diced leeks

1 carrot, scraped and diced

2 tablespoons minced
parsley

2 cups vegetable or chicken
broth

½ cup dry white wine

¼ teaspoon fine sea salt

Grinding of black pepper

2 tablespoons freshly
squeezed lemon juice

Farro is extremely nutritious and versatile, perfect in many recipes. In this version poached cod is added to the cooked farro at the last minute. Viewers who request really healthy food will enjoy this well-balanced dish that is high in essential vitamins and nutrients. It makes a good main course served with a side dish of steamed Swiss chard and a green salad.

Simmer the codfish in the water in a sauté pan just until the fish turns milky-white and easily flakes. Drain the fish with a slotted spoon and transfer to a bowl. With a fork, flake the fish and set aside.

Melt the butter over medium heat in a copper or heavy-clad 2-quart pot. Stir in the farro, leeks, carrots, and parsley, and cook the mixture, stirring frequently to coat all the grains. When the leeks are wilted and soft, slowly pour in ½ cup of the broth and stir the mixture until all the broth is absorbed. Continue adding small amounts of liquid, allowing the grain to absorb each addition. Add the wine and cook the mixture just until the grains are no longer hard; they should remain firm but cooked. Gently stir in the cod and cook slowly just until the mixture is hot. Stir in the salt, pepper and lemon juice. Serve immediately.

Variation: Cook cod separately and add to farro cooked in fish broth or chicken broth; add peas and celery.

Emilio's Kitchen

No one believed me when I told them that Emilio's Italian grocery store was just a little hole-in-the-wall operation. Ever since he had become a regular on the series, people have been charmed by his no-nonsense approach to cooking Italian food and his hilarious sense of humor. Viewers from all over the country have come to his venerable store just to say hello. One visitor actually flew her private plane from Cleveland, Ohio, just to go shopping in Emilio's store; when she arrived she was disappointed to find that he was closed!

Emilio is a southern Italian who can make a tasty dish out of nothing, a trait that is innate in Italian cooks. At noontime hungry patrons flock to his stand-up lunch counter to buy his homemade bean soups, pasta dishes, and calzones. Never mind that his store is located in an area of Portsmouth, New Hampshire, where upscale restaurants abound and lunch for many people is *the* event of the day, Emilio packs them in in a steady stream. This gregarious guy with trimmed mustache and perennial beret has welcoming words for everyone, usually beginning with the question, "So what's happenin'?"

Each season I allow for one show remote to be filmed in Emilio's homey storefront kitchen. Walking into it is a leap back into a 1950s kitchen. The shelves are lined with staples such as olive oil, anchovies, tomatoes, spices, and pasta. The pots and pans have seen lots of wear, and the floor still has the original linoleum, now threadbare in spots. The old gas stove is where we usually work together making soup or sauces and philosophizing about our mutual heritage.

Emilio puts fun into cooking and that is why I like to work with him. One of the aspects of our cooking together is the fact that we never agree on how things should be done, and our on-camera

Ciao, Mary Ann, Do You Have . . . ?

exchanges become lighthearted as we cook. One of the funniest programs in recent memory was one that we devoted to making dishes using only three or four ingredients. That was no problem for Emilio. In a matter of minutes he had created linguine with a jalapeño and garlic sauce with olives that was as delicious as the finest dish on a gourmet restaurant's menu.

I know his appearances make an impact, because invariably when I am out at a book signing or some other gathering, the first question I get is, "How is Emilio?"

Pane di Fichi Secchi ed' Anice
(Dried Fig and Anise Bread)

Makes 2 loaves

I am keenly aware that a lot of people are afraid to work with yeast, so over the years we have made a lot of regional breads on the series to demystify the process. A few years ago I wrote a book entitled What You Knead, *which took the novice bread baker step by step into breadmaking. This recipe for Dried Fig and Anise Bread is easy to make and produces two wonderful loaves, and the whole process can be done in an electric mixer. Start the dough early in the day, or the night before. Wheat gluten is available by mail order (page 347) or can be found in the baking section of some grocery stores. It helps to develop a better-rising dough. Be sure to use pure anise extract and not just a weak, watered-down imitation.*

½ cup warm water (110°F)

1 tablespoon active dry yeast

7½ cups (approximately) unbleached all-purpose flour

5 ounces dried Calamyrna figs (about 13 whole), stemmed

1½ cups plus 1 tablespoon warm milk

6 tablespoons unsalted butter, softened

⅔ cup sugar

1¾ teaspoons pure anise extract

2 large eggs, slightly beaten

1 tablespoon wheat gluten

2½ teaspoons salt

½ cup confectioners' sugar

Pour the water into a small bowl and stir in the yeast. Stir in ½ cup of the flour to make a loose dough. Cover the bowl tightly with plastic wrap and let it rest at room temperature for 2 to 3 hours or overnight; the dough will look spongy with lots of holes.

Place the figs in another bowl, cover them with water, and let stand at room temperature for 1 hour to soften them. Drain the water, dry the figs and dice them. Set aside.

When ready to make the dough, transfer the yeast mixture to the bowl of a large electric mixer. Add the milk, reserving 1 tablespoon, then add the butter, sugar, 1½ teaspoons of the anise extract, eggs, wheat gluten, and salt to the bowl and combine the mixture on medium speed using the paddle attachment. Begin adding the remaining flour 1 cup at a time and mix on high speed to allow the ingredients to combine. Add only enough flour until the dough begins to come away from the side of the bowl and is not sticky on your hands.

Ciao, Mary Ann,
Do You Have . . . ?

Transfer the dough from the mixer to a lightly floured surface. Push the dough down with your hands to flatten it. Place the figs on top of the dough, then fold the dough over to cover the figs. Knead the dough with your hands to evenly distribute the figs in the dough. Shape the dough into a large round and place it in a lightly buttered large bowl. Cover the bowl tightly with plastic wrap and allow the dough to rise for 2 hours, or until it is double in size.

Preheat the oven to 375°F. Line 2 baking sheets with parchment paper.

Punch the dough down with your hands and transfer it to a work surface. With a knife divide the dough into two equal pieces and work with one piece at a time. Roll each piece under the palm of your hands into a 46-inch-long rope. Starting at one end of the rope, coil the dough up tightly and place it on one of the parchment-paper-lined baking sheets. Repeat with the second piece of dough.

Cover the baking sheets and allow the dough to rise for 30 minutes.

Bake for 40 to 45 minutes, or until the crust is evenly browned on the top and bottom of the bread. Use an instant-read thermometer inserted in the center of the bread to determine if it is cooked. If the thermometer registers between 200° and 210°F, remove the bread to a cooling rack and cool until warm.

Meanwhile in a small bowl combine the confectioners' sugar, the remaining 1 tablespoon milk, and the remaining ¼ teaspoon anise extract. Stir the ingredients together to make a glaze. Use a spoon to drizzle the top of the breads with the glaze. Serve the bread warm or at room temperature.

Note: To freeze the bread, allow it to cool completely, then wrap it well in aluminum foil.

Panettone
(Christmas Bread)

Makes 2 loaves

Panettone is the bread of Christmas, enjoyed all over Italy. I introduced viewers to this candied-fruit-studded symbol of the holidays on one of my very first shows. Since then many viewers have written and sent along photos of their own panettone. I have changed the original recipe that appeared in my book Ciao Italia *somewhat, suggesting the addition of wheat gluten, which helps dough rise higher and keeps the final product fresher longer. I have also changed the baking procedure by eliminating the use of a high-sided mold or pan and instead use panettone waxed papers, available in cookware stores or by mail (see page 347). But even these are not necessary because brown paper bags also work well, and the panettone can be left in the paper for gift giving. Because of the multiple risings, it is best to start the dough a day ahead. You will also find another version of panettone from my fellow baker Gary Rulli on page 305. I like that one very much, too, but it is more time-consuming. Try them both.*

1 tablespoon active dry yeast

1 cup warm water (110°F)

1 cup unbleached all-purpose flour

4 large egg yolks

2 whole eggs

¾ cup sugar

5 tablespoons butter, softened

¼ cup orange liqueur

1 tablespoon vanilla extract

4½ to 5 cups unbleached all-purpose flour

1 tablespoon wheat gluten

1 tablespoon salt

¾ cup diced candied lemon peel

½ cup diced candied citron

Grated zest of 2 large oranges

In a medium-size bowl dissolve the yeast in the water and stir in the flour. The mixture should be the consistency of pancake batter. Cover the bowl tightly with plastic wrap and let rise in a warm place for 6 hours or overnight.

In a large mixer or large bowl beat the egg yolks, whole eggs, sugar, butter, liqueur, and vanilla together. Blend in the yeast mixture. Beat in 1 cup of the flour and the wheat gluten until well blended. Add the remaining flour 1 cup at a time plus the salt, lemon peel, citron, and orange zest and continue beating until a ball of dough forms and moves away from the side of the mixer or bowl. You may not need all of the flour, or you may find that you

Ciao, Mary Ann,
Do You Have . . . ?

303

need to add more; only add enough to develop a ball of dough that is soft but not soupy and not sticking to your hands.

Remove the dough from the mixer or bowl and knead it for a few minutes by hand on a lightly floured surface until it is smooth. Transfer the dough to a lightly buttered large bowl. Cover the bowl tightly with plastic wrap and allow to rise until double in size, about 4 hours.

Preheat the oven to 425°F. Spray two 6×4-inch-deep panettone papers with vegetable oil or fold the top of two brown paper lunch bags over twice to make a collar and spray the inside of the bags.

Punch down the dough and divide it in half. Knead each half for 2 to 3 minutes and form each piece into a round. Place each round in the panettone papers or bags. Cover with a clean towel and let them rise for 35 to 40 minutes, or until the dough is two-thirds up the sides of the paper.

Cut an X with a scissors in the center of each dough. Bake the panettone for 5 minutes, reduce the heat to 375°F, and continue baking for 35 to 40 minutes, or until a cake skewer inserted into the center of the bread comes out clean. If the top of the bread begins to brown too quickly, cover it loosely with a piece of aluminum foil.

Let the bread cool completely on a rack. To give as a gift, simply wrap the panettone as is in clear cellophane and tie with a bow.

Panettone can be made ahead and frozen for up to 3 months if well wrapped in heavy-duty aluminum foil.

Did you know that it is an Italian tradition to have the head of the house cut the panettone on Christmas Day and serve it to all family members?

Ciao, Mary Ann, Do You Have . . . ?

Panettone Emporio Rulli
(Gary Rulli's Panettone)

Makes 2 large or 4 smaller panettoni

One year I decided to film some of our remotes in Napa Valley, California, because if you were taken there blindfolded and sat on a verdant hillside overlooking vineyards and olive trees, you would swear that you were in Italy; in fact, a lot of Italian immigrants settled in the Napa and Sonoma Valley areas because of the similarity in landscape and climate to their native countryside. I went there to tape a program about wine and Italian varietals and to scour the hillsides high above Napa Valley for porcini mushrooms. I traveled to Emporio Rulli, a fabulous pasticerria (pastry shop) in Larkspur, to make Italian fruit tarts with owner Gary Rulli, who studied pastry making in Italy and then opened his own authentic—right down to the Italian woodwork—pastry shop. It became a tremendous success. Gary is a true pastry artist and one of his signature traditional breads is panettone, the dense, sweet golden raisin and candied-fruit bread of Milan. It is far superior to the packaged version, commercially made months ahead of time and bearing not even a hint of resemblance to the homemade. The following is Gary's recipe. Read the recipe first, as I recommend that you begin the biga (starter) the night before. Bake the panettone directly in heavy-duty waxed panettone paper molds available in a variety of sizes (see mail order section, page 347). I have also baked the dough in regular size brown lunch bags by folding the top edges down to make a collar and spraying the inside with vegetable spray before adding the dough.

To make the biga, in a 5-quart mixer fitted with a dough hook, dissolve the yeast in the water; add the sugar and let rest 5 minutes. Add the flour; mix on low speed until smooth. Cover with

BIGA (STARTER)

1 teaspoon active dry yeast

⅓ cup warm water (110°F)

¼ teaspoon sugar

⅔ cup unbleached all-purpose flour

FIRST DOUGH

1 teaspoon active dry yeast

¼ cup warm water

Biga

2 egg yolks

1 tablespoon sugar

1⅓ cups unbleached all-purpose flour

SECOND DOUGH

All of the first dough

3½ cups unbleached all-purpose flour

2 tablespoons honey

20 tablespoons (2½ sticks) unsalted butter, plus extra for greasing molds and bowls

*Ciao, Mary Ann,
Do You Have . . . ?*

¾ cup sugar

9 egg yolks

⅓ cup plus 1 teaspoon milk

2 teaspoons sea salt

1 teaspoon vanilla extract

1 teaspoon lemon extract

Grated zest of 1 orange

1⅓ cups golden raisins

⅓ cup diced candied citron

⅔ cup diced candied orange peel

Did you know that almost every region of Italy makes a sweet bread similar to the panettone of Milan? They just call it by another name. In Venice, it is called fugasse.

plastic wrap and let rise until tripled in volume (3 to 6 hours, or overnight).

To make the first dough, dissolve the yeast in the water; set it aside for 5 minutes. Add it to the *biga* in the mixer bowl; mix with the dough hook until the *biga* is well blended. Add the egg yolks, sugar, and flour; mix for 5 minutes on medium speed, or until the mixture is shiny and smooth. Cover the bowl with plastic wrap and let rise until tripled in volume (it is important that the dough be kept slightly warm but not hot, about 70°F).

To make the second dough, add the flour, honey, 9 tablespoons of the butter, ⅓ cup of the sugar, the egg yolks, and the milk to the first dough. Beat on medium speed for 5 minutes; add the remaining sugar, salt, vanilla and lemon extracts, and orange zest. Beat on medium speed for 5 minutes. Beat in another 8 tablespoons of the butter 1 tablespoon at a time; the dough should pull away from the sides of the bowl and be shiny, smooth, and elastic. Add 1 more tablespoon of the butter, then by hand mix in the raisins, citron, and orange peel. The dough will be very heavy. Flour your hands and shape the dough into a ball. Place the dough in a large 8-quart plastic tub or pan; cover the tub with plastic wrap and allow the dough to rise until doubled.

Punch down the dough with your hands and turn it out onto a floured work surface. Divide the dough into two 2-pound 4-ounce pieces or four 1-pound 2-ounce pieces. Butter your hands and turn each piece into a tight ball.

Preheat the oven to 360°F. Butter the baking molds or brown paper bags.

Place each dough piece in a baking mold. Cover with a clean towel and let rise for 1 hour, or until the dough has risen past the rim of the mold and springs back when poked. Cut an X in the top of each panettone and fold the four cut corners of dough back on themselves to allow for air to escape and prevent the bread from splitting.

Melt the remaining 2 tablespoons of butter and brush the tops of the panettoni.

Bake the panettoni for 45 minutes, or until a cake skewer inserted in the center comes out clean; larger loaves will take longer to bake than smaller loaves. If the top of the panettone browns before the bread is completely baked, place a loose sheet of aluminum foil over the top.

Cool the panettoni completely on a wire rack.

Biscotti ai Pinoli
(Pine Nut Cookies)

Makes 4 dozen cookies

1½ cups sugar

1 tablespoon prepared almond paste (Odense brand is readily available)

4 eggs

⅛ teaspoon salt

2 cups unbleached all-purpose flour

½ teaspoon baking powder

2 teaspoons almond extract

½ cup pine nuts

¼ cup confectioners' sugar

One day a large manila envelope chock full of family heirloom recipes arrived from Joe Infantino, a viewer from California. I could tell by the lovingly typed recipes and the notes that accompanied them that Joe was proud of his Italian heritage. This recipe for almond-flavored pine nut cookies was tested in my kitchen, and when I was through, I could not keep these delicate and light-tasting cookies away from my family; they literally melt in your mouth. The preparation begins in a double boiler; make sure the water only heats to lukewarm or the eggs will curdle while they are beaten. Do not be in a hurry to remove the cookies from the baking sheet. Let them cool and set or they will crack.

Preheat the oven to 350°F. Butter and flour 2 baking sheets and set them aside.

Fill the base of a double boiler with just enough water so the bottom of the top pan does not touch the water. Add the sugar, almond paste, eggs, and salt to the top pan. Barely bring the water to a simmer and with a hand-held electric beater beat the mixture until it is frothy like a milkshake and feels lukewarm.

Remove the top pan from the double boiler and continue to beat for another 5 minutes, or until the mixture is cool.

Transfer the mixture to a bowl. Sift the flour and baking powder together and add it to the egg mixture along with the almond extract. Mix the batter well; it will have the consistency of cake batter. Drop heaping teaspoonfuls of the batter onto the baking sheet, spacing each 1 inch apart as the batter will spread. Sprinkle

Ciao, Mary Ann, Do You Have . . . ?

308

each cookie with a few pine nuts and dust each one with confectioners' sugar. Let stand 5 minutes.

Preheat the oven to 350°F.

Bake the cookies on the middle rack of the oven for 10 minutes or just until the edges begin to turn golden brown. The cookies should remain pale in color. Remove the baking sheets to cooling racks. Let the cookies cool 5 minutes before removing them to wire racks to cool completely.

Did you know that pine nuts come from the stone pine tree and are time-consuming to extract? That is one reason for their hefty price tag. Today most pine nuts come from China.

Ciao, Mary Ann,
Do You Have . . . ?

Ossi di Morto
(Cookies of the Dead)

Makes at least 14 dozen cookies

5 large eggs

1½ tablespoons freshly squeezed lemon juice

2 tablespoons grated lemon zest

4 cups unbleached all-purpose flour

4 teaspoons baking powder

1 pound confectioners' sugar

Ossi di morto *(literally, bones of the dead) seems like a cryptic name for a sweet confection that is made in Italy for the feast of All Souls' Day. From town to town, region to region, this cookie looks and tastes completely different. This version is from Tuscany. The texture of this cookie is crisp and brittle like old bones. Make the dough and shape the cookies the day before baking. Use a mixer to make this heavy dough, then finish kneading it by hand before cutting it into pieces. As the cookies bake they will separate, creating something that looks like little pillows on a meringue-like base. These cookies are very chewy with a delicate flavor from the lemon zest.*

In a heavy-duty mixer or large bowl beat the eggs just to break them up and combine with the lemon juice and lemon zest.

In a separate bowl stir together the flour, baking powder, and confectioners' sugar. Add to the egg mixture and mix until a dough is formed, which should be stiff but not dry.

Remove the dough to a lightly floured board and knead it with your hands until smooth. Cut the dough into 4 equal pieces and work with one piece at a time, keeping the rest covered. Roll each piece on a lightly floured surface under the palm of your hands into a rope that is 44 inches long and ½ inch wide. Cut each into forty-four 1-inch pieces and place them on lightly greased baking sheets, not too close together. You will need several baking sheets for this. Cover the cookies with clean towels and allow them to rest overnight in a cool but not cold place. They will feel hard when ready to bake, but this is important in order for them to separate.

Ciao, Mary Ann, Do You Have . . . ?

310

Preheat the oven to 350°F.

Bake the cookies for 15 to 20 minutes, or until they are the color of light brown eggshells. Remove the cookies to a wire rack with a spatula to cool completely. Store any cookies not immediately used in airtight containers.

Ciao, Mary Ann,
Do You Have . . . ?

Pizzelle Colorate
(Colored Pizzelle)

Makes about 4½ dozen cookies

3½ cups unbleached all-purpose flour

2 teaspoons baking powder

⅛ teaspoon salt

12 tablespoons (1½ sticks) unsalted butter, at room temperature

1¼ cups sugar

5 extra-large eggs, at room temperature

1 tablespoon vanilla extract

3 cups multicolored sugar sprinkles

Everyone loves pizzelle. One of the all-time favorites, this waffle-like cookie is made on a pizzelle iron. Originally these cookies were made one at a time, using a single-handled pizzelle iron with a personal design etched in the center. My grandmother Saporito had one that sported two individuals toasting with wineglasses. The idea was to hold the iron over a gas flame, turning it once to create the cookie. Over the years I have experimented with many variations of pizzelle, changing their look and taste with the seasons of the year. For Christmas my family loves this version, which is a standard vanilla-flavored dough; before each little ball of dough is put onto the form, it is coated with multicolored sprinkles. When the lid is pressed down on the dough, a pretty stained-glass look is created that is unusual and very festive. Chill the dough for several hours before rolling the balls in the sprinkles. I prefer to use a non-coated pizzelle iron, as the weight of the lid helps to create a thinner cookie.

In a medium bowl sift the flour, baking powder, and salt.

In another bowl, beat the butter and sugar together with an electric mixer. Beat in the eggs one at a time until well blended. Add the vanilla extract. On low speed, blend in the flour mixture a little at a time until well blended. The dough will be soft.

Cover the bowl and chill the dough for at least 2 hours.

(Note: You can make the dough in a food processor, combining the butter and sugar first, then eggs and vanilla, and last the flour mixture.)

Heat a pizzelle maker according to the manufacturer's direc-

Ciao, Mary Ann, Do You Have . . . ?

tions. If it is nonstick, spray it with a baking spray or lightly brush with vegetable oil.

Pour the sugar sprinkles into a shallow dish. Using 2 teaspoons scoop up a spoonful of the dough, and using the spoon as a guide, roll the dough in the sugar sprinkles, coating it well. Place the dough in the center of the form; if you have a 2-form maker, or 4-form maker, roll the balls first before putting them on the form.

Close the lid and latch it for a count to 30. Lift the lid and remove the pizzelle with the edge of a fork and place them on cooling racks in single layers to cool completely. For darker-colored pizzelle hold for a longer count. Continue making pizzelle until all the dough is used.

The pizzelle should be thin and have a crisp texture. When completely cool, wrap them in groups of 6 in plastic wrap and place them in airtight containers. Pizzelle can be made ahead and frozen for up to 3 months.

Variation: When just removed from the pizzelle form, the waffles can be rolled around cannoli forms, or pressed between two small custard cups to form shapes that can be filled with cream, custard, or fruit. Scoop softened ice cream between two pizzelle to make delicious ice-cream sandwiches.

Tortine di Pesche
(Little Peach Cakes)

Makes 16 individual cakes

DOUGH

⅓ cup unsalted butter, cut into bits

1 cup sugar

2 eggs

1½ cups unbleached all-purpose flour

½ teaspoon salt

2 teaspoons baking powder

6 tablespoons milk

1 tablespoon peach brandy or ½ teaspoon vanilla extract

CUSTARD

3 egg yolks

½ cup sugar

¼ cup unbleached all-purpose flour

1 cup milk

2 teaspoons peach brandy or ½ teaspoon vanilla extract

1 tablespoon butter, optional

Ciao, Mary Ann, Do You Have . . . ?

314

Whenever I travel to various cities, people with the name Esposito ask if I am related to them, and I like to think that we are all related in some cosmic way. In Philadelphia while shooting some footage for Ciao Italia, *I did two introductory pieces at Fante's, a wonderful kitchen store in the Italian neighborhood of south Philadelphia. I met Mariella Esposito, who with her brother, Nick Giovanucci, owns the store. You can find just about any cooking item you could ever need, including peach cake molds to make traditional peach cakes. When I spotted the molds I was ecstatic, because so many viewers have asked me to provide a recipe for cakes with a custard filling that look like freshly picked peaches. Here is the recipe, courtesy of Fante's. You will need a peach ball mold, nail heads, and leaves (see mail order sources on page 347). You will also need time. I recommend that you make the custard several days ahead and refrigerate it.*

Preheat the oven to 350°F. Butter and flour the peach mold and set it aside.

To prepare the dough, in a bowl blend together the butter and the sugar with a hand-held mixer. Beat in the eggs one at a time. Sift the flour, salt, and baking powder together. Combine the butter and flour mixture, add the milk and brandy, and mix well. Drop 1 heaping teaspoonful of the batter into each peach cake cavity.

Bake for 12 minutes, during which time you can grease and flour the nail heads. As the cakes are baking, a slight white "crust" will begin to form. Insert the nail head cup down into the center of each cake and bake for 2 or 3 minutes longer. The nail heads form the "pit" area of the peaches.

The cakes are done as soon as they start to pull away from the edge of the cavity. Remove the mold from the oven before the edges of the cakes begin to brown. This will give the best coloration results.

Combine all the custard ingredients in a saucepan and cook over medium-low heat, whisking continuously until the custard thickens and coats the back of a spoon. Transfer the custard to a bowl and cover it with a sheet of buttered wax paper and allow it to cool.

Remove the peach cakes from the mold and remove the nail heads.

In a small bowl combine the gelatin with water as directed on the package. Stir in the brandy and food coloring. Set aside.

Using a toothpick or small brush, add color streaks to the center (pit) of each peach cake with a little food coloring.

Brush the insides of the cakes with the coloring mixture.

Fill the pit with about 1 teaspoon of the custard and join two halves together, positioning them slightly off center to form the peach.

Brush the outside of the cake with the gelatin mixture, being careful not to soak them too much. This will give them a light color, and when dry, some firmness.

In another small bowl combine the ½ cup granulated sugar, the ½ cup confectioners' sugar, and a drop of red and yellow food coloring. Mix the ingredients together to obtain a peach color.

Roll the "peaches" in the colored-sugar coating mixture, pressing gently to allow the sugar to adhere. This will bring out the coloration.

Insert a paper, plastic, or edible leaf and allow the cakes to dry before serving.

COLORING

1 package (3 ounces) peach-flavored gelatin, prepared according to package directions

2 tablespoons peach brandy

Small drop red food coloring (optional)

COATING

½ cup sugar

½ cup confectioners' sugar

Red and yellow food color to obtain peach color

Ciao, Mary Ann,
Do You Have . . . ?

315

Cuppelle
(Molded Wafer Cookies)

Makes 6 cookie cups

2 egg whites at room
temperature

2 ounces (¼ cup) sugar

4 tablespoons unsalted
butter, softened

½ scant cup unbleached all-
purpose flour

¼ teaspoon almond extract

Cuppelle are delicate, crisp molded cookies that serve as containers for fresh fruits, ice cream, or pudding. You have to work fast, while the cookies are still warm, to successfully mold them over an inverted cupcake pan or small custard cups.

Line 2 cookie sheets with parchment paper. Use a 6-inch round cardboard template to draw 3 circles on each piece of parchment, leaving 2 inches between each circle.

In a bowl whisk the whites until foamy. Whisk in the sugar a little at a time. Whisk in the butter. Whisk in the flour 1 tablespoon at a time. Whisk in the almond flavoring. The batter will be thin and should be homogeneous and fluid.

Preheat the oven to 375°F. Position the oven racks in the middle of the oven.

Turn a standard 12-cup cupcake tin upside down and set aside.

Place 2 tablespoons of the batter in the center of each circle and with a rubber spatula spread the batter to fill in the circles.

Bake 1 sheet at a time, as these must be watched carefully to prevent them from burning. Bake the *cupelle* for about 7 minutes, or just until the outer edges turn golden brown.

With a metal spatula carefully remove the cookies from the parchment paper and with your hands mold each one over a cupcake form, placing each one in a separate row so as not to touch one another. Let the cookies cool for 10 minutes, then remove them to a cookie rack. As they cool they will become very crisp.

Repeat the baking and molding process with the second sheet of cookies.

Fill the cooled *cupelle* with ice cream, fruit, mousse, or sorbet.

*Ciao, Mary Ann,
Do You Have . . . ?*

316

Primi Piatti

Zuppa di Pomodorini, Porri e Riso (Cherry Tomato, Leek, and Rice
   Soup)
Crema di Zucca (Cream of Squash Soup)
Conchiglie con Finocchio (Pasta Shells with Fennel)
Lasagne alle Bietole (Swiss Chard Lasagne)
Broccolini e Spaghetti (Broccolini and Spaghetti)

Secondi Piatti

Rombo con Radicchiella e Patate (Halibut with Mustard Greens
   and Potatoes)
Peperoni Ripieni Sottosopra (Upside-Down Stuffed Peppers)

Contorni

Bietole con Fior di Latte (Chard with Fresh Mozzarella Cheese)
Cipolle Ripiene (Stuffed Onions)
Radicchiella con Olive e Formaggio (Mustard Greens with Olives and
   Cheese)

Insalate

Insalata di Barbabietole e Carote (Marinated Beet and Carrot Salad)
Insalata d'Aragosta dal Corsaro (Lobster Salad Corsaro Style)
Sformato di Pane Stratificato (Molded Tomato Bread Salad)

Guy's garden is zucchine lunghe *(long squash)*, Costoluto Genovese *(tomatoes)*, *Roma beans, antique arugula, radicchio, broccoli rape,* cippoline *(little disk-shaped onions)*, *Italian flat-leaf parsley, basil, fennel, zucca gialla (yellow squash)*, pomodorini *(cherry tomatoes)*, *favorite lettuces including Romaine, Giulio, and Rosanna, shallots, garlic, beets,* cavolo nero *(black cabbage)*, *artichokes, cauliflower,* borlotti *beans, mustard greens, peppers, escarole, carrots, sunflowers, pumpkins, fava beans, radishes, cucumbers, and gratitude for Mother Earth.*

"*A*ll good things must come to an end" sums up how I feel when my sojourns in Italy are over and it is time to part company, but I always bring Italy home with me in my impressions of the places I have visited, the new friends that I have made, the diverse foods that I have enjoyed, and the glorious vegetable and fruit gardens that are the inspiration for my home garden. So it seems fitting to me to continue this culinary tour here in Guy's garden.

Winter likes to linger in New Hampshire, reminding its residents that they are to take nothing for granted, no false hopes of an early spring, or soothing, warm rays of lasting sunshine, or rapidly fading memories of shoveling snow. Still, Guy and I hope that with the arrival of April we will be blessed by the weather gods and be able to get a head start with spring planting in our vegetable garden.

By design, the garden has evolved from growing the most generic of plants into an almost exclusively Italian vegetable garden. This has been the result of our long stays in Italy, where gardens entice us everywhere, even those tucked into the tiniest of spaces. We covet the vibrant green and ruby red lettuces that grow so lushly in Italy, and with so many varieties, we want to try them all. But my desires do not stop at leafy greens. I must also plant those tiny disk-shaped onions called *cipolline* that are perfect for pickling, as well as those plump and creamy fava beans that are one of the first vegetables to announce that spring has arrived in Italian gardens. They make the best antipasto, eaten raw with a wedge of sharp Pecorino cheese and a good Pinot Grigio wine.

I am hopeless in Italian seed stores, ducking into garden shops in each town that I visit, searching for seeds to bring home. It takes a stern comment from Guy to remind me that we already have a boxful of seeds purchased in previous years that still need to be planted. But how can I possibly turn my back on the likes of *cavolo nero* (black cabbage), *zucchine lunghe* (long baseball-bat-size zucchini), and *zucca gialla,* Italy's answer to our pumpkins, except that theirs are wonderfully brown and knobby on the outside, with thick, almost wood-like stems that when cut open reveal a flesh as orange as any jack-o'-lantern.

As long as we have been married we have had a garden. Guy considers it sacred ground, a tranquil place away from the workplace, where he is free to commune with and manipulate the earth, coaxing it to do his bidding, sometimes willingly and sometimes just unyieldingly. And it always amazes me how the microscopic seeds that we gingerly sprinkle in straight-as-an-arrow rows can muster enough energy to send firmly rooted stems crashing through the earth's crust to claim their place in the sun.

On quiet Sunday mornings in May while our neighbors dream or sip coffee and read the Sunday paper, we are crouched knee-deep in dirt, planting seeds and giving seedlings their first taste of tilled, fresh soil. All that I know about gardening I have learned from Guy. Among other things, he has taught me how to conquer weeds, how to thin plants and pinch them back for bushier growth, and the benefits of planting through black plastic. He has taught me about the need to rotate crops from year to year so as not to exhaust the soil, and he has taught me that a vegetable garden takes patience and careful watching.

One of the nice things about our garden is its location on a sunny hill. From its vantage point we can see meadows, hills, and stands of oak, pine, and apple trees. And sometimes we have company while we work—like the family of red-tail foxes that romp in the grass by the garden and live by the driveway in a drainpipe. We also share our garden with woodchucks, rabbits, and deer. These three have necessitated the installation of an electric fence around the entire perimeter of the garden. I always remark that our vegetables are the most expensive in the area, even if they are homegrown, because of the enormous electrical bills we pay in garden season! More than once when I have accidentally stepped too close to the fence I have been cruelly reminded by its stinging jolt of electricity. I tell myself that this is part of the price a gardener must pay in order to reap the harvest.

We built a little garden shed next to the garden to house hoses, wheelbarrows, tools, and a host of other supplies. We also use the shed to dry onions, garlic, and shallots, which we hang in bunches from the rafters. When dried, I braid them and give them as little kitchen gifts to my cooking friends. But I especially like the garden shed as a cool resting spot, a place away from the heat of high summer and the merciless mosquitoes that lay claim to us.

Guy is always covered from head to toe in long-sleeved shirt, pants, and a wide-brimmed hat when he is spending hours in the garden. I take precautions, too, especially since we are prone to picking up deer ticks, a real worry for country dwellers like us. It is when we are working together in the garden's defined and confined space that our hearts really open up to each other and we talk about everything from our children to how best to care for our aging parents to the best way to rid the eggplant of Japanese beetles.

The best time for me to be in the garden is late afternoon when the intensity of the sun begins to wane. That is when I enjoy the garden most, especially the corner that is reserved for sunflowers. I love just looking at them and am content to leave them in their happy places until Guy says, "Why don't you cut some for the house." Once I do, I know that their beauty, like summer, will not last.

One year while I was driving through the countryside of Cortona in eastern Tuscany, a sea of sunflowers just past blooming appeared over a large expanse of farmland. Their gigantic heads were bent as if in prayer. I took out an envelope and gathered some of the dried seeds and tucked them away in my bag in anticipation of the next garden season, when I would plant them in new and foreign earth. To my surprise the seeds did not disappoint me and sent out a regal display of golden yellow flowers with chocolate brown centers. They stood erect and proud like tall guardians of the garden.

July Fourth comes and with it parades and picnics, but more important, it signals for me the first taste of fresh summer tomatoes. Of all the vegetables in our garden, the variety of tomatoes is the most numerous. There are several types of plum, including the meaty Roma and the San Remo varieties. There is Taxi, a yellow-orange tomato that we love for salads, and Brandywine, an heirloom beefsteak variety with a pinky-red skin and flesh that is my very favorite and is harvested late in the season. Nothing beats a tomato sandwich made with them and a few leaves of fresh basil on slices of coarse Italian bread. When I want to be more creative I make my Molded Tomato Bread Salad (page 345), which always gets rave reviews and is the perfect summer lunch on a hot day. There is the ridged-looking Costoluto Genovese, a multi-purpose tomato that I once tried to sell at a farmer's market but no one would buy because it "did not look like a tomato." And there is the disease-resistant Sicilian tomato, the seeds of which were sent to me from Palermo by my friend Gianfranco. And I could never be without those pop-'em-in-your-mouth, eat-'em-like-candy cherry tomatoes called Sweet 100.

Hard work eventually rewards us. Each evening I climb the path to the garden with my basket to gather radicchio, arugula, lettuce, parsley, and basil for our dinner salad; I like the freedom of making a decision on the spot as to whether to pick Swiss chard or green beans for dinner that night. It makes me feel good too, when I *must* go to the grocery store for staples, to walk by the produce section and say to myself I need nothing.

Making a salad has become an art in my kitchen. There is no meal without it, period. There must be a variety of just-picked greens in the salad bowl, such as Romaine, oak leaf, escarole, and two varieties my husband loves called Rosanna and Giulio. I dislike cleaning salad greens, so Guy bought one of those fancy salad spinners a few years ago, and it is standard equipment in the kitchen for hydrating the leaves and then eliminating the excess water from them before they are dressed with extra-virgin olive oil and vinegar. Once when my mother was visiting, she remarked about how much salad I was preparing for three people. "Guy loves salad," I told her, and when he consumed most of the contents of the big red salad bowl, my mother commented that she thought it was unhealthy for him to eat so many greens!

All summer long I watch the garden for signs of the best time to film a segment or two for my television series. I want the zucchini blossoms to be perfect for picking so I can show viewers how to stuff them or dip them into a batter and fry them. I am hoping that the eggplants will grow a little larger in the next few days so I can feature them as well. Bringing the viewer into the garden with me to see the produce that we grow and will use in the studio kitchen has led to lots of requests for seeds!

By August I am beginning to have my fill of zucchini and green beans. We become produce peddlers to our neighbors, bringing them neatly arranged, boxed still-lifes of vegetables. Some of our neighbors have come to expect our produce and I tease Guy that he should have a truck with "Guy's Garden Delivery" painted on the sides. The cherry tomatoes are bursting in clusters on the stem, but the plum varieties are in various stages of greenness. I know that in a few weeks I will have my work cut out for me as I deal with most of the tomato harvest coming due at the same time. My dehydrator and freezer will help me. I dry a lot of the plum tomatoes and put them up in olive oil; some get crushed for tomato sauce, and cherry tomatoes are thrown into zipper-type plastic storage bags and frozen for use in soups, stews, and sauces. One of my favorite ways to use them is for Cherry Tomato, Leek, and Rice Soup (page 326).

The days are getting shorter by the time the middle of August rolls around, and the predictable and shrill hum of the cicada is not as prevalent anymore. Some of the maple trees have jump-started fall, with their leaves changing from green to gold to red, and the light is different, too; it's hard to explain, but it's just different. The nights are getting a little cooler as well, and we throw the winter quilt back on the bed.

In the garden the pumpkin vines have started to yellow and turn brittle and the squash foliage is withering. Soon we will be watching for the first frost of the season. Each night I listen to the weather report; and when it is nippy, I run up and throw newspaper over the basil plants. Any green tomatoes are harvested and kept under newspaper in the garage, where they ripen slowly and extend the tomato-eating season for us into November.

By the time October comes there are still some die-hard crops of Swiss chard, parsley, arugula, and lettuces left. A few overlooked tomatoes are withering on the ground and it is time to clean and prepare the garden for the long winter lull. So another weekend finds us ripping out exhausted plants and removing rotting vegetables to a compost heap. It is sad in a way to put the garden to bed; we realize that we have been spoiled so royally by such an abundance and variety of vegetables. Oh, the freezer is full of vegetables to get us through winter, but we will dearly miss those showy, vine-ripened tomatoes. And I will reluctantly resort to buying lettuces in the grocery store to satiate our need for nightly salads.

Finally Guy turns the electric fence off and we clean and put away the garden tools. We sort seeds, label them, and tuck them away like good-luck charms. We close and lock the garden shed door. Guy hangs the key on the big oak tree and walks down the hill to the house. The anticipation of next year's garden soothes my temporary disappointment and gives me something to look forward to. But for now I look forward to the fall and winter months, when I can pull the quilt snugly over my shoulders and dream a little longer on Sunday morning, sip a cup of tea, and read the Sunday paper, too.

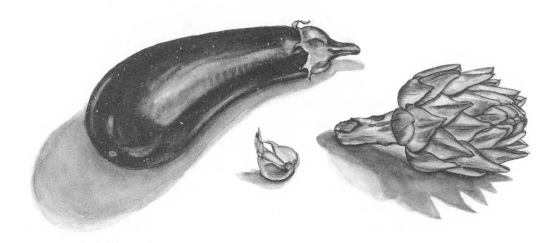

Zuppa di Pomodorini, Porri e Riso
(Cherry Tomato, Leek, and Rice Soup)

Makes 1¼ quarts

1 pound leeks, dark green tops removed and discarded

¼ cup water for cooking the leeks

2 pounds whole cherry tomatoes, stemmed and washed

Fine sea salt to taste

½ cup long-grain rice

1¼ cups water for cooking the rice

Even though only a few ingredients are necessary for this soup, it is very important that the tomatoes be in season for the best flavor. Many episodes of Ciao Italia *have featured my Italian vegetable garden. In those episodes I show how the vegetables grow, are harvested, and cooked. In the case of cherry tomatoes, I plant a variety called Sweet 100, a prolific and sweet-as-sugar tomato that is excellent for this soup. There is such a bumper crop that I can harvest the tomatoes, stem, wash, and dry them and pop them whole into heavy-duty zipper-lock plastic bags, freezing them for winter use. There is no fat in this soup. Make it in a nonstick soup pot for best results.*

Cut the leeks in half lengthwise, wash them well to remove any dirt, and cut them into thin slices. Put the leeks in a nonstick soup pot and add the water. Cook the leeks, covered, over very low heat and stir them occasionally until they are very soft; this will take about 20 minutes. Stir in the tomatoes and cook, covered, over medium-low heat for 30 minutes.

Transfer the mixture to a food processor or blender (in batches if necessary) and whirl or blend until smooth.

Pour the soup into a fine-mesh strainer set over a bowl. With a wooden spoon stir the soup and press on the solids to extract the juices. When the remaining pulp in the strainer is solid and dry-looking, discard it.

Transfer the soup to the soup pot. Stir in salt to taste and set aside.

Meanwhile in a small saucepan combine the rice and the water and bring to a boil. Lower the heat to simmer, cover the pot, and cook the rice until it has absorbed all the water. Transfer the rice to the soup and stir it in. Reheat the soup until hot and then serve.

Variation: Add fresh minced herbs such as parsley, basil, mint, or dill, or add diced mozzarella cheese to the soup just before serving.

Did you know that the ancient Romans revered leeks (*porri*) for their health benefits? It is said that the emperor Nero, who loved to sing, ate them every day to improve the quality of his voice.

Crema di Zucca
(Cream of Squash Soup)

Makes 2½ quarts

4 pounds (2 large) butternut
squash

⅔ cup water

⅔ cup heavy cream

3½ cups nonfat half-and-
half

2 teaspoons fine sea salt

¼ cup honey or brown sugar

¼ teaspoon ground ginger

¼ teaspoon fresh grated
nutmeg

Did you know that squash and pumpkin are used so much in the cooking of the city of Mantua in Lombardia that they are symbols of the city?

Traditional Italian cooking has always been the central focus of Ciao Italia. *That is not to say that I am not open to* alta cucina, *or more refined Italian cooking that incorporates rich ingredients like cream to raise the level of sophistication of a dish. I like to observe the new trends in food and I often experiment with what I see. This recipe for delicate and velvety-tasting creamed squash soup is one of my very favorites and so easy to make when lots of ripe butternut squash is sitting in my garden.*

Preheat the oven to 350°F.

Cut the squash into quarters. Remove the seeds and discard them. Place the squash pieces cut-side down in a large baking pan. Pour in the water. Cover the pan tightly with aluminum foil and bake the squash until it is very tender, about 1 hour.

When cool enough to handle, scoop the flesh from the squash into the food processor bowl. Discard the skins. Puree the squash until it is very smooth, then transfer it to a 3- or 4-quart soup pot. There should be approximately 4½ to 5 cups of pureed squash.

Stir in the heavy cream, half-and-half, salt, honey or brown sugar, ginger, and nutmeg. Cook the soup slowly over medium-low heat until bubbles begin to appear around the outside edges. Ladle the soup into soup bowls and serve immediately.

If you prefer a thinner soup, use a little milk or additional half-and-half to thin it down.

Conchiglie con Finocchio
(Pasta Shells with Fennel)

Serves 4 to 6

I don't understand why so many Americans shy away from eating fennel (finocchio). *This licorice-tasting, celery-like vegetable is an icon in the Italian kitchen. Italians use it as a* digestivo, *a vegetable that is offered with the salad course at the close of the meal to settle the stomach. But fennel can be stewed with tomatoes, stuffed and baked in a cream sauce, or used as a sauce for pasta as in this recipe for* conchiglie (shell-shaped pasta). *In this recipe, bacon can be substituted for the pancetta, but the flavor isn't quite the same.*

1½ pounds fennel, washed

1 tablespoon plus 1 teaspoon fine sea salt

1 pound #93 conchiglie (shell-shaped pasta)

½ pound pancetta, diced

1 medium onion, diced

4 tablespoons extra-virgin olive oil

1 teaspoon dried red pepper flakes

⅔ cup Pinot Grigio or Riesling wine

¼ teaspoon coarsely ground black pepper

2 tablespoons finely diced fennel leaves, reserved from chopping the fennel

Grated Pecorino cheese for sprinkling over the pasta

With a knife cut the stems of the fennel, leaving only the white bulbous part. Cut the feathery leaves off the tops. Dice enough of the leaves to make 2 tablespoons and reserve them. Use the remaining tops and leaves when making soup.

Cut the fennel bulb(s) in half lengthwise; cut out the woody center core and discard it. Slice the fennel into ¼-inch-thick slices and set aside.

Fill a pasta pot or large pot with 4 quarts of water and bring it to a boil. Add 1 tablespoon of the salt and the fennel. Boil the fennel for about 5 minutes, or until it is soft but not mushy. With a slotted spoon remove the fennel to a dish and set aside.

In the same pot cook the shells until they are al dente, cooked but firm and holding their shape.

While the pasta cooks, sauté the pancetta and onions in the olive oil over medium heat until the pancetta begins to brown. Stir in the red pepper flakes and the fennel. Raise the heat to high and pour in the wine. Cook 2 minutes on high heat, stirring occasionally, then lower the heat to medium and cook for another 3 minutes. Stir in the remaining salt and the pepper. Cover the pan and keep the sauce warm while the pasta is cooking.

Drain the pasta, reserving 2 tablespoons of the cooking water. Transfer the shells to the sauté pan with the fennel; add the reserved water, sprinkle on the fennel leaves, and toss the mixture over medium heat until well mixed. Transfer the mixture to a serving dish. Sprinkle the cheese over the top of the pasta and serve immediately.

Lasagne alle Bietole
(Swiss Chard Lasagne)

Serves 8

One of the most frequent requests that I get on Ciao Italia is for meatless lasagne, and the variations are endless. And one of the most surprising discoveries for viewers who have watched me make various lasagne, both with homemade pasta sheets and with boxed lasagne sheets, is that the boiling process can be completely eliminated when using a good Italian no-boil lasagne brand. I prefer Del Verde. I have made grilled vegetable lasagne, seafood lasagne, and cheese lasagne this way, and now comes this wonderful Swiss chard lasagne, which I make often because my crop of chard lasts all season long. I harvest it frequently, steam it, and freeze it so I can make this dish whenever I want to. If you do not like Swiss chard, substitute spinach.

2 pounds Swiss chard, stemmed and washed

1 tablespoon extra-virgin olive oil

1 medium onion, peeled and diced

2 pounds skim ricotta cheese

2 teaspoons fine sea salt

Grinding of coarse black pepper

2 egg whites

2 tablespoons minced fresh parsley leaves

2 teaspoons dried oregano

4 ounces shredded mozzarella or scamorza cheese

½ cup black olives in oil, pitted and diced

2½ cups homemade tomato sauce (see page 256)

8 sheets no-boil lasagne

Fill a soup pot with water and bring it to a boil. Add the Swiss chard and cook, uncovered, just until the leaves wilt, about 5 minutes. Drain the Swiss chard, let it cool, then squeeze out as much water as possible and coarsely chop it. Transfer the chard to a large bowl and set it aside.

In a small sauté pan heat the olive oil and cook the onion over low heat until it is very soft. Add the onion to the Swiss chard. Stir in the ricotta cheese, salt, pepper, egg whites, parsley, oregano, cheese, and olives.

Spread ¼ cup of the tomato sauce in the bottom of a 13½×8×2-inch-deep pan. Lay 2 of the lasagne sheets side-by-side in the pan. Spread one-third of the filling evenly over the top of the lasagne sheets. Spoon a few tablespoons of the tomato sauce over the filling. Cover with 2 more sheets of lasagne and spread

Guy's Garden

another third of the filling over the top, spooning a few more tablespoons of tomato sauce over the filling. Add 2 more lasagne sheets and spread the remaining filling over the top and spoon a few more tablespoons of tomato sauce over the filling. Top with the final layer of lasagne sheets and pour all the remaining sauce evenly over the top of the lasagne.

Preheat the oven to 350°F.

Cover the pan with a sheet of aluminum foil, making sure to tightly seal the pan, and bake for 45 to 50 minutes, or until the lasagne is piping hot and the lasagne sheets are soft.

Remove the lasagne to a cooling rack and let rest 10 minutes before serving. Cut into squares and serve immediately.

Broccolini e Spaghetti
(Broccolini and Spaghetti)

Serves 4 to 6

Broccolini is similar to broccoli but with smaller and looser florets; the stem is totally edible, leaving no waste. The delicate florets and slender stems have a hint of sweetness and can be cooked just like broccoli or eaten raw. In this recipe, broccolini is flavored with pancetta and tomatoes, providing a nice flavor contrast with the spaghetti.

¼ cup extra-virgin olive oil

¼ pound pancetta (Italian bacon), diced

1 pound broccolini, washed and drained

3 cloves garlic, minced

1 pound fresh tomatoes, skinned, seeded, and coarsely chopped

½ cup water or chicken broth

1¼ teaspoons fine sea salt

Grinding of black pepper

1 pound spaghetti

¼ cup reserved pasta-cooking water

Grated Pecorino cheese for sprinkling over pasta

Heat 2 tablespoons of the olive oil in a large skillet, add the pancetta, and cook, stirring over medium heat, until the pancetta begins to render its fat. Stir in the broccolini and continue cooking for another 3 minutes. Stir in the garlic and continue cooking until the garlic softens. Stir in the tomatoes, chicken broth, ¼ teaspoon of the salt, and the pepper. Cover the pan and cook over medium-low heat for 5 minutes. The broccolini should remain al dente, or have a bit of crunch to it. Set the broccolini aside and keep it warm while the spaghetti is cooking.

In a pasta pot with insert bring 4 to 6 quarts of water to a boil. Stir in the remaining tablespoon of salt and the spaghetti. Stir the spaghetti once or twice. Cover the pot and bring to a boil, then remove the cover and cook until the spaghetti is al dente.

Drain the spaghetti into a colander, reserving ¼ cup of the cooking water. Return the spaghetti to the pasta pot. Stir in the broccolini, the reserved water, and the remaining 2 tablespoons of olive oil and mix well over medium-low heat. Transfer the mixture to a platter, sprinkle the top with Pecorino cheese, and serve immediately.

Did you know that it is best to grate hard cheeses such as Parmigiano-Reggiano and Pecorino when they are at room temperature?

Guy's Garden

Rombo con Radicchiella e Patate

(Halibut with Mustard Greens and Potatoes)

Serves 2

1 pound mustard greens,
stems removed, leaves
washed and drained

¼ pound pancetta, diced

2 yellow-gold or red skin
potatoes, scrubbed and
thinly sliced

¼ teaspoon black pepper

2 halibut steaks (1 pound),
cut ¾ inch thick, skin on

Fine sea salt to taste

2 teaspoons extra-virgin
olive oil

2 tablespoons freshly
squeezed lemon juice

Since I crave mustard greens, here is a wonderful way to present them . . . with fish! I took my inspiration for this dish from the restaurant trend of serving fish on a bed of something green. Halibut steak is my choice, a delicate fish with a mild taste that is a nice foil for the sharp mustard taste of the greens. This is a nice dinner for two with a green salad and crusty rolls.

Cook the mustard greens as described for the Mustard Greens with Olives and Cheese on page 341. Set the mustard greens aside and keep warm.

Preheat the oven to 400°F.

In a sauté pan cook the pancetta until it begins to render its fat. Add the potatoes, in batches if necessary, and cook them until they are golden brown. Stir in the pepper. As they cook, transfer the potatoes to a serving dish and keep them warm.

Smear a large sheet of aluminum foil with the olive oil. Place the halibut steaks on the foil, sprinkle them with the salt, and coat them in the olive oil. Place the halibut on the foil. Pour the lemon juice over the top and seal the foil.

Put the package on a small cookie sheet and bake the fish for 10 to 15 minutes, depending on the thickness of the halibut. When done the fish will look uniformly white all over and easily flake with a fork.

Spread the potatoes on a serving platter. Place the halibut over the potatoes and top with the mustard greens. Serve immediately.

Peperoni Ripieni Sottosopra
(Upside-Down Stuffed Peppers)

Makes 9 stuffed peppers

One of the most magical dishes of southern Italy, especially from around the province of Avellino in Campania, is peperoni ripieni *(stuffed peppers). I have often grown sweet bell peppers in my garden, but the sweetness of those I have had from Campania far outshines anything I have ever tasted here. It is the variety, the intensity of the Mediterranean sun, and the long growing season that accounts for this. Or maybe it is the proximity of grumpy Mount Vesuvius that has lent richness to the soil over the centuries. Whatever the reasons, these delicious peppers and the variety of seasonings and stuffings they encase are a favorite of many. My mother makes hers with ground beef, ground pork, and ground veal, and keeps this meat mixture moist by baking the stuffed peppers upside down. They can be baked a day ahead and are even better as leftovers. They make a great entree for a party. Serve a salad and crusty bread and let the party begin!*

To make the sauce, in a sauce pot heat the olive oil and cook the onion until it softens. Stir in the pork butt chunks and Italian sausage and brown on all sides. Stir in the garlic and cook until the garlic softens. Lower the heat and stir in the crushed tomatoes, tomato puree, salt, and pepper. Cover and simmer the sauce for about 1 hour. Stir in the basil. The sauce is now ready to use.

Preheat the oven to 350°F.

Cut ¼ inch off the tops of the peppers. Carefully remove the seeds with a spoon, then rinse the peppers and set them aside.

In a large bowl combine the sirloin, pork, veal, rice, cheese, onions, eggs, parsley, salt, and pepper. Mix gently with your hands. Fill the cavities of the peppers with some of the mixture, being

MOM'S TOMATO SAUCE

4 tablespoons extra-virgin olive oil

1 medium onion, peeled and minced

3 pounds boneless pork butt, cut into 1-inch chunks

½ pound sweet Italian sausage

2 large cloves garlic, minced

2 (28-ounce) cans crushed tomatoes

1 (28-ounce) can tomato puree

2 teaspoons fine sea salt

½ teaspoon coarse black pepper

5 or 6 leaves fresh basil, shredded

9 large sweet bell peppers, washed and dried

Guy's Garden

FILLING

1 pound ground sirloin

1 pound ground pork

1 pound ground veal

2 cups cooked rice

1 cup grated Parmigiano-Reggiano cheese

1 large onion, peeled and minced

4 eggs

2 tablespoons minced parsley leaves

3 teaspoons sea salt

1 teaspoon coarse black pepper

careful not to overpack them or they will split in the oven while baking.

Ladle 1½ cups of tomato sauce in each of 2 large baking pans. Arrange the peppers upside down in the pans. Ladle 2 cups of sauce over each pan of peppers.

Cover the pans tightly with aluminum foil and bake for 45 minutes to 1 hour, or until the peppers are soft. Remove the pans from the oven, remove the foil, and carefully turn the peppers right-side up. Serve the peppers immediately with additional sauce on the side.

Don't be impatient if you grow peppers in your garden. They need a lot of heat. I cover them with a gauze-like material available in garden stores called Reemay to keep the heat in and the bugs out. Want red peppers? Some varieties of green pepper will turn red if left long enough on the stem. Other varieties will turn yellow, orange, or purple.

Bietole con Fior di Latte
(Chard with Fresh Mozzarella Cheese)

Serves 4

I don't know why Swiss chard is called Swiss chard; it has nothing to do with Switzerland. Chard is really a beet plant that is easily grown in the garden. For variety I plant white, yellow, and red chards. Their beautiful and strong quilted-like leaves look impressive. I usually cook the leaves in boiling water, then squeeze-dry them before chopping and cooking them with Italian bacon (pancetta) or olive oil. Here the boiling step is eliminated and the chard is cooked raw in a little olive oil with garlic. Fresh mozzarella cheese, called fior di latte, is made from cow's milk and rennet and is formed by hand into balls and sold in water. It is very different in taste and texture from its more expensive cousin—mozzarella di bufala, made from the milk of the water buffalo. It is the finishing touch, making this an elegant side dish to any meat or poultry course. Do not discard the chard stems; they are delicious as well and take a little longer to cook either by boiling or sautéing them.

2 pounds Swiss chard

1 tablespoon extra-virgin olive oil

1 large clove garlic, minced

Fine sea salt to taste

Fresh ground black pepper to taste

4 ounces fresh mozzarella (*fior di latte*), diced

Remove the stems from the chard by bending them and pulling them away from the leaves. Save the stems for another use. Place the leaves in a bowl of cold water and let them soak for a few minutes, then drain the leaves and wash them under cold running water. Dry the leaves with a towel, then stack them 6 to 8 leaves thick, and roll them up tightly like a newspaper. With a knife cut them into ½-inch pieces. Set the leaves aside.

In a 12-inch sauté pan heat the olive oil, stir in the garlic, and cook for 1 minute. Add the chard, cover the pot, and let the chard cook over medium heat for about 5 minutes, or until the leaves are wilted. Stir in the salt and pepper. Turn off the heat and sprinkle the cheese over the chard. Cover the pan and allow the cheese to melt. Stir with a wooden spoon to distribute the cheese. Transfer the mixture to a serving plate and serve immediately.

Variation: Tomato sauce (page 256) is also good poured over the top of the melted cheese.

Did you know that chard will discolor if prepared in aluminum cookware? Use stainless-steel cookware if possible.

Cipolle Ripiene
(Stuffed Onions)

Serves 4

Cipolle (onions), once considered a poor man's meat, are one of the four evangelists of Italian cooking (see page 124), which is to say that along with parsley, celery, and carrots they form the flavor structure and point of departure for cooking a variety of delicious-tasting foods. For this recipe use large white onions, which are hearty enough to be a meal in themselves. The filling can vary with the whim of the cook, but I like this bread stuffing flavored with sweet Marsala wine. Good-textured bread should be used.

2 cups torn bread pieces

¼ cup diced raisins or currants

½ cup sweet Marsala wine

4 large white onions, peeled

4 tablespoons extra-virgin olive oil

⅓ cup pine nuts

2 tablespoons minced parsley leaves

½ teaspoon fine sea salt

Grinding of coarse black pepper

Grease a casserole dish with olive oil and set aside.

Place the bread cubes in a bowl with the raisins or currants. Pour the wine over the mixture and toss with a spoon to coat everything well. Set the mixture aside.

Cut the onions in half widthwise and scoop out the center with a spoon, leaving a ¼-inch-thick wall.

Finely chop the scooped-out onion sections and set them aside.

Heat 2 tablespoons of the olive oil in a sauté pan, add the chopped onions, and cook them over low heat until they begin to brown. Stir in the pine nuts, reserved raisins, and the parsley and cook for 1 minute. Stir in the salt and pepper.

Transfer the onion mixture to the bowl with the bread and combine well.

Preheat the oven to 350°F.

Divide and stuff the hollowed-out onions with the bread mixture and place the onions in the casserole dish. Drizzle the remaining olive oil over the onions, cover the dish with a sheet of aluminum foil, and bake for 30 minutes. Uncover the dish and bake for another 15 minutes, basting the onions occasionally with any juices that accumulate in the pan. Serve the onions hot as an accompaniment to poultry, meats, or fish.

Radicchiella con Olive e Formaggio
(Mustard Greens with Olives and Cheese)

Serves 6

Mustard greens were popular in Italy in the Middle Ages and have all but disappeared today. A check of many of Italy's best markets, including the one in Padova, did not yield a trace of this ruffled-edge, green leafy vegetable, but that did not discourage me from reintroducing them on a garden segment of Ciao Italia. *I learned how to cook them from my mother. She cooked mounds of this pungent, mustard-tasting vegetable in large amounts of boiling water, then drained and squeezed the greens dry. She mixed them into scrambled eggs and put them between slices of coarse bread for lunch. They were never a requested food from me. Now older and wiser, I can't wait to plant mustard greens each year in my home garden, and I like them sautéed with dark-as-midnight, pungent black olives and cheese.*

1 teaspoon salt for cooking the greens

2 pounds mustard greens, leaves only, washed

¼ cup extra-virgin olive oil

2 large cloves garlic, minced

¼ cup black oil-cured olives, pitted and cut in quarters

Fine sea salt to taste

Grinding of coarse black pepper

¼ cup grated Pecorino or crumbled Sardinian feta cheese

Fill a soup pot with water and bring to a boil, add 1 teaspoon of salt and the mustard greens, and cook, uncovered, for 3 to 4 minutes. Drain the mustard greens in a colander and when cool enough to handle, squeeze out all the excess water. Chop the greens coarsely and set them aside.

In a sauté pan heat the olive oil, add the garlic and olives, and stir until the garlic softens but does not turn brown. Add the mustard greens and cook for 3 to 4 minutes, stirring occasionally.

Transfer the mixture to a serving dish and add salt and pepper to taste. Sprinkle the cheese over the top and serve immediately.

Did you know that if green vegetables such as mustard greens, broccoli, and green beans are boiled uncovered, they will retain their green color? The acids in the vegetables evaporate during the cooking process, and when vegetables are cooked with a lid, these acids are trapped and can turn green vegetables a dull gray-green color.

Note: This dish can also be used as a sauce for dressing one of the hollow-tube pastas cut into short pieces, such as rigatoni, penne, or ziti.

Guy's Garden

Insalata di Barbabietole e Carote
(Marinated Beet and Carrot Salad)

Serves 6 to 8

3 large red beets with tops attached (about 1¼ pounds)

1½ cups beet tops, torn into pieces

⅓ cup plus 2 tablespoons extra-virgin olive oil

3 tablespoons cider vinegar

2 large cloves garlic, minced

1 teaspoon fine sea salt

¾ teaspoon celery salt

1 tablespoon sugar

2 large carrots, scraped and julienned into matchsticks

½ cup minced fresh mint

2 tablespoons minced fresh chives

This is a jewel of a salad, in more ways than one. Made with beets, carrots, and tender beet tops, its vibrant colors sparkle on any dinner table. When I started cooking beets on my television program, I first showed viewers how they were grown in my garden. Many viewers were fascinated by the yellow beets and the striped red and white beets that we used in some of the programs. And they were amazed at the idea of turning pureed beets into colorful beet-flavored pasta. This salad using red beets is inexpensive to make, but it looks like a treasure when ready to serve. Buy beets with the leaf tops attached. If you can't find them, substitute spinach leaves in this salad. Be sure to make the salad early in the day and allow the flavors to mingle at room temperature for several hours before serving.

Wash the beets well to remove tough surface dirt. Cut the beet tops off and reserve the leaves but leave about 3 inches of stem attached to each beet. Place the beets in a large saucepan and cover them with cold water. Boil the beets until a knife is easily inserted all the way into the beets. Depending on the size of the beets, they will cook in about 30 to 35 minutes.

Drain the beets and set aside to cool.

Tear the beet leaves into bite-size pieces and set aside.

In a bowl whisk together the olive oil, vinegar, garlic, salt, celery salt, and sugar. Set aside.

When the beets are cool enough to handle, peel the skin, and cut off the remaining stems and discard them. Cut the beets into thick round slices and cut each slice into ¼-inch-wide strips.

Place the beet strips in a large rectangular dish. Gently mix in the carrots, beet top greens, mint, and chives. Pour the dressing over the beet mixture and toss gently to coat well. Cover the dish tightly with plastic wrap and allow the salad to stand at room temperature for several hours before serving.

Did you know that it is easier to mince herbs with a kitchen scissors than a knife? After stemming the herbs, roll them up tightly together and snip.

Insalata d'Aragosta dal Corsaro

(Lobster Salad Corsaro Style)

Serves 2

½ pound cooked lobster tail meat

10 cherry tomatoes, stemmed, washed, and cut in half

1 tablespoon finely minced Italian parsley leaves

Grated zest of 1 large lemon

3 tablespoons extra-virgin olive oil

1½ tablespoons freshly squeezed lemon juice

¼ teaspoon fine sea salt, or more to taste

¼ teaspoon ground white pepper

8 whole arugula leaves, washed, dried, and refrigerated

I enjoyed this cold lobster salad in Cagliari, the port capital city of the island of Sardinia, in a beautifully appointed restaurant called dal Corsaro on Viale Regina Margherita, 28. The lobster, which is called aragosta, *is smaller, clawless, and sweeter than what we are used to in New England. Served with the unusually sweet cherry tomatoes from nearby Santa Margherita, it was a perfect dish with a simple dressing of olive oil and fresh lemon juice. To get close to the original taste, I pick a variety of cherry tomatoes from my garden called Sweet 100. My advice is to make this wonderful salad in the summer when tomatoes are in season. Be sure to make the salad at least a few hours ahead of time and then allow it to come to room temperature before serving.*

Cut the lobster meat up into bite-size pieces and place in a bowl. Gently mix in the tomatoes, parsley, and lemon zest.

In a small bowl whisk together the olive oil, lemon juice, salt, and pepper. Pour the dressing over the lobster mixture and toss gently with two spoons. Cover the bowl and refrigerate for at least 2 hours. When ready to serve, allow enough time for the lobster mixture to come to room temperature.

Line each of the 2 plates with 4 arugula leaves. Divide the lobster mixture and spoon half of it into the center of the arugula on each plate. Serve immediately with crusty rolls.

Sformato di Pane Stratificato

(Molded Tomato Bread Salad)

Serves 6 to 8

One of the early episodes of Ciao Italia *dealt with how to make tradi-tional salads using slightly bitter greens like escarole and chicory. Since then, I have demonstrated a number of other salads, including bread salad, made with chunks of dense and slightly stale bread that had been soaked in vinegar and combined with wedges of juicy tomatoes and pungent basil leaves. In the following version of bread salad, a loaf pan is used to create a molded, layered salad of red and yellow tomatoes and peppery arugula leaves. When the salad is unmolded it makes a festive presentation for a summer dinner party. Use the best-tasting tomatoes you can find, and good sandwich bread that will absorb the tomato juices and not crumble when cut. The salad is best made several hours before serving. For variation, top with a chiffonade of fried leeks, which give a complementary sweet taste and crunch.*

Line an 8½×3½×5-inch loaf pan with a sheet of plastic wrap, leaving an overhang all around the pan. Set aside.

To make the dressing, combine all the ingredients in a jar, shake well, and set aside. The dressing can be made several days ahead and stored in the refrigerator. Bring to room temperature before using.

To prepare the filling and assemble the salad, make a design with a few of the arugula leaves placed in the bottom of the pan. Save the rest to place between the layers.

Trim the bread slices to fit neatly in the bread pan (about 7½×4 inches if using the called-for bread pan). Place one of the bread slices over the arugula in the bottom of the bread pan. Brush the

DRESSING

½ cup extra-virgin olive oil

⅓ cup cider or white wine vinegar

2 tablespoons sugar

½ teaspoon fine sea salt

1 tablespoon finely minced oregano or 1 teaspoon dried

1 large clove garlic, finely minced

FILLING

2 ounces arugula leaves, stemmed, washed, dried and left whole

Five ¼-inch-thick bread slices, cut lengthwise from a 1-pound-4-ounce loaf of white bread

1 large (about 4 ounces) red beefsteak tomato, cut into thin rounds

1 large (about 4 ounces) yellow beefsteak tomato, cut into thin rounds

Guy's Garden

bread with some of the dressing. Make a layer of red tomato slices over the bread. Cut up a few slices to fill in any gaps along the sides. Brush the tomatoes with a little of the dressing. Place a layer of arugula leaves over the tomatoes and brush them with a little of the dressing. Lay a second bread slice over the arugula leaves and repeat brushing with the dressing. Add a layer of the yellow tomatoes, filling in any gaps with pieces of cut tomatoes, and brush them with the dressing. Add another layer of arugula leaves and brush with a little of the dressing. Continue to make two more layers in the same manner, ending with a bread layer. Brush the top of the bread with any remaining dressing.

Cover the pan tightly with a piece of plastic wrap and bring the overhanging edges over the top. Press down on the loaf with your hand to make sure that it is compacted and even with the top edges of the pan. A brick wrapped in aluminum foil and placed on top of the loaf makes a perfect weight—or use some other type of weight to compress the loaf. Refrigerate the loaf for several hours.

Unwrap the top of the loaf, place a platter over the top and invert the loaf onto the platter. Carefully lift off the loaf pan, remove the plastic wrap, and discard it. Use a tomato knife to cut the loaf into slices. Serve immediately.

Tip: A tomato knife has a serrated blade that cuts tomatoes without tearing them. Tomato knives are available from kitchen and cutlery stores. See the mail order section for a list of sources (page 347).

Mail Order Sources

These suppliers carry many of the authentic specialty ingredients used in the recipes in this book.

Balducci's
424 Avenue of the Americas
New York, NY 10011
800-225-3822 or
1-800-BALDUCCI/Catalog
www.balducci.com

All kinds of Italian products: cheeses, farro, pancetta, chickpea flour, semolina flour

Ciao Times
P.O. Box 891
Durham, NH 03824
603-868-5824
www.ciaoitalia.com

Mail order and Web site orders for Ciao Italia products, including personalized aprons, wooden dough scrapers, T-shirts, and mugs

Claudio's King of Cheese
929 South Ninth Street
South Philadelphia, PA 19147
215-627-1873

Wide variety of Italian imported cheeses, pasta, prosciutto, olives, and olive oils, Gorgonzola dolce and piccante cheese

Colavita USA
2537 Brunswick Avenue
Linden, NJ 07036
800-665-4731/Catalog
www.colavita.com

Extra-virgin olive oils, pasta, gourmet items, balsamic vinegar, tomatoes, olives

Dairy Fresh Candies
57 Salem Street
Boston, MA 02113
800-336-5536/Catalog
dairyfreshcandies.com

Candied citron peels, mostarda di frutta, *nuts, olive oils, chocolate for cooking and eating, extracts, pine nuts, Amarena cherries, jam. One of largest selections of regional and holiday specialty items.*

Dean & DeLuca
Catalog Orders
P.O. Box 20810
Wichita, KS 67208-6810
800-221-7714
www.deandeluca.com

Italian meats, cheeses, cookware, Arborio rice

DiBruno Brothers
109 South Eighteenth Street
Philadelphia, PA 19103
215-665-9220/Catalog

Del Verde pasta, Italian cheeses, fresh mozzarella, olives, olive oils, prosciutto di Parma cured meats, pancetta

Draeger's
P.O. Box C
Menlo Park, CA 94026
800-642-9463

Cookware, cheese graters, rolling pins, bakeware, Italian ceramics, complete gourmet food store

Fante's
1006 South Ninth Street
Philadelphia, PA 19147
800-878-5557

Pasta machines and motor attachments, ravioli forms, cookware, bakeware, peach molds, parchment paper, panettone papers, serving bowls, platters, chitarras for making pasta, food processors, tomato knives

Gallucci's Italian Foods
6610 Euclid Avenue
Cleveland, OH 44103
216-881-0045/Catalog

A comprehensive Italian grocery store featuring cheeses, olive oils, cured meats, buffalo mozzarella, marmalades, preserved fruits, wines, pasta, flours, baking supplies, dried beans, cannellini beans, ricotta salata, pizzelle irons, dried figs, dried oregano

Joe Pace and Sons
42 Cross Street
Boston, MA 02113
617-227-9673/Catalog

Italian meats, cheeses, breads, durum flour, mostarda di frutta, pasta, dried cod, salted sardines, fresh ricotta, pancetta, mortadella, prosciutto di Parma, olive oils, wine vinegars, Italian candies, ladyfingers, mascarpone cheese, Arborio rice, Carniroli rice, Gorgonzola cheese, pancetta, Amarena cherries, Amarena cherry jam

King Arthur Flour
P.O. Box 1010
Norwich, VT 05055
802-649-3881 or
800-827-6836/The Baker's Catalogue

Semolina and durum flours, wheat gluten, yeast, unbleached all-purpose flour, pastry flour, sea salts, extracts, baking equipment, candied fruits, dried fruits, turbinado sugar

Kitchen Etc.
32 Industrial Drive
Exeter, NH 03833
800-232-4070/Catalog
www.kitchenetc.com

Pasta pots, pasta machines, motor attachments, pasta boards, rolling pins, bakeware, cookware, small appliances, kitchen gadgets, cutlery, glassware, linens, utensils, tomato knives

Pennsylvania Macaroni Company
2010-12 Penn Avenue
Pittsburgh, PA 15222
412-471-8330/Catalog

All types of pasta, no-boil lasagne sheets, cheeses, olive oils, cured meats, flour, imported cookies and candies

San Francisco Herb Company
250 Fourteenth Street
San Francisco, CA 94103
800-227-4530/Catalog

Complete line of nuts, spices, candied citron and peels

The Spice Corner
904 South Ninth Street
Philadelphia, PA 19147
800-SPICES-1 or 215-925-1661
www.thespicecorner.com

Semolina flour, spices, and nuts

Zabar's
2245 Broadway
New York, NY 10024
212-787-2000 or
800-697-6301/Catalog
www.zabars.com

Gadgets, kitchenware, salad spinners, cured meats, cheeses, pâtés, cheesecloth, pasta pots, colanders, kitchen scales, handle scoops, ravioli forms, pastry brushes, bakeware

English Index
——————

English Index

English Index

English Index

English Index

Italian Index